IDAHO
AND THE
MAGIC CIRCLE

Copyright © 2000 by Betty Bever
All rights reserved. This book, or parts thereof, may not be reproduced or publicly performed in any form without permission.

Second Printing January 2001

Printed in the United States of America by
The Caxton Printers, Ltd.
Caldwell, Idaho 83605

I.S.B.N. 1-885101-79-1

To My Family

*My son Tim,
Grandson Brady,
Granddaughter Erin,
and in memory
of my son Bill.*

Dear Reader:

A long time ago I was a "Stringer" for the Idaho Statesman. A "Stringer" is a free-lance writer who submits stories for publication. If the paper finds them interesting, they print them.

We were at Magic Reservoir, west side, and this was my first "Opening Day" of fishing. It was Memorial Day weekend, and there was a steady stream of pick-ups, cars, and assorted vehicles, many with boats trailing behind, coughing their way over the dusty, narrow road to the resort area. Many pulled in early to ready up their cabins for the season, others to get settled and "be out on the water first thing in the morning, or maybe even one minute after midnight!" Nobody dared put a line in the water until fishing was legal.

The air crackled with excitement, and greetings were noisy and spirited. "Hey, there's — and the kids!"; "You ole fool, thought you'd be dead by now!"; "Stop by later....etc." There was a lot of laughter, back-slapping, "remember whens", and beer.

I thought it was all pretty wonderful, and decided to write a story about "Opening Day at Magic" and send it to The Statesman. I wanted outsiders to know what they were missing.

But, I never did. That story turned into this book.

First, I needed some background information about the dam and its beginnings. I checked newspapers, books and other sources. No luck. One newspaper reporter decided to do a story about Magic Dam way back in the 50's but gave up— said the dam history was shrouded in mystery.

And so my search began. I covered libraries, court houses, old newspapers, Idaho history books, irrigation offices and interviewed lots and lots of wonderful, friendly Idahoans. All of which kept me reaching back,

back in time. In order to tell you why "this" happened, I had to find out what, or who brought it about.

Several years later I was up to my ears in bits and pieces of information about Idaho, how it came to be Idaho, and what went on in those early days to bring us to Magic Dam. When one day (so help me this is the truth) right in front of me on the desk was a compass — the metal kind with a pencil attached. I placed the metal point in Magic Reservoir and drew a circle... a circle around Magic Dam... A Magic Circle!! Aha! Sun Valley on the North; Carey on the East; Shoshone on the South; and Hill City on the West.

Now, I could focus my research on "The Magic Circle," even though sometimes I have to tell you what happened OUTSIDE in order to explain what happened INSIDE.

And, that's how it became "Idaho And The Magic Circle."

We go all the way back to the Indians, who were the first people to live in "The Magic Circle" 10,000 or more years ago.

Now, don't let that stop you from reading this book. The chapters are short, the top outside corner of every page shows the time covered, and, you can start anywhere. It's reader friendly and it's all there.

Sincerely,
Betty M. Bever

p.s. In 1980 Magic opened on Memorial weekend as it always had, and closed November 30th.
In 1981 the Idaho Fish and Game opened the "Winter Season" (February and March) to ice-fishing.
In 1985 Magic was opened for year-round fishing.

TABLE OF CONTENTS

The First People	9
The Claimers	17
Oregon Country	19
Camas Prairie - Discovered!	22
Rendevous	25
The Missionaries	27
The Northwest Ordinance	30
Oregon Trail	32
Measles	35
State of Oregon	37
Goodale Cut-Off	38
Gold!	40
Idaho?	45
The Politicians	50
Idaho Territorial Governors	54
First Magic Circle Mines	58
Fort Bridger Treaty	59
Farmers and Ranchers	62
Transcontinental Railroad	64
Progress	67
Indian Wars	69
The Promoters	73
Newcomers	75
A New Decade-A New Land	78
Claiming and Naming	81
How to file a Mining Claim	85
Ketchum	87
Bullion	90
Bellevue	92
Hailey	94
Other Magic Circle Towns	99
Alturas County Seat	102
Hailey - SOLD!	104
Growing Pains	106
Camas Prairie	110
Shoshone, The Railroad Town	114
What's in a Name?	117
Oregon Short Line RR	124
Wood River Branch of OSL	126
The Constituancy	130
The Damphools	135
Chinese	137
Girls! Girls! Girls!	141
Camas Prairie Settlers	144
Other Homesteaders	146
The Mormons	148
Ice Caves	151
S. D. Boone	155
The State of Idaho	157

A Time of Change	160
Irrigation and the Government	163
Go West! Go West!	167
Wood River Valley Irrigation Ass'n	171
Men, Money and Harry Wilson	174
Idaho Irrigation Co., Ltd.	178
Arvada - Alberta	180
Alberta	182
Alberta Land Opening	189
Summer of 1907	193
Fall of 1907	196
The Panic of 1907	200
Gooding Land Opening	203
Small Town Newspapers - 1907	205
1907 News	208
Did You Ever See a Bald-Headed Indian?	212
Nightmares and Dreams	215
Barnum and Bailey	218
1908 - Out with the Old - In with the New	221
Magic Dam - 1908	227
Magic Dam Diary	229
The Company Promotion	246
Richfield	250
Dietrich	254
How to Farm 101	258
Sign of the Times - 1910	259
J. O. Jones at Magic Dam	264
R.I.P. Harry Wilson	271
Tidings of 1911	272
Central Idaho Railroad	276
The Turbulent Teens	281
The Roaring Twenties	297
The Great Depression	306
The Successes	318
Wood River Valley	320
Sun Valley	322
Magic Valley	330
World War II	332
Sun Valley Goes Navy	337
Gleason's Landing	344
Magic City	353
The North Shore of Magic	355
The Seiche	356
Baja Magic	359
Update - Sun Valley and Elk Horn	361
Westshore Lodge	362
Magic Dam Electricity	364
Dam fools	365
Burren West	367
The End	369

Pre History

HOW THE FIRST PEOPLE GOT HERE

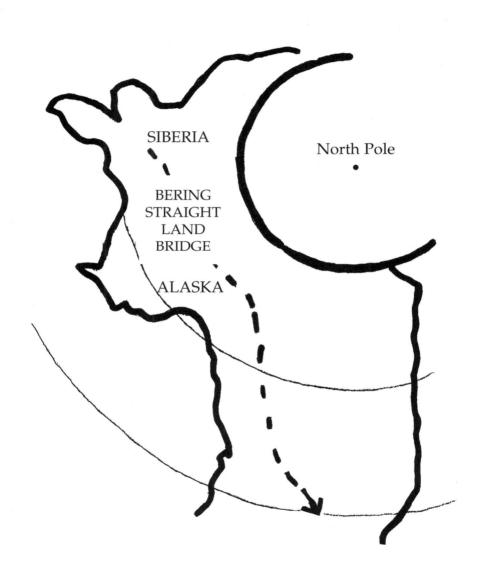

Pre History

THE FIRST PEOPLE

Thousands of years ago in the murky shadows of prehistory, the first "huddled masses" picked their way from Northeast Asia (over the Bering Strait Land Bridge) into North America. Primitive Asian Nomads, they were, huddling together for safety and warmth and scrounging the countryside and rivers for food. Some say they brought domesticated dogs with them, which were occasionally used as pack animals.

These people managed to survive, and thrive, and centuries later their descendants were all over North and South America.

Ten thousand years ago some of them were living part-time on Camas Prairie, inside "The Magic Circle."

They stayed together in small family groups, and stoned rabbits and other small living things for food. Eventually, one of them twisted together some grass and made a pretty decent string. Before long they were all doing it and soon had ropes and nets, and even crude shelters woven out of grass and brush.

Somewhere along the line they discovered fire, and the women learned to cook. It was easy for the men to catch small animals, but the women were usually pregnant and not able to get around fast enough. When he brought his catch back to camp, she would de-fur or de-feather it to cook with the roots and berries she'd gathered while he was out hunting. This was womens' work.

Much, much later - in 1492, those first Americans were mistakenly named "Indians" by Columbus. You know the story - he was looking for the East Indies and thought he'd found it, so named the people "Indians."

Later, another Italian sailor, Amerigo Vespucci, hit South America, explored up and down the coast, reported back, and they named the entire land after him - "America", North and South.

1500 - 1800

So much for the naming.

About 1517 the Spanish Conquistadors landed in South America with a boatload of horses. While they were out conquering, some of the horses got loose, and centuries later, the horses' descendants showed up on Camas Prairie. They had been traded from tribe to tribe until nearly everyone had some. The name our Camas Prairie people gave to the horse meant "big dog."

The horse was a giant step for the people on Camas Prairie. Now the men could ride around chasing larger animals. They developed special "killer weapons" for hunting on horseback, and the women learned to clean and rub and tan the big hides to make decent clothes for the family, and the large hides were sewn together and draped over upright poles to make a "tipi." She learned to dry all that meat to keep for later use. She kept the horns, and cleaned the bones to make tools, and strung the teeth on twisted grass to make a dandy necklace for herself. Before long, everybody wanted one.

They were warmer, better fed, prettier, and a lot more comfortable generally. Besides, now that they had horses, they were able to range out farther in search of food, and if things got bad, they could always eat the horse and wear his hide.

They contrived a trailing vehicle that worked well. Later called a "travois" by French trappers, it was simply two long poles tied over the horse's neck and bound together with hides to make a platform in the rear. It trailed along nicely over any kind of terrain - rocky, sandy, muddy or mountainous. They could pack up all their food and supplies, go to the Snake River in the spring to fish for salmon, back to Camas Prairie in the summer to harvest the Camas, and in the fall, join a big game hunting party in the mountains. They wintered wherever they were most comfortable.

Loosely organized tribes stayed together during this annual migration in search of food. They lived with the land

1500 - 1800

and respected all of nature. They learned by watching and listening to everything around them - birds, animals, trees, water, sun, moon, rain and earth. They knew intuitively that everything in nature vibrated with a kind of sacred energy, and their everyday lives were mixed with the spiritual.

They evolved into a proud, intelligent, self-sufficient people. For the most part they lived in peace, but occasionally would raid another camp to steal a horse or a woman. For entertainment, the men enjoyed gambling, horse racing, ceremonial dances, and hunting. They developed bows shaped out of wood and mountain sheep horn, and stone-tipped arrows and spears; made shields of buffalo hides, and put together heavy, war-like clubs. They painted their horses with white clay, decorated them with feathers, and held ceremonial dances. There were "shamans" who cured the sick, conducted the ceremonies and controlled the weather!

The dead were buried among the rocks dressed in their best garments and wrapped in a fur blanket with the head pointed west. They believed the soul went along the Milky Way on its journey to the land of the dead. The favorite horse of the deceased was killed, and the mourners cut their hair, gashed their legs, and observed a year of mourning.

Every generation became more proficient than the last. They developed remarkable weaving skills, and could weave practically anything out of grasses, reeds or fibers from the sagebrush. Baskets were woven so tightly they could carry water, and they wove excellent sandals out of grass. The women learned to make warm blankets by carefully removing the rabbit skins, cutting them into long strips, and wrapping them around sticks to dry. The spirals were then woven together to make furry robes for the whole family. They also wove soft, fluffy duck-feather blankets.

They called themselves "weaver people", and when any

1500 - 1800

one of them spotted a nice stand of grass he would shout "shawnt shaw-nip", which, in their language meant "abundant grasses."

Eventually, they fashioned some crude pottery, but weaving was their forte. Still later, they made durable bags out of salmon skins to hold fish oil, and beautiful gloves, bags, and clothing of finely-tanned deerskin. The men wore moccasins, leggings and fringed shirts, and carried eagle feather fans for ceremonial occasions. The women wore dresses, moccasins, knee-length leggings, and necklaces of elk teeth. In cold weather, both wore robes of buffalo, elk, or wildcat.

They were fond of games and sports and laughter.

These people were later called "Shoshonee" by the first French trappers who heard their excited cries "shawnt shawn-nip." The trappers made maps and marked the area "Shoshonee Country" because that's the way their cries sounded to the Frenchmen.

The Shoshoni and Bannock tribes are those most closely associated with Southern Idaho. The Bannock called themselves "Southern People" and were of the Paiute tribes. They migrated into Shoshoni territory and became friends. They were taller, more slender, and lighter complexioned than the Shoshoni, but they lived in Shoshoni territory and their language was similar. The Bannock word for themselves was "Panaita" meaning Southern People, and also "Panakwate" meaning "partners with the Shoshoni." The name "Bannock" came from the word "bamp" (meaning hair) and "nack", meaning a backward motion, alluding to the manner in which the tribe wore a tuft of hair thrown back from the forehead. Somehow, the name "bamp-nack" turned into "Bannack" and eventually, to the Scotch word "Bannock" which is used today.

The two tribes remained separate, but their traditions were much the same. They lived in three-generation families where everyone helped in the care and education of the children. They were surrounded by grandparents, aunts,

1500 - 1800

uncles, parents, cousins and siblings. They called all of their adult relatives "father" and "mother." There were no orphans. The children were given names in infancy without any special ceremony, and nicknames were given later in their development as were special names for feats of bravery.

Customs and traditions which had been established down through the ages were their tribal laws.

At the onset of puberty, the young maiden was isolated in a small shelter which contained its own fire and special furnishings. She was kept there for about ten days under the care of a knowledgeable older women who instructed her in matters relating to marriage and family life. At the end of her isolation, she donned new clothes and courtship began.

The young man experienced a more gradual transition into adulthood. There was a special ceremony for his first big game kill, after which he would spend more and more time hunting, fishing, and traveling with adult males. He would join raids, and hopefully would be invited to join a warrior society in his later teens. Boys usually married at about 20 years of age.

After puberty, courtship became an almost constant preoccupation of boys and girls. There were many formal dances where boys and girls formed trysts, and adult supervision was minimal at such times. At night the boys sometimes played reed flutes within hearing of a girl's tent, and if she were interested, she would come out to meet him. Courtship did not last long as the girls usually married shortly after puberty. Infant betrothals and other family-arranged marriages were also common. If the girl accepted, the prospective groom gave the father of the bride-to-be a gift of horses, which was reciprocated at the marriage ceremony.

Life was orderly and structured, and except for an occasional raid on another tribe - peaceful.

As time went on, Camas Prairie became the vacationland for many tribes. Every summer they came from

1500 - 1800

far and near to gather the camas bulbs and join in a gigantic reunion - the first real Idaho "harvest festival."

They would greet old friends, show off new clothes and ornaments, strut, gossip, play games, race horses, hold contests, sing, dance, gamble, hold serious religious ceremonies, and trade, trade, trade – and this was just the men! They were all lively traders, and Camas Prairie quickly became the official regional trading center. There were lovely, pastel seashells from tribes on the Pacific Coast; superb horses from the Nez Perce; neatly flaked arrowheads of obsidian from the Glass Buttes of Oregon; baskets and fancy sandals from the locals, and beautiful buckskin clothing. They all brought special things to trade.

Camas Prairie was also an important information center. It was here they heard news of happenings all over the country. Even though few of them spoke the same language, they all understood sign language which was their intertribal means of communication. They could easily converse, no matter how different their spoken language was.

Sign language developed the same way human speech developed - from the necessity to communicate. Both hands in motion, and when used by experts in conversation, its fluid grace of movement is beautiful to see. There are 48,000 combination gestures in the Indian sign language, and is so much like the language of the deaf, there would be little trouble conversing. The Indian name for deaf mute means "people who talk with their hands and arms."

The camas bulb was one of the Indians' most important staples; without it, they would go hungry for much of the winter. A member of the lily family, the bulb is small and round, about an inch-and-a-half in diameter, with a dark outer coating and white meat resembling an onion. It was harvested from mid-July through September, after the blue flowers were gone and the seeds had dropped.

1500 - 1800

The women did the work of the harvest. First, a pit was dug, lined with rocks, and a fire built to heat the rocks. They dug the bulbs from the ground with a slightly curved stick, sharpened on one end with the point made hard in a fire. The handle was of bone, or antler, tied cross-wise on the other end. They carried the bulbs to camp in baskets, cleaned them, and when the rocks were hot, the bulbs were spread over them between layers of grass. The grass and bulbs were then covered with earth and left to cook for several days. The heat from the rocks baked the bulbs, and baking made them sweet and tasty. Some were eaten on the spot, and some were mashed into flat cakes and dried for winter use.

While the bulbs were cooking, the women had a chance to socialize. They talked about their husbands, the kids, the in-laws, the out-laws, and checked out the newest weave in blankets, baskets and sandals. They exchanged housekeeping hints and recipes, and learned new techniques from each other, like how to keep the baby dry and clean in the "tekat" (cradleboard). How? Before you drop the little critter in, line the tekat with soft, tender leaves of sagebrush. When it is time for a change, simply dump everything out (except the babe), reline the tekat, and you're in business again. This could well have been the fore-runner of the modern disposable diaper - and it was biodegradable!

Every six or seven years, swarms of grasshoppers and crickets would descend upon Camas Prairie, and the Indians considered them a special treat. They gathered them up to pound into a kind of flour for future use. They recognized protein when it hopped by.

These Camas Prairie harvesters and their ancestors, had made many adjustments down through the centuries just to stay alive; soon, they would be forced to make the most

1500 - 1800

disruptive adjustment of all - their land was about to be invaded by white men.

1800 - 1840

THE CLAIMERS

White men around the world greedily looked upon America as a vast, unclaimed territory, and whoever got there first could claim it for himself. So, while the Indians were going about their business of survival, white men were sailing around in ships "claiming" land. When they found a place they wanted, they would jump off the boat, plant their flag, bury some coins from their country, and say "I claim this land for England - or Spain - or France - or Russia - or whoever", and THAT WAS IT! They owned it! They could sell it, or trade it, or live on it, or plunder it!

Sometimes two or three countries would "claim" the same land, or parts of it, and vast sections would pass from one to another as a result of war, purchase, trade or larceny.

After the Revolutionary War in America, the brand new Colonies became eligible to claim, buy, settle, plunder and trade along with the big boys. There was a great spread of land between those Colonies and the Pacific Ocean, and the Colonies aimed to have it all. So they hopped right in to wheel and deal and do some claiming on their own.

In 1792, when the new Colonial government was only sixteen years old, the American Sea Captain Robert Gray sailed around Cape Horn and up the Pacific Coast to the Oregon River (which he immediately named "Columbia" after his ship). He sailed about thirty miles up the river, got out of the boat, raised the flag, buried some coins, and claimed for America, "all the land drained by the Columbia River and its tributaries."

Now, this was a pretty big claim, because the Columbia River drains much of Washington, Oregon, Idaho, and parts of Montana and Wyoming! He didn't know this when he made his claim, but it turned out to be a pretty good move.

Before Captain Gray showed up, the Columbia River was known by the Indian name "Oregon", which meant "River

1800 - 1840

of the West", and whenever reference was made to "Oregon Country", it covered all of the land between the Continental Divide and the Pacific Ocean.

Idaho was once "Oregon Country."

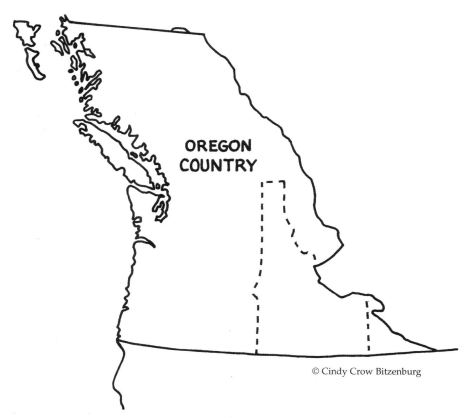

© Cindy Crow Bitzenburg

OREGON COUNTRY 1820-1848

1800 - 1840

OREGON COUNTRY

No white man ever even considered that the land belonged to the Indians. The wide-spread Oregon Country extended way up into Canada, and was also claimed in part by England, Spain, Russia, and America. In 1812, England had control, but six years later agreed to occupy it jointly with America. Spain got out in 1813, and Russia in 1824.

While all this struggle over ownership was going on, white men were streaming in from everywhere on sailing ships. Traders, merchants, fur trappers, explorers, adventurers, all found a country rich in furs, lumber, and good land, rugged and untouched.

The first white men to venture inland were the fur trappers, mostly French and English, filtering down from Canada. Solitary men they were, roaming the country, scrambling for pelts, exposed to hunger, thirst, heat, snow and Indians. Many lived in self-imposed isolation, while others made friends with the Indians, moved right in with them and even married Indian maidens. They took on all the paraphernalia of Indian life and even dressed like them. Often, it was difficult to distinguish a "white Indian" from your regular basic Indian.

The marrying made the trappers acceptable to the tribes. The trappers found safety in joining a tribe, and it made for good bartering. The maidens were often quite ambitious to become the wife of a white trapper because in addition to the finery he could give her, it freed her from camp drudgery and other heavy work expected of Indian women. As for the trapper - he knew well that his life would be a whole lot better with a willing, efficient, obedient, respectful Indian woman to cook his meals and make his clothes and keep him clean and tan his hides and tend his horses and have his babies and always be there when he wanted her. Not only that, the

1800 - 1840

Indians considered trapping to be "woman's work", so she did that, too. The trapper who married an Indian maiden was no dummy.

It was the white trapper who gave "white man names" to people and places, many of which we still use today. For example, the French-speaking trappers named many of our Indian tribes such as "Nez Perce" ("pierced nose"); "Siksika" "(black feet"); "Pend Oreilles" ("ear bobs"); "Coeur d'Alene" ("pointed heart" or "heart of an awl"); "Grosventres" ("big bellies"), etc. It is supposed that perhaps one member of a tribe had a pierced nose so a French trapper identified the entire tribe that way - and from then on.

Early trappers named "American Falls" after American Fur Co. trappers who lost their lives there. Another mighty falls was first named "Canadian Falls" but was later changed to "Great Shoshone Falls", to honor the Shoshoni Indians.

The early trappers communicated with the Indians in a curious dialect called "Chinook", a growling, spluttering, put-together jargon widely used by both whites and Indians in those early days. It was a mixture of French, English and Indian. Other things were named from this strange language, such as the "Chinook Winds", which referred to the warm winds blowing from the direction of a tribe of Indians named "Chinook." Also, there are Chinook salmon, etc.

The word "Camas" is a Chinook word meaning "sweet", and is sometimes spelled Kamas or Quamash. The Indians called the bulbs "Pahsego", "pah" meaning water, and "sego" meaning bulbous root that grows in swampy places, but it is the Chinook word "Camas" that we still use today. Instead of "Camas Prairie", it could have been "Pahsego Prairie."

Remember that.

It was the white trapper who taught the Indian still another linguistic skill - profanity. There was no profanity in the Indian language.

1800 - 1840

It was the white trapper who introduced the Indian to goods of European manufacture, such as metal knives, tools, traps, fish hooks, cloth and glass beads.

It was the white trapper who introduced the Indian to guns and whisky.

It was the white trapper who introduced society to a new category of people - the half-breed.

So, that's the way it was between the white trapper and the Indian. Some got along and some didn't, but their association made a profound impact on the Indian way of life. When the tribes gathered now on Camas Prairie for the harvest, the bulbs might be dug with metal tools, "cuss words" might be heard, and the sound of gun shots might disturb the horses, women and children, and disrupt the once-peaceful gathering.

So might the drunken Indians.

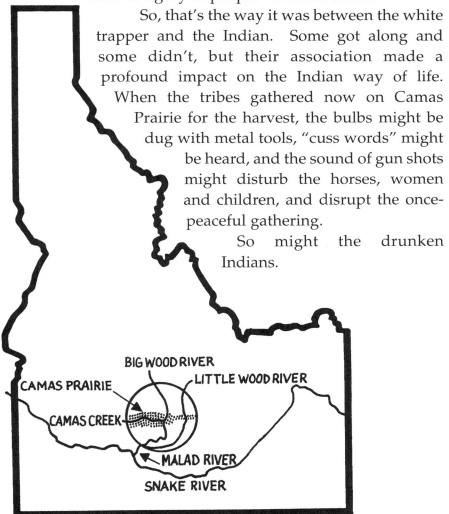

© Cindy Crow Bitzenburg

1800 - 1840
CAMAS PRAIRIE – "DISCOVERED"

In the early 1800's beaver hats were all the rage for fashionable gentlemen around the world. The tall, elegant hats were much in demand - prices soared - and the race for furs was on!

Large fur companies began to send out expeditions of trappers in search of beaver, and trading with the Indians became lively, indeed. Beaver were slaughtered by the hundreds-of-thousands.

In 1810, John Jacob Astor of New York, set up a fur company and financed an expedition to explore the Snake River region for new beaver sources - except - it was not known as the "Snake River" until his men, headed by Wilson Price Hunt, met up with some local Indians. One of the Hunt party was trying to find out the name of the tribe, and the Indian made a serpentine movement with his forefinger, indicating they were "weaver people." However, as fate would have it, the Frenchman, mis-read the sign, and took it to mean "snake", so called them the Snake Indians, named the river after them, and wrote it on his map. "Les Serpentes."

One of the men in that first Hunt party was Donald MacKenzie, a big, powerful Scotsman, known for his ability to walk far and fast, shoot straight, and manage all sorts of men, both red and white. He was a huge, grizzly-bear of a man, six-feet-four weighing about 320 pounds. He had a wild shock of red hair you could spot a mile away. He seemed to be always bursting with energy, and his men nicknamed him "perpetual motion." He was intelligent, had the insatiable curiosity of an explorer, and the courage to venture anywhere. He rode a big horse.

In 1818 MacKenzie headed up his own expedition which was also financed by Astor. It included 55 trappers, 195 horses and 300 beaver traps. He left Oregon moving east along the

1800 - 1840

Snake River clear up to the headwaters. The trip took two years, and when he was ready to return to Oregon, he decided not to retrace his route along the Snake River, but to follow an uncharted trail that led north then west.

It turned out to be one of the old Indian trails leading to Camas Prairie!

So - it was Donald MacKenzie, a Scotch trapper with a burr in his speech and one under his saddle, who DISCOVERED CAMAS PRAIRIE IN 1820!

Never mind that people had been living there for thousands of years. Never mind that hundreds of Indians came each year to harvest the camas and trade and dance and vacation. Donald MacKenzie "discovered Camas Prairie." The history books all say so. Why? Because he drew a map of his trail, and the rivers and mountains. It pays to write things down.

Four years later, another party of 140 trappers led by Alexander Ross were trapping the Lemhi and Salmon Rivers southward, and they, too, ended up inside the Magic Circle. Some say it was Ross who named the river "Malade", or "Malad." Early maps show that both the Big Wood River and Camas Creek were at one time called Malade, and for good reason - a party of early French trappers had become violently ill while camped on a river somewhere in Southern Idaho. They decided that the fresh beaver they had eaten had, itself, been eating some kind of poisonous root. They named the river "River Aux Malades", which in French, means "River of Sickness." They wrote the name on their maps as a warning, and after that, several other maps of Southern Idaho showed up with the same warning name.

A reed, called water hemlock, a member of the parsley family, grows in the moist ground in many places in Idaho, so the sickness hit more than one trapping expedition. Consequently, several rivers ended up with that same name.

1800 - 1840

The records show that in 1832 another Scotsman named John Work and his party, camped on "the North Branch of the Sickley River" (Big Wood) where it joins what we now call Camas Creek.

And again, in August of 1834, Nathaniel Wyeth and others, when they finished building the trading post at Fort Hall, came up to Camas Prairie where they camped on a branch of the Malad, and feasted on camas.

Old maps call the rivers "Big Woody", "Little Woody", and Little Wood was once called "McCormick Creek." Never did find out who McCormick was. Probably some trapper who drew his own map and named it after himself.

All of this information about what the rivers were once called is obsolete, because now they are clearly identified as the "Big Wood River", the "Little Wood River", and when they meet each other they become the "Malad." The name just seemed to slip on downstream until it caught at the junction. It is often referred to as the shortest river in the world - has been recorded at 2.5 miles long, and drops into a deep, deep gorge - 250 feet or more in spots. The Malad is a mean, mad river.

So, according to the records, there were at least three trapping expeditions inside the Magic Circle before 1840, plus Wyeth and his group. We may never know for sure how many individual trappers were there, but we do know thousands and thousands of "Indians" were...

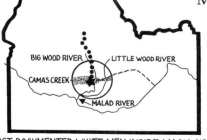

FIRST DOCUMENTED WHITE MEN INSIDE MAGIC CIRCLE
- - - - - - ROUTE OF DONALD MacKENZIE IN 1820
• • • • • • • ROUTE OF ALEXANDER ROSS IN 1824
★ ⌈ CAMP OF JOHN WORK IN 1832
  ⌊ CAMP OF NATHANIEL WYETH IN 1834

© Cindy Crow Bitzenburg

1800 - 1840

RENDEZVOUS

There were trappers, and there were traders. The early traders sometimes set up "trading posts" where they could collect furs on a day-to-day basis in exchange for supplies or doo-dads. Indians and trappers both did business at the trading posts with their "hairy bank notes", which is what they called the pelts.

But it was the big fur companies, with the help of men like Donald MacKenzie, who pioneered the "Rendezvous."

"Rendezvous" is a French word meaning "a place appointed for a meeting." They would set a time and place, and advertise it a year in advance. The company would bring in tons of supplies for the event, and hundreds of trappers, traders, and Indians would come from far and near to trade their furs for powder, lead, knives, traps, blankets, fish hooks, salt and other necessities for the coming year. Entire Indian tribes would arrive in full tribal costume, with colors flying, to present impressive displays of horsemanship and pageantry.

Trappers often got Indian wives at Rendezvous. It was unquestionably the BIG EVENT of the year! A magnificent gala for those solitary souls, many of whom had seen few humans in the past year. It went on night and day. There were races - (horse and foot) - shooting contests, singing, dancing, fighting, and drinking, drinking, until there was no more.....

The fur company stores were always well supplied with plenty of whisky, which was usually shipped in as raw alcohol, and then "improved" with lacings of chewing tobacco, red pepper, molasses, and river water. More water was added as the revelers got drunker, and the final product was mostly flavored water, but by that time no drinker was sober enough to notice.

After nine or ten days of feverish trading, gambling, fighting, and drinking, the badly hung-over Indians and

1800 - 1840

trappers drifted back to the wilds to spend another year trapping.

The fur companies took off with the loot.

The last Rendezvous was in 1839.

Few of the white folks who came later ever heard of, or cared, about the names of those extraordinary men, the trappers, who opened the way for them. Their simple maps showed rivers and trails, and they were the first whites to meet the Indians. They changed the course of the Indian culture by introducing European goods, and started the sad, in-between off-spring who were outcasts never really accepted by Indian or white - the half-breed.

The risk of life in the hey-dey of the fur trapper was so great that two-fifths of all trappers were killed in one decade - either by accident - or by Indian.

By 1840, when the demand for furs vanished - so did the trappers.

1800 - 1840

THE MISSIONARIES

The Rendezvous was an annual event in 1836 when the New England Presbyterian Church Elders decided it was time for their missionaries to "go into the western wilderness and "Christianize the savages." The church agreed to provide supplies and transportation, and two young, newly-wedded couples accepted the assignment - Dr. Marcus Whitman and Narcissa, and the Rev. Henry Spaulding and Eliza. Dr. Whitman, a medical doctor who wanted to be a minister, had made the trip overland to Oregon the year before, and was convinced they could make it with wagons.

Up to this time, no one had ever crossed the continent in a wagon. The biggest obstacle was the Continental Divide.

The little group started out with three wagons, eight mules, twelve horses, and sixteen cows. In the wagons were farming utensils, blacksmith and carpenter tools, seeds, clothing, and other necessities to help them to become self-supporting, and to establish a mission.

When they reached the Great Plains, they joined a pack-line of fur company representatives headed for rendezvous in Wyoming. Actually, the fur company men were not too happy about having them, but agreed to let them trail along behind, warning that they must "keep up." There was safety in numbers, and the missionaries needed all the safety they could get, so they trailed along in the dust. It was an extremely difficult trip, especially for the dedicated, gently-bred young women. Most of the way they rode side-saddle, which was the only way a "respectable" woman would ride in those days. Occasionally, they did get to ride in a wagon, but only when things were really rough for them.

The Rendezvous was the end-of-the-line for the fur company men, so the missionaries had to find another group bound for Oregon. They did, but those men in charge insisted

1800 - 1840

that the wagons be abandoned because it would be impossible to get them over the Continental Divide. Finally, in desperation, Dr. Whitman agreed to leave all but one - the smallest wagon - and swore he would take full responsibility for it, he argued that it was important "for the ladies", and at last they agreed.

Those two women, Narcissa Whitman and Eliza Spaulding, were the first white women to cross the Divide.

The little wagon was in bad shape after the long trip over the Plains, and soon began to disintegrate rapidly. The determined Dr. Whitman somehow managed to salvage the box and two wheels and made a kind of two-wheeled cart. They actually got it as far as Fort Boise, where it just fell apart.

Even though Dr. Whitman failed to prove that wagons could cross the continent, he did prove they could make it over the Continental Divide, which had been the greatest obstacle, both physically and psychologically. He was certain others would follow.

The Whitmans went on into what is now the State of Oregon to set up their mission among the Cayuse Indians, and the Spauldings went to the Nez Perce in what is now Idaho.

The Spauldings were responsible for an incredible number of "firsts" in Idaho: they founded the first mission, and began to teach God, the Bible and agriculture to the Indians; they planted the first garden and turned the water from Lapwai Creek to water it - the first

© Cindy Crow Bitzenburg

✝ ELIZA SPAULDING WAS THE FIRST WHITE WOMAN IN IDAHO

1800 - 1840

irrigation ever, in Idaho. Mrs. Spauding was the first white woman to settle in Idaho and gave birth to the first white child born here - a girl, named Eliza. Mrs. Spaulding was part of the group to bring the first wagon over the Divide, and was part of the reason for bringing it. The Spauldings planted the first apple tree in Idaho, and brought in the first printing press.

It was, in fact, the first printing press on the entire Northwest coast. Mrs. Spaulding was trying to teach her Indian charges to read, and managed to convince the elders of her church, back in New England, that she must have a printing press to print religious tracts for the Indians. It arrived from Honolulu in 1839.

So, Idaho had a printing press twenty-one years before the first permanent white settlement was established!

****

In 1843 - seven years after the missionaries hauled that rickety wagon-cart over the mountains - nine hundred people left Independence, Missouri by wagon train, headed for the fertile fields of Oregon.

The "Oregon Trail" was open.

Eliza Spaulding's Printing Press, the first in the Northwest. 1839

1840 - 1860
THE NORTHWEST ORDINANCE

When our Founding Fathers set up the American government, there was a vast, unexplored wilderness between those Easterners and the Pacific Ocean, which they knew would someday be part of them. In order to be certain it would be governed according to their laws, they established the Northwest Ordinance in 1787. It was an orderly, step-by-step system for taking new lands under their wing, with a guarantee of gradual self-government.

The plan was based on population - adult white male population. Nobody else counted - not women, children, or any other "foreigners." If you were white and male, you counted.

First: When there was a goodly number of adultwhitemales in an area, it could become a "territory." The American government would outline the borders, appoint a governor, secretary, and three judges to administer it, and a Federal Marshal to keep the peace.

Second: When the adultwhitemale population reached 5,000, they could elect their own legislature, which would then share power with a "council" selected by the Feds. They would also be permitted to send a delegate back to Congress who would have the privilege of speaking before that body - but could not vote.

Third: When the adultwhitemale population reached 60,000, the territory could frame its own constitution, and ask Congress for admission to the Union as a full-fledged "State."

The Northwest Ordinance was a nice piece of work.

In 1846, when the United States and England decided to split the Oregon Country, the United States got everything south of the 49th parallel (the Canadian border). There were 5,000 or more adultwhitemales already in the area, having come in either by ship, around Cape Horn, or over the Oregon Trail, and two years later it became "Oregon Territory."

1840 - 1860

Idaho was no longer called "Oregon Country", it was now "Oregon Territory."

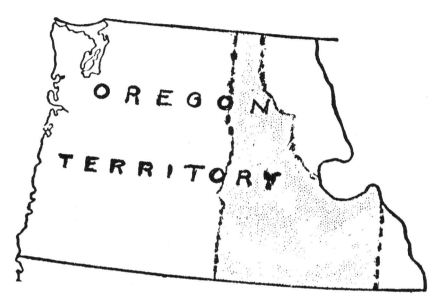

Idaho as part of Oregon Territory, 1848 to 1853.

1840 - 1860
THE OREGON TRAIL

The Oregon Trail was nothing more than a series of trails which had been used by the Indians for hundreds of years. When the trappers, traders and explorers showed up, they followed the Indian trails already there, and so did the missionaries. When the wagon trains started in 1843, the Oregon Trail remained virtually the same, but more and more traffic made it deeper and wider and messier.

The Oregon Trail brought America to Oregon, and Oregon to America. But even though Idaho was part of the Oregon Territory when the covered wagons first started to roll, nobody stopped in Idaho. They hustled right on through the barren Snake River Valley as quickly as possible to get to the rich farm land in the Willamette Valley.

Idaho served only as a "bridge country" for the great migration.

In 1840, Southern Idaho was still a place where the buffalo roamed, and so did the Indians.

THE OREGON TRAIL THROUGH IDAHO
© Cindy Crow Bitzenburg

The bottom had dropped out of the fur market when the fancy gentlemen around the world turned to silk top-hats instead of beaver. The trappers had wasted and plundered the animals for furs, and then drifted away like ghosts. The Spauldings were

1840 - 1860

quietly missionary-ing up in Nez Perce country, there were still two old fur trading posts - (Fort Hall and Fort Boise) - and that was about it, in 1840.

But not for long.

Those who had reached the Oregon Coast first by sailing around the Horn, were happily building and farming, and interest in the area was definitely picking up. Writers and promoters were sending back glowing reports about how wonderful Oregon was, and for everybody to come on out "where the soil is fifty feet deep, and soft as a woman."

* * * * * * *

The two old trading posts became Idaho's first "rest stops", but the travelers stayed only long enough to regroup, freshen up, repair the wagons, and pick up a few supplies. Even though those places were called "forts", they were really just settlements made by white men who followed the fur business. They had been built for safety and protection, and served as a meeting place to do business. There was plenty of grass, game, fuel and water – a welcome sight indeed, for the weary wagon train folks.

At first, there were only a few wagons struggling over the route taken by the Whitmans and Spauldings. Then, more and more until a great wave of humanity swept through Southern Idaho. White-topped wagons, heavily laden, drawn by weary oxen, mules and horses, creaked and groaned through blinding clouds of dust, leaving an unbelievable amount of litter in their wake - broken wheels, tools and furniture, dead animals, goods that had to be discarded when a wagon fell to pieces and there was no way to carry it further. Ashes and messes from hundreds of camps and fires were spread over the trail - and many human graves marked the passage of the wagons.

1840 - 1860

The Indians became more and more perplexed and angry at these travelers who were fouling the land so terribly, tearing up their pastures with the big, ugly wagon wheels and killing the wildlife. The heavy traffic interfered with their annual migration in search of food, and when the Indians met the travelers face-to-face, the fighting was vicious and many atrocities ensued. The Indians fought desperately to drive them away and stop the desecration of the land, but as many Indians were killed as whites - and the wagons continued to roll.

And it was certainly not an easy time for the courageous, determined people in the wagon trains. Daily, they faced unbelievable hazards on the trail - wagon breakdowns, rattlesnakes, accidents and broken bones, exposure and disease. Small-pox, cholera, mountain fever, measles, and dysentery were common. One cholera epidemic killed thousands even before they reached the Rocky Mountains. The Indian attacks, plus the natural hazards of drought, hunger, blizzards, floods, heat, all took their toll. It is estimated that approximately 34,000 people died on the Oregon Trail.

It was 2,000 miles from Independence, Missouri to the Columbia River on the Oregon Trail.

The Oregon Trail people named our highest Southern Idaho mountain range. As they moved along from east to west, they could see the jagged, snow-covered peaks to the north, and to those hard-working folks who were users of tools, the mountains looked like a giant-sized saw lying on its back. The "Sawtooth Mountains" became theirs - when they named them.

The Oregon Trail through Idaho covered a distance of approximately 415 miles, most of which was flat, barren, sage brush desert. No wonder they hurried through. . .

MEASLES

The year 1847 was a nightmare for the missionaries and the Indians. It all started at Dr. Whitman's mission when about sixty Oregon Trailers asked to spend the winter there. The Whitmans agreed, and the people began to settle in. However, as luck would have it, some of them were sick with measles, and before anyone realized what was happening, a full-blown measles epidemic had spread like wildfire through the Indian tribes. Measles and small-pox were white man's diseases unknown to the indians, and they were extremely vulnerable. Furthermore, the Indian remedy for a high fever was to lower it in a cold water bath, but when they did this in the case of measles - they died! Dr. Whitman tried desperately to help them with proper treatment, but they would not listen. They were sick and angry and frightened, and began accusing the good missionaries of purposely bringing the diseased emigrants in to take their land and poison them.

They turned on Dr. Whitman and Narcissa, and murdered them both, along with eleven of the people staying at the mission. The others ran for their lives, hiding in the brush, but two sick little girls were left uncared for in an upstairs bedroom of the house, and they, too, perished.

The Indians were of the Cayuse tribe that had befriended the Whitmans when they first set up the mission.

After demolishing the Whitman mission, they stormed up to Lapwai after the Spauldings. They took as prisoners Mrs. Spaulding, her children, and several others, and for some unknown reason did not kill them, but left them with some Nez Perce several miles away at a small camp. When the Rev. Spaulding, who had been away on business, was returning, he got word of the Whitman massacre, rushed home to his own mission, and was led to his family by the friendly Nez Perce. He gathered them up and fled - never to return.

1840 - 1860

Both missions were completely destroyed.

The dreaded measles continued to spread from tribe to tribe and hundreds of Indians died. Their hatred and suspicion of all white people increased, and they retaliated in the only way known to them - they fought. Grisly massacres of lone wagon trains - many white men killed, and women and children captured and tortured.

All throughout Southern Idaho Indians were on the warpath. A small group of Mormons had moved up into the Lemhi Valley to farm, and were irrigating their crops from Pattee Creek. Brigham Young himself had paid them a visit, but three years after they arrived the Bannocks attacked the settlement, killed two of them, and drove the rest back to Utah.

By the 1850's, Idaho had pretty much been given back to the Indians. . .

1840 - 1860

THE STATE OF OREGON

Meanwhile, over in the Willamette Valley of Oregon Territory, things were going along pretty well, people were settling and farming when out of the blue, the cry of GOLD! was heard out of California, and half the population seemed to rise up and take off for the gold fields!

To counteract the exodus, the U.S. Congress stepped in and passed the "Donation Land Act of 1850", offering large tracts of land free, to settlers in the Oregon Territory. Then, for the next few years, they had a struggle trying to decide where the borders should be, and in 1853, decided to put Northern Idaho and Washington into "Washington Territory", and the Southern part of Idaho would remain in "Oregon Territory."

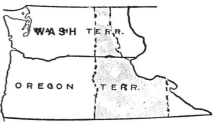

By 1859 there were enough adultwhitemales settling down to qualify the area for Statehood, and Oregon became a State. They sliced out that portion, and named everything that remained "Washington Territory."

So - then all of Idaho became "Washington Territory."

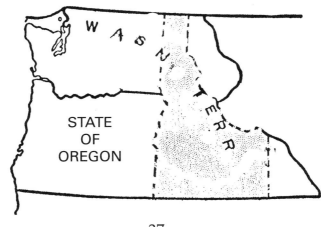

1860 - 1870
THE GOODALE CUT-OFF

In 1862 a wagonmaster named Timothy Goodale was leading a large wagon train to Oregon. While the train was resting at Fort Hall, Goodale sent his scouts out to explore an old Indian trail he'd heard about. The scouts reported the trail to be passable, and Goodale turned his wagon train north and west out of Fort Hall, instead of taking the Oregon Trail along the Snake River.

That trail was the same one taken by Donald MacKenzie forty-two years before - and it led directly to Camas Prairie!

Can you imagine what a lovely surprise it was for those weary travelers to come upon such a magnificent place? Nearly half-a-million acres of flat, splendid land, fifty miles long and fifteen miles wide; the best of water, plenty of excellent grass, timber stands nearby, an abundance of fish, and abounding with game of all kinds. Compared to the Snake River desert, it was heaven!

But - it was also "Indian Country" and nobody was brave enough to settle down and stay.

When it was time to move on, they descended into the valley on the west to rejoin the original Oregon Trail.

It didn't take long for the "Goodale Cut-Off" to become a popular route. The people in the wagon trains loved Camas Prairie and called it their "Blue Valley." One of the many who crossed the prairie even wrote a lovely, soft, sweet song about "Blue Valley." . .

The Indian attacks on wagon trains continued, and finally, the people petitioned the United States Government for military protection. The Cavalry moved into Forts Hall and Boise, and the soldiers began to use the "Goodale Cut-Off" when they traveled from Oregon to Fort Hall to escort the wagons back over the Oregon Trail.

1860 - 1870

In 1865, a company of 250 soldiers under the command of Captain Ephriam Palmer set up camp on Soldier Creek (named after them). The camp itself was named "Camp Wallace" after the territory's first governor. They stayed from early June to September, 1865, to protect the wagon trains on the Goodale Cut-Off from the Indians. There was one woman in that camp - the wife of Captain Palmer. She was afraid to stay at Fort Boise without her husband, so mounted her pony and went along with the troops to spend the summer on Camas Prairie.

The Goodale Cut-Off was the first real "highway" through the Magic Circle, and coincides surprisingly with the present Highway 26.

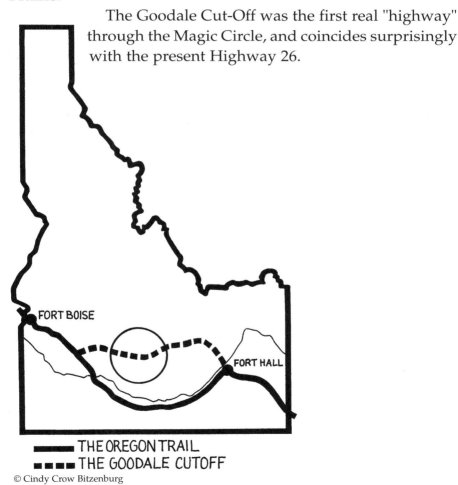

▬▬ THE OREGON TRAIL
■ ■ ■ ■ THE GOODALE CUTOFF

© Cindy Crow Bitzenburg

1860 - 1870

GOLD!

While it was land that attracted white settlement to Oregon, it was GOLD! that attracted white settlement to Idaho.

In 1860 gold was discovered up in the Clearwater country, and the city of Lewiston was quickly established as a supply center for the mines. Prospectors flooded in - and then filtered out into the surrounding areas to stake claims and get rich! Within two years, some of them were busily panning away in the Boise Basin.

Gold Fever could hit anybody. There was no such thing as a "typical" prospector. Sailors deserted their ships, farmers deserted their fields, clerks deserted their desks. There were young adventurers, immigrants from the old country, lawyers, doctors, preachers, teachers, and creatures.

The victim of Gold Fever was usually "street wise" because he traveled a good deal and mingled with a considerable cross-section of society. He frequently suffered from malnutrition because there was always more whiskey available than food, and he did his own cooking. A big spender, he would blow his hard-earned gold dust on booze at the local saloon and/or "wicked city women", if available.

It didn't cost much to go into prospecting - all he needed was a shallow-sided pan to scoop up gravel from a stream, swish it around, and the heavy gold particles would sink to the bottom. When he found gold, he would stake a claim and maybe build a sluice box to make the operation more efficient. The sluice box, rocker and Long Tom were all used. Each was a long wooden box with ridges on the bottom. River gravel and sand were shoveled into the box, flushed with a steady flow of water, and the heavy gold would collect behind the ridges in the bottom. It usually took two men working together to operate a sluice, and this method could produce anywhere from $10 to $100 a day - hopefully.

1860 - 1870

This was called "placer mining" and considered easy pickin's. Sometimes a prospector would find a "nugget", a piece of pure gold - could be the size of a seed or an egg - and when this happened, everybody yelped and yelled and yahooed around, and if more than one was found, it could set off a full-fledged gold rush! Finding a nugget meant that the Mother Lode was not far away because a nugget was part of a "vein of pure gold" that had broken loose.

So, at the first cry of GOLD! in Idaho, prospectors appeared out of nowhere, and stories of gold were traded and nourished. They carried what supplies they could, and in some cases were on foot, so didn't have much. A few had a horse or burro, but even at that could not carry much food. They lived in any kind of rough shelter to keep warm and dry - tent, cave, or under a bush. But, when one of them hit a strike that turned out to have promise, they were quickly joined by more prospectors and the place would turn into a mining camp. Then came the "camp followers" - saloon keepers, shop keepers, livery stables, merchants, pack train outfits, builders, robbers, gamblers, and ladies of the evening. They were all there for the gold, and fortunes could be made quickly - and lost. Some mining camps grew into towns, but others were abandoned as soon as the gold was gone.

Most of the gold ended up with the camp followers.

Every single item had to be packed into the camp on the backs of horses and mules - at first. Even when freightlines began to operate, the cost was exorbitant. Some of the supplies were actually worth more than their weight in gold - flour, for example, could cost between $25 and $150 for a 100-lb. sack, depending upon the cost to get it to camp. The prospector's main food supply was flour, bacon, beans, lard and salt. All easy to carry, and would not spoil. They rarely killed wild game because they were too busy working for gold.

1860 - 1870

Consequently, they were often sick with scurvy and other diseases brought on by such meagre diets.

Life in a mining camp was an adventure in itself. At any moment, a prospector might explode into the saloon bellowing GOLD! GOLD!. He got everyone's attention and they would all celebrate. On the other hand, most of those already in the saloon were drowning their sorrows because they hadn't had a strike. The saloon was the social center of the camp, and it was open day and night. Yes, there was always a saloon - it was the first business to be set up. Sometimes it was only a barrel of whisky with a community cup. Sometimes just a board across a couple sawhorses. Later, a tent, and if it looked like the camp might become a town, the first real building was the saloon. It was the miners' home. They needed a place to gather, get drunk, tell lies, fight, gamble, and mingle. It was the heart of every mining camp.

The saloon business was more profitable than the prospecting business - even the bartender had a scam. Remember the old-time bartender we often see in yellowed photographs? Handle-bar moustache, greasy, slicked-back hair parted in the middle, sleeve garters, bow-tie, wrap-around apron? Well, that greasy hair-do was a real money maker. The prospector usually paid for his whisky with gold dust carried in a small leather pouch on his belt, and it was the bartender who carefully measured out and weighed the dust pinch-by-pinch. After each careful pinch, or so, he would casually stroke his hair with the pinching hand, and deposit any clinging gold dust in the hair grease. Later, all he had to do was wash his hair and pan his own gold. That was only one of the fancy tricks he had up his gartered sleeve, and he was hardly ever caught!

Might mention that saloons and whisky were not unique to the prospectors. Wherever people migrated in those days, the saloons went with them. Whisky was often carried by the Oregon Trail folks "for medicinal purposes" like rattlesnake bites, rashes, etc. and many enterprising merchants loaded their wagons with whisky and set up improvised barrel saloons along the way - and business was good! When military expeditions met the emigrant trains, a bar would evolve as if by magic, and there were many other occasions that called for a nip or two.

When the prospectors rushed into the Boise Basin, the camp followers were not far behind. First, pack trains bringing in supplies, followed by freight wagons, and soon a town was shaping up. The supplies had to be brought down the Columbia River by boat, deposited at Lewiston, and packed from there to the miners. It was awfully expensive.

And the law? Where was the law? At that time, remember, Idaho was still Washington Territory, and the seat of government was far, far away, so it was up to the miners to make their own laws. The first miners to arrive promptly drew up a set of rules and everybody who came later was bound to follow them, or be tossed out - or worse. They elected a Miners' Judge who would hear the case and make a decision (some of the cases were even argued by lawyers who were often to be found in camp). If a petitioner felt the judge rendered an unfair verdict, he could call for a trial by jury - provided he was willing to pay the jury enough to make up for the lost time at their claims. If the jury verdict was still unacceptable, he would take his complaint to the Miners' Meeting, and that was the last stop.

Pioneer mining was wasteful and inefficient, and many prospectors picked up the easy loot and left for greener pastures. But, some liked the country and turned to farming to supply the needs of other miners and the community, and many of the camp followers stayed on and did the same.

In 1860, when gold was first discovered in Idaho, there were very few people around. In the southeast corner on the boundary line between Idaho and Utah, thirteen Mormon

1860 - 1870

families were living in wagon boxes. They thought they were in Utah, but they weren't, and that little settlement was the first permanent settlement in Idaho - they called it "Franklin."

To the north, on the Coeur d'Alene River there were a few Catholic priests - but other than that, there were only six or eight other whites. Maybe.

So, it was gold that brought enough adultwhitemales into the area to meet the requirements to become a territory.

Back east the Civil War was starting, (1861 - 1865) and the United States Union Army needed all the gold it could get.

On March 3, 1863, President Abraham Lincoln signed the "Organic Act" - part of the Northwest Ordinance - which cut off a piece of Washington Territory on the west, added what later became Montana and Wyoming, and named it "Idaho Territory."

IDAHO TERRITORY FROM MARCH, 1863 TO MAY, 1864

© Cindy Crow Bitzenburg

1860 - 1870

IDAHO?

There are tales and legends, misquotes and downright lies about the origin of the name "Idaho", and even to this day it is shrouded in mystery. Here are a few facts and fancies about the name, and you are free to accept whichever one makes sense to you:

The word "Idaho" is an Arapahoe Indian word meaning "sweet water." The Arapahoe had been inhabiting the area around Pike's Peak in Colorado for centuries, and referred to a certain spring by that name. When gold was discovered in that area in 1858, prospectors flooded in and picked up the name "Idaho" from the Arapahoe. Soon, the Pike's Peak gold rush brought in enough adultwhitemales to qualify for a territory, and the first step was to elect a delegate to send to Congress to get the territory started. The delegate turned out to be a slick St. Louis physician named Dr. George Willing who was traveling around the gold fields at that time. There was some question as to whether he had really even been elected "delegate", but he went to Washington D.C. nevertheless.

Sometime later, in December of 1875, the following letter, written by a friend of Dr. Willing, a Mr. William O. Stoddard, was published in the New York Daily Tribune, telling about an event that had happened back in 1859:

"My eccentric Friend, the late Dr. George M. Willing, was the first delegate to Congress from the young mining community in the Pike's Peak region, when the subject of the organization of a new territory was under debate on the floor of the House of Representatives in Washington. Various names had been proposed without any seeming approach to agreement, and the Doctor, whose familiarity with the Indian dialects was pretty well known, was appealed to by some of his legislative friends for a

1860 - 1870

> *suggestion. One of them said "something round and smooth, now, with the right sort of meaning to it." Now it happened that the little daughter of one of these gentlemen was on the floor that morning with her father, and the Doctor, who was fond of children, had just been calling her to him with "Ida, ho - come see me." Nothing could be better, and the veteran explorer promptly responded with the name "Idaho."*
>
> *"But, what does it mean?"*
>
> *"Gem of the Mountains", replied the quick-witted Doctor with a glance at the fresh face beside him, and the interpretation, like the name, has 'stuck' to this day. Dr. Willing told me about it at the time, or soon afterward, and with the most gleeful appreciate of the humor of the thing, and I have often heard him repeat the story."*

So, according to Mr. William O. Stoddard, it was Dr. Willing who introduced the word "Idaho" to Congress in 1859 and threw in his own interpretation "Gem of the Mountains." Dr. Willing was a crafty, intelligent, witty man, and the little "Ida" incident probably popped the name Idaho into his head because he was certainly familiar with the name used in the Pike's Peak area. I think he was delighted with his own cleverness and promoted the name from then on. At least, no other definite explanation or claim has been made for the sudden appearance of the name "Idaho" before a Congressional Committee.

The following year, a Colorado Senator proposed the name "Idaho" for the territory that instead became "Colorado." <u>He</u> said that Idaho meant Gem of the Mountains. (Had he been one of those the year before who had heard the smart-alecky Dr. Willing's story about little Ida?) Others disagreed with the Senator saying "Idaho" wasn't even an Indian word, and they finally ended up with "Colorado." But even though the name

1860 - 1870

"Idaho" was not used at that time, it had been noised around enough to become familiar to Congress, and that it meant "Gem of the Mountains."

* * * * * * *

Of course, the name had always been a familiar one around Colorado. About 1860 there was an "Idaho Restaurant" at the corner of Lawrence and F. Streets in Denver, and there was "Idaho Hall" in Nevada City, Colorado, which was described as "one of the handsomest buildings in the region." And, there were the "Idaho" springs identified by the Arapahoe, and also an "Idaho City" in Colorado.

* * * * * * *

Meanwhile, out in the West, the Washington Territorial Legislature (which included the present State of Idaho) created "Idaho County", and when gold was discovered in the Clearwater and Salmon River Country they just naturally became known as the "Idaho Mines." On top of that, a steamboat river captain named J.S. Ruckles christened his boat "Idaho" because he was delivering supplies on the Columbia River to the Idaho Mines.

By this time, everybody just took it for granted that "Idaho" meant "Gem of the Mountains." Thanks to Dr. Willing.

* * * * * * *

Moving right along to when Congress was considering a name for our new Territory, the U.S. House of Representatives decided to call it "Montana", but the Senate amended the bill by striking out "Montana" and inserting "Idaho." A Senator from Massachusetts convinced them that "Montana" didn't mean

1860 - 1870

anything, but that "Idaho" meant "Gem of the Mountains", and since the new Territory was in mountainous country, the name "Idaho" would be well understood.

* * * * * * *

But, that's not all - the following letter was written by W.W. Wallace, son of the first Governor of Idaho Territory, William H. Wallace. The letter is dated February 12, 1902:

> *"I wish to make the following statement which may be of some historical value. When the bill was being prepared for the organization of the territory (Idaho), a committee of three from the Pacific Coast met at my father's rooms in this city, and among other things considered was the name the territory should bear. My mother was present during this conversation. The names 'Lafayette', 'Montana', and 'Idaho' were mentioned. My mother immediately became interested in the proceedings and said, 'I hope you will conclude to name it "Idaho."*
>
> *'One of the committee, a Dr. Henry, spoke up and said ' "Idaho" it shall be!'*
>
> *'I will give you the reason why mother selected Idaho as the name of the territory. The year before, in the summer of 1862, my mother was visiting in Iowa and met a sister of hers whose home was in Colorado, near Pike's Peak. She had a little daughter about one year old with her, whose name was Idaho Jackson. Mother thought that there never was just quite as sweet and pretty a little creature in all the world and was talking about her all the time, to the amusement of father and myself. So that when the names above mentioned were being canvassed, you can readily understand why Mother selected "Idaho." The name, an Indian one signifying "Gem of the*

1860 - 1870

Mountains" was always used by mother in singing her little niece's praises.

signed: W.W. Wallace

It is interesting to note that Mrs. Wallace's niece lived in Colorado where there was a stream, near Pike's Peak, which the Indians called "Idaho." It is also interesting that Mrs. Wallace accepted the fact that it meant "Gem of the Mountains" which was the meaning generally accepted by Congressmen.

* * * * * * *

But, there is still another version of the origin of the name, not connected to any of the above. Some say "Idaho" is a Shoshoni word, based on a story about several miners who were awakened one morning by nearby Indians calling out "E-da-how!" and pointing to the rising sun just coming over the mountain. The miners decided their words must mean something like "The Rising Sun!", or an exclamation like, "Behold, the sun coming down the mountain." This story was told again and again and many became convinced that "Ed-dah-how" somehow turned into "Idaho."

* * * * * * *

Whatever. The first "Idaho Territory" was bigger than Texas. It took in all of Idaho, Montana and Wyoming, and covered 325,000 square miles!

It would be a monster to rule - particularly when the capital, which was established in Lewiston on the far western edge of the territory, was completely cut off from the mining camps on the other side of the Bitterroot Range, and miles and mountains away from the Boise Basin.

1860 - 1870
THE POLITICIANS

President Lincoln appointed William H. Wallace to be the first governor of the new Idaho Territory. Wallace came out and established the capital at Lewiston. He said it was the only "real town" in Idaho, even though there were more adultwhitemales in the Boise Basin at that time.

The first things that needed to be done were to take the census, and lay out districts within the territory so that representatives could be elected to serve with the "council" appointed by the President.

When that First Idaho Territorial Legislature met in 1863, their first act was to raise their own salaries! True! Absolutely!

The Act of Congress that organized the Territory set the salaries as follows: Governor, Chief Justice and two Associate Justices of the Court - $2,500 each, per year. Territorial Secretary, $2,000 per year. Members of the Legislature and Chief Clerks - $4 per day, plus 20 cents per mile each way for members traveling. Assistant Clerk and Attaches - $3 per day.

The assessable property in the Territory was less than three million dollars, but those rascals claimed they needed more money, so they passed an act taking an appropriation out of the Territorial Treasury to pay themselves certain amounts <u>in addition</u> to those paid by the United States.

The <u>additions</u> were as follows: Governor and Justices - $2,500 each per year. Territorial Secretary - $1,500 per year. The per diem compensation of the members and Attaches of the Legislative Assembly - $6 per day, and to each Chief Clerk - $6 per day. To each Assistant, Engrossing and Enrolling Clerk - $5 per day, and to the Chaplains of each branch of the legislative assembly - $3 per day. To each Sergeant-at-arms and Doorkeeper - $4 per day, and to each Page - $3 per day.

That first humble, honest, dedicated group of Idaho politicians also seemed to be religiously inclined, for they

1860 - 1870

passed an act which stated, "No person shall keep open any play house or theatre, race ground, cock-pit, or play at any game of chance or engage in any noisy amusement on the first day of the week, commonly called the "Lord's Day." Punishment: Not less than $30, nor more than $200.

And, they passed another Purity Act to "Prohibit marriages and cohabitation of whites with Indians, Chinese, and persons of African descent. Punishment: One year in the Territorial Prison."

That first all-adultwhitemale Territorial Legislature was determined to keep Idahoans virtuous, pure, and lily white, by golly!

They established the Boise Barracks, and soon after, the townsite of Boise was laid out under the direction of Cyrus Jacobs who believed that the Boise Valley would become "the storehouse and kitchen garden" for the Boise Basin and the Owyhee mines.

The first Territorial Legislature was required to establish counties and they did - the first was Owyhee, the second, Oneida. Then, they turned their attention to the land east of the Rocky Mountains and set up ten counties: Missoula, Deer Lodge, Beaver Head, Madison, Jefferson, Choteau, Dawson, Big Horn, Ogalala and Yellowstone.

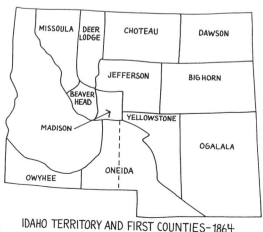

© Cindy Crow Bitzenburg   IDAHO TERRITORY AND FIRST COUNTIES—1864

1860 - 1870

The act creating these counties was approved on January 16, 1864, but, sixty days later, the United States Congress took all of them away from Idaho Territory and made Montana Territory out of them - plus a little more. It helped to solve the "large area" problem, but it also shaped another problem when the piece to Montana did not include the panhandle.

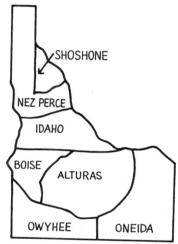

IDAHO TERRITORY AFTER MAY, 1864
© Cindy Crow Bitzenburg

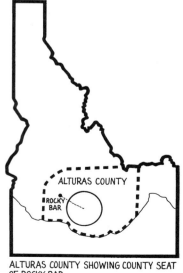

ALTURAS COUNTY SHOWING COUNTY SEAT
OF ROCKY BAR
© Cindy Crow Bitzenburg

1860 - 1870

So, the great Idaho Territory had shrunk considerably, and was left with only two counties - Owyhee and Oneida. The Legislature immediately set up Nez Perce, Shoshone, Idaho, Boise, and No. 7 - Alturas, with the Alturas County Seat at Esmeralda. However, the 2nd Legislature moved the County Seat of Alturas County to Rocky Bar.

Alturas County had one Councilman, and two Representatives.

Those first two sessions of the Idaho Territorial Legislature did a remarkable amount of work during the limited time they were in session. In fact, when printed, their works had the greatest number of pages on record of any lawmaking body at that time.

But then...they were also drawing double pay...

1860 - 1870
IDAHO TERRITORIAL GOVERNORS ETC.

It was not exactly easy for the President of the U.S. to entice anyone accustomed to living in the heavily populated, civilized, "settled" part of the United States to move out to a wild, raw, new Territory to be governor of a region so vast, it was beyond his comprehension. However, it was the President's job to make these appointments and he forged ahead.

1863 - President Abraham Lincoln appointed William H. Wallace to be the first governor of the new Idaho Territory. Wallace arrived, set up the capital at Lewiston, resigned as governor, got himself elected as Idaho's delegate to Congress, and on October 31, 1863 returned to Washington D.C. and William B. Daniels became "Acting Governor." Daniels couldn't get along with anybody in Lewiston. There was a big fight going on about moving the capital to Boise where there were more adultwhitemales, and Daniels was in the middle. He was not a happy man.

1864 - on February 26th, Lincoln appointed as governor, a strange person named Caleb Lyon of Lyonsdale, New York. He showed up in Lewiston on August 8th finally, and he couldn't get along with the Territorial Legislature either. The fight over moving the capital to Boise was getting hotter and hotter, and one fine morning Caleb announced that he was going duck hunting - and then just disappeared, never to be seen in Lewiston again!

So again, Idaho had an Acting Governor - Clinton DeWitt Smith. It took Smith eight months to get to Idaho. The Plains Indians cut off overland travel on his first attempt to get through, forcing him to go all the way back to the East Coast and take a boat down to Panama where he crossed the Isthmus on the Panama Railroad there. However, when this determined man finally arrived in Lewiston, he snatched the Territorial Seal

1860 - 1870

and Archives right out from under the guards' noses and hightailed it down to Boise City, which then became the official capital of Idaho Territory!

Governor Smith, and the capital, arrived in Boise on April 14, 1865 - the same day that President Lincoln was assassinated.

It should be mentioned that William H. Wallace, Idaho's first Governor, had been a close personal friend of President Lincoln's, and served as pallbearer at his funeral.

The rivalry between Lewiston and Boise continued, and after the Capital was officially seated in Boise, the denuded Lewistonians acidly dubbed Boise City "Bossey Sitty."

1866 - A fella named Horace Gilson absconded for Hong Kong with the Idaho Territorial treasury amounting to $41,062, which had been at his disposal as Secretary. Also that same year, Caleb Lyon of Lyonsdale was again appointed Governor! This time, Caleb didn't even announce that he was going duck hunting - he just up and left the country altogether - with $47,000! The entire fund of Indian money not yet disbursed to the tribes! Again - the Territory was without a governor.

Sometimes the appointees never arrived in Idaho at all. Sam Bard was appointed in February, 1869 but was busy running a radical newspaper in Atlanta, Georgia and never even left Atlanta!

Gilman Marston was appointed Governor of Idaho in May, 1869, but never got out of New Hampshire, and ultimately declined to serve.

In December, 1869, Alexander Conner of Indiana was appointed, and he never showed up either.

Next came Ebenezer Dumont of Indiana who was appointed in April of 1871, and he actually got to the Idaho Territory - but resigned on September 5th.

Finally, finally, Thomas Warren Bennett was appointed on December 6, 1871, arrived in Bossey Sitty on December 24th,

1860 - 1870

and entered his duties as Governor of the Territory of Idaho. Mount Bennett, and Mount Bennett Hills, located just south of Camas Prairie, were named after this governor.

In spite of these incredible efforts to find someone willing and able to act as Governor, the system continued to work, and Idaho Territory was getting organized. Counties were set up, surveys were made, schools were built, the Legislature was meeting regularly, Ben Halliday's stage lines were operating, and Ben was given the contract to transport the U.S. Mail by stage coach. The military was still escorting wagon trains over the Oregon Trail, farmers around Boise were doing a brisk business raising food for man and beast, and were even forming their own "canal companies" to help each other get irrigation water to land farther and farther away from the rivers.

The initial point of the survey was 19 miles southwest of Boise, and Camas Prairie was the first land in the Territory to be surveyed. The office of Surveyor General for the Territory was created in 1866, and no surveys were made of any part of the territory until the following year. In 1867 a party of surveyors came to Camas Prairie to establish the Base Line; most of the Township lines to the South; and a few to the North. Four years later, another survey party made rectangular surveys to determine the section, half-section and quarter-section lines. Other surveys were made - but much later.

In 1868, the United States Congress established Wyoming Territory and another piece of Idaho Territory was whisked away!

That's when Idaho got into the shape it's still in to this day.

1860 - 1870

IDAHO TERRITORY IN 1868
© Cindy Crow Bitzenburg

1860 - 1870
THE FIRST MAGIC CIRCLE MINES

Gold was discovered in the Boise Basin in 1862, and by the following year a few prospectors were seen poking around inside the Magic Circle. They didn't stay long because the Indians on Camas Prairie made them pretty nervous, and when somebody got the word that gold had been discovered over the mountains in Montana, they all hustled over there to have a look.

The next spring - 1864 - a few stopped again, briefly, but quickly departed. There was one, however, named Warren P. Callahan, who found a galena lode near Goodale's Cut-Off south of later Bellevue. He marked the spot and went on to Montana with the others. Too dangerous to explore at the time - but Callahan planned to return. . .

In 1865 a few prospectors set out from Rocky Bar and actually found some claims worth filing on. They were the first claims in the Magic Circle and were named "Big Camas" and "Black Cinder." Both were located on what later became known as the "Hailey Gold Belt." The first tunnel inside the Magic Circle was dug at "Big Camas."

Callahan and his brother kept coming back to check his galena lode, and finally in 1873 they located a claim there, and filed another in 1874. They did their annual assessment work regularly for the next few years, but the Indian threat kept them away. All during that time, they displayed galena samples from their lode at Rocky Bar, but nobody paid much attention. Prospectors got excited about gold - but lead and silver? - never!

1860 - 1870

THE FORT BRIDGER TREATY

Meanwhile, the Indians on Camas Prairie were becoming more and more desperate and threatened by the white invasion of their lands. The trappers had slaughtered the beaver; the missionaries had decimated their people with measles and small-pox; hundreds of heavy wagons had gouged the land and killed the foliage, and the U.S. Military protected these vandals with soldiers and guns. Gold-seekers were crawling all over the area, and a steady stream of traffic was moving back and forth from the Boise Basin to the Montana mines. Fewer tribes gathered on Camas Prairie for the harvest now, and those only out of desperation for the camas bulbs which were such an important part of their diet - without which they would starve.

They felt helpless and frustrated and knew not how to put a stop to the white man's desecration of the land and their people.

Not to worry! Back in Washington D.C., the government was fixing to take care of this "Indian Problem" the way it had taken care of all the others - they would simply draw up a treaty. Everything would be neat, clean and "legal" - according to white man's laws. This one would be called the "Fort Bridger Treaty."

After all, the U.S. Government had been clearing Indians off the land for a good many years, and was an old hand at writing treaties by the time they got to Idaho. They wanted that land so that white men could settle, or mine, or whatever, without being hassled by the Indians, and they did not want to have to continue sending troops to protect them. So - the Indians must go.

The terms of the Fort Bridger treaty were carefully explained to representatives of the Bannock tribe, who clearly understood the promises of the government:

1860 - 1870

> "It is agreed that whenever the Bannocks desire a reservation to be set apart for their use, or whenever the President of the United States shall deem it advisable for them to be put on a reservation, he shall cause a suitable one to be selected for them in their present country, which shall embrace reasonable portions of <u>Portneuf and Camas Prairie</u> countries."

The Bannocks would never have agreed to a treaty that would require them to give up their precious Camas Prairie.

The rough draft was sent back to Washington D.C. for the full "official" treatment - to be printed on official parchment with official scrolls, official seals, and official ribbons, all in the proper form and wording. But, somewhere along the line through the bureaucratic mill, a "correction" was made. The word "Camas" was changed to "Kansas", and nobody noticed. Whoever made the "correction" was probably familiar with "Kansas", but who in Washington D.C. would ever had heard the Chinook word "Camas"?

When the official treaty on the official parchment was officially signed, the original white men and Indians who had agreed to the terms, were not present - this "signing" was only a formality that needed to be taken care of, so since both sides supposedly knew what was in the treaty - there was no problem. The Indians couldn't read the white man's words anyway.

The Fort Bridger Treaty was signed in 1868.

The following year, President U.S. Grant set aside, by executive order, the Fort Hall Indian Reservation in the "Portneuf Country."

"Kansas Prairie" was ignored.

And Camas Prairie was officially thrown open to white settlement.

1860 - 1870

But nobody told the Indians. . .whose rights to Camas Prairie had been granted by treaty. . .

1860 - 1870
FARMERS AND RANCHERS

In 1862 when gold was first discovered in the Boise Basin, Congress passed the "Homestead Act" which gave 160 acres of land to each "Head of Family", if he would cultivate it and live on it for five years. This was called "proving up", and if he could accomplish it without starving to death in the process, the government would give him the land free. The "Head of Family" was a nice touch, because that meant he had to have a "family" and "family" meant wife.

Congress well knew that if the West would ever be settled, it would take women to do it. "Women" meant children, a home, stability, culture, education, and having a 24-hour-a-day helpmate who would bear the children, cook, clean, plow, build, wash, iron, scrub, hang curtains, make rugs, etc. etc.

So they gave the land to the Dad.

The high cost of food for man and beast in the mining camps had turned many disillusioned miners to farming and stockraising. Some were settling in the Boise and Payette valleys raising grain, vegetables and hay, and several orchards were soon producing. These farmers had a terrible time at first, grubbing sagebrush to plow the land, and having to build houses, barns, corrals, and fences. Seed was extremely expensive and hard to come by, and in order to get water to the land they had to dig long irrigation ditches. But, somehow they managed, and soon, patches of green began to appear along the streams and rivers.

All of the early businesses had been connected directly to mining, but little by little, it began to change, and farming, fruit raising and stock raising grew steadily.

Cattlemen had been operating in Texas, Wyoming, Montana, and the Dakotas, long before they showed up in Idaho. Their rangeland had begun to suffer from heavy grazing and they had to look for new land. Idaho turned out to be good cattle country, and the Snake River area soon became part of what we call the "romantic old West." Texas longhorns came up through Utah, and some of those herds helped to start Idaho's first ranches. Large cattle companies from other parts of the west brought huge herds into Idaho to graze, and cattle roamed the open country. There were very few wire fences, and lots of open range. Cowboys became part of Idaho's population - calves were branded and turned loose and a few years later, fat cattle were rounded up. Mining camps paid well for beef, and many cattlemen were better off than the miners.

Camas Prairie, and the lower valleys of the Big and Little Wood rivers were running cattle by the late 1860's. Shortly thereafter, sheep raisers began to build up large flocks.

1870 - 1880
THE TRANSCONTINENTAL RAILROAD

Up until 1869, there were three ways to get from the eastern states to California and the west coast: You could hop on a sailing ship which would take you around Cape Horn in approximately 196 days, or you could travel overland like the wagon train folks, or you could sail down to the Isthmus of Panama, take the rickety railroad across, and then hopefully get another ship to take you up the west coast.

But, in 1869 the Central Pacific and Union Pacific Railroads met at Promontory Point, Utah, and the first transcontinental railroad was completed. Now one could travel from coast to coast on the train!

When the last tie was laid and the golden spike was driven home and the big celebration was over - hundreds of railroad workers were thrown out of work. Many of them had heard the rumors about the gold discoveries in Idaho, so they came on up to get theirs.

Most of the laborers on the Union Pacific were Irish, and on the Central Pacific, mostly Chinese, and by 1870 the Idaho Census showed 3,853 Chinese and only 2,726 whites. Don't know how many of those whites were Irish, because they were classed "white", but the Chinese were considered "foreigners."

The whites in Idaho were as rotten to the Chinese as they were to the Indians. Chinese were permitted to buy only the mines that had been all worked out that no one else wanted, but they worked harder and longer, and somehow managed to scrape out a profit - even from the worst mines.

They were forced to pay a special "Chinese Miners' Tax" that applied to them alone, and even the Chinese prostitutes were subject to extra taxation. Massacres were frequent - Chinese were not allowed to testify in court - were frequently robbed and beaten, and the robbers had no fear of being punished. They worked long, grueling hours, and had no protection from anyone. They were ridiculed relentlessly because they wore long pigtails, had yellowish skin and slanted eyes, and were easy to identify.

****

Immediately after the completion of the Transcontinental Railroad, large commission houses for the reception of freight, were built at Kelton, Utah. Freighters then organized teams with as many as 14, 16, and in some cases, 18 mules or horses, to pull great lead wagons to which were attached as many as three trailers, and began moving freight to the increasing population of the Idaho mining camps.

A young man named John Hailey started a "42 hour stage service" running between Bossey Sitty and Kelton.

The Mormon Leader, Brigham Young, had desperately wanted the Transcontinental Railroad to cross south of Salt Lake City, but when he found that it elected to cross to the north, he just up and decided that the Mormon Church would build its own railroad line to connect with it, so the Utah Central Railroad was established and construction was started immediately. A narrow-gauge, built by property owners and farmers along the line, using their own teams and equipment. They took stock in the little railroad, in lieu of wages. Not only did the Mormons build the Utah Central, they built the Utah Southern, Utah Western and Utah Eastern. Truly, an astounding accomplishment. Nevertheless, the northern part of the Utah territory was still out in the cold and those folks were anxious to have a railroad, too. So, after a conference or two, the Utah Northern was finally organized in August of 1871.

The Utah Northern was the very first railroad to poke its nose into Idaho Territory - but as far as Idaho was concerned, it was only a bridge to the mines in Western Montana.

1870 - 1880

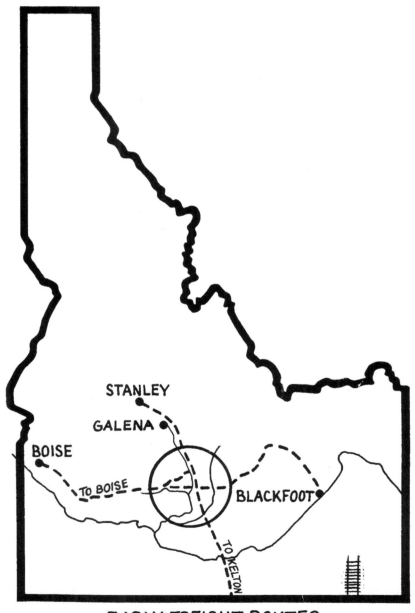

EARLY FREIGHT ROUTES

© Cindy Crow Bitzenburg

1870 - 1880

PROGRESS

Mining fostered all other industries. The discovery of gold brought attention to the new Idaho Territory, but none of the gold stayed in Idaho. It all went back to the Union Army during the Civil War, and into the pockets of war profiteers on the East Coast. When the gold finally began to peter out, the miners took off for easier pickin's and those left behind fell on hard times.

Everything had been going so well! A few farmers around Boise were irrigating, and their crops flourished. Stage lines, freighters, livery stables, saloons, and other businesses that grew from the mining boom had been thriving, but when the miners left, over-production brought prices down. It was too far and too expensive to freight fresh produce to the railroad at Kelton, and too far to drive the livestock. So, even though they were stuck with their own over-production, those early farmers and stockmen proved that the land, and the range, in Idaho, were good.

The politicians in Bossey Sitty were still struggling, but making progress in spite of themselves. The land was being surveyed, the census taken, and a U.S. Marshal was in charge of the new penitentiary.

Telegraph and World News Service came to Silver City, and Idaho's first daily newspaper was being published there. Telegraph lines were started from Silver City to Boise. . .but, forget that. . .the company went bankrupt and the line was never completed.

In 1873 there was a nationwide "Panic" and things went from bad to worse all across the country. The railroads in general had over-extended themselves in many places, maintenance costs were very high, floods and fires took their toll, and Utah farmers were plagued by drought and seven consecutive years of grasshopper infestations. Their Utah

1870 - 1880

Northern narrow-gauge was inching its way north through Idaho, but was still a long way from those Montana mines, when Jay Gould, a big railroad promoter with Union Pacific, stepped in and bought the Utah Northern for forty cents on the dollar! He talked other financiers into joining him, and the Utah Northern was reorganized, refinanced, and renamed the "Utah and Northern."

Immediately, Gould and his partners got busy with plans to build the line quickly to the Montana Mines and on December 17, 1878 Blackfoot became the construction terminus.

One more important event happened - in 1877, Congress passed another land give-away. Uncle Sam was anxious to have people settle down in the West, even though much of it was dry desert land. This new act, titled "The Desert Lands Act" awarded 640 acres of land to the head of the family and his wife - IF THEY COULD GET WATER TO IT!

1870 - 1880

THE INDIAN WARS

The condition of the Bannock Indians on Camas Prairie was worsening. The tribe had been depleted by small-pox and measles, their pastures practically destroyed by the wagon trains, and many of the young men had been killed in attacks and skirmishes with the whites. So, the Indians were gradually being rounded up and herded onto the reservation at Fort Hall. The only remaining shred of their traditional way of life was Camas Prairie, which they knew belonged wholly to them because the United States Government said so in the Fort Bridger Treaty.

That government, as usual, was bungling and unprepared when it came to handling Indian Affairs. They never seemed to get the hang of it. They appointed inept agents - none of whom stayed around very long - and each new replacement was in the dark as to what he was supposed to do, or what had gone before.

The Bannocks were deposited at Fort Hall with promises of good land, stock, subsistence, shelter, everything they would ever need, supposedly. All empty promises! No clothes, no blankets, no shelters or food, no money, and no one to turn to for help. They were harassed, victimized and ill-used by whites wherever they went, and were forced to spend most of their time hunting and digging camas off the reservation, in order to survive.

To make matters even worse, one of those miserable "Indian Agents" "confiscated" three hundred of their best horses.

The hapless Bannocks were bewildered and frustrated and tried desperately to follow their old migratory cycle in search of food. They were stopped and abused at every turn, and all the while they were trying to cope with their terrible upheaval, white stock raisers were moving onto Camas Prairie.

1870 - 1880

The straw that broke the camel's back came in the Spring of 1878 when three young Bannock braves came across a large number of hogs on Camas Prairie ROOTING OUT THE LUSH BULBS! They could destroy the Camas forever! Besides that, hogs, cattle and horses were grazing all over the rich bottom land!

Convulsed with rage, they routed the white men tending the stock, and then sent word of this violation back to the tribe. Chief Buffalo Horn quickly rallied 300 warriors, and the Bannocks were on the warpath!

After clearing all of the animals off Camas Prairie, they swept down along the Snake River viciously striking scattered ranches, ferry crossings and travelers. They captured and sank Glenn's Ferry, then advanced westward. As they moved along, they were joined by other tribes, and by early July, there were 2,000 Indians on the move!

At South Mountain, near Silver City, Chief Buffalo Horn was killed, and Chief Egan of the Paiutes took over the leadership. Egan and Buffalo Horn both were confident from the outset, that they could depend on help from the Umatillas in Oregon. However, when they got there, the Umatillas backed out and said they did not want to fight because they had been friendly with the soldiers for too many years.

On July 13th, the Bannocks and soldiers met in a fierce battle near Pendleton, Oregon. Two days later, Chief Homily of the Umatillas approached the Bannock "for a conference." The Bannocks granted his request, but as soon as their guard was down, 90 Umatillas ambushed Egan and 30 of his braves, killing them all.

The rebellion died with them.

The Bannock War of 1878 began in late May - and was over in August.

Those still living spent the summer dejectedly filtering back to the reservations.

1870 - 1880

This was not the only Indian War in Idaho in the late 1870's. The Nez Perce under Chief Joseph, with 500 warriors, went on the warpath after the government opened the Wallowa Valley in Oregon, to white settlement - an area those Indians claimed as an inheritance. It started with the "Battle of White Bird" on June 14th and ended on October 5th with the surrender of Chief Joseph. In his famous speech he said:

"I am tired of fighting. Our Chiefs are killed. Looking Glass is dead. Toohulhulsote is dead. The old men are all dead. It is the young men who say no and yes. He who led the young men is dead. It is cold and we have no blankets. The little children are freezing to death. My people, some of them, have run away to the hills and have no blankets, no food. No one knows where they are - perhaps they are freezing to death. I want to have time to look for my children and see how many of them I can find. Maybe I shall find them among the dead. Hear me, my chiefs, I am tired. My heart is sad and sick. From where the sun now stands I will fight no more forever."

And there was the "Sheepeater War." Renegade Bannocks and Tukuarika Indians went on the warpath when the government refused to furnish them with the promised supplies. They hid out in the hills near the Magic Circle and lived on mountain sheep during their raids. They fought at Big Creek and Loon Creek during the summer. They surrendered on September 1, 1879.

It was the last of the Indian Wars.

The Idaho Indians would cause no more trouble for the white people who invaded their land.

For many years after the wars, the lonely Bannocks continued to visit Camas Prairie to dig the Camas that were left, and to hunt squirrel and other small animals for food.

1870 - 1880

Indians had lived for thousands of years in these Southern Idaho mountains and deserts. Then came the white man, and in less than a century, they were forced onto reservations, compelled to accept the ways of the white man, controlled by the calculating policies of the United States Government thousands of miles away, and administered by a constantly changing succession of inept, politically appointed "Indian Agents."

Upon first meeting the white man, the Indian generously extended to him the warmest hospitality, shared his women, food, clothing and tipi, and provided whatever the white man wanted. He was an excellent and willing guide through unchartered, rugged country, and many times helped the white man to survive. Lewis and Clark and the early trappers testified to that.

The Indians and whites held widely opposing concepts about the land - the Indians believed that the power was in the land itself and that no one could "own" it. The white man believed the European concept that owning the land was a symbol of power for the owner.

The Indians therefore, could not understand why the white man would move onto the land and settle there, usurping his hunting and camas fields. Little by little, the most fertile valleys and best grazing lands were occupied by whites, and the Indians were expected to retire gracefully to the barren reservation lands set aside for them. They had no legal rights, and were treated as children. The white man took away their entire culture, but did not replace it with an educational system.

Not one treaty made with Indians, has been kept by the United States Government.

The Indian removals are indeed a shameful, sorry chapter in our history. . .

1870 - 1880

THE PROMOTERS

Robert Strahorn was a writer who started his career by covering the West for the New York Times and Chicago Tribune. He was a flowery, colorful writer, often prone to exaggeration, and his stories were widely read by thousands in the East who were fascinated by the Wild West. Others who followed Strahorn's stories, were wealthy capitalists who might just be interested in investing in the development of the raw, new country.

In 1877, Robert Strahorn married Carrie Adell, a well-educated, lively, independent woman who requested that the word "obey" be left out of their marriage ceremony. (Carrie was deeply involved in the woman's suffrage movement in Wyoming where they planned to make their home). Robert happily agreed to her request, and suggested to the minister, "if you don't want to leave it out entirely, just put it in my part, I've been running wild for so long I just want to be obliged to obey somebody."

It was shortly after the wedding that Robert was hired by the Union Pacific Railroad to take charge of their publicity department and to establish a Literary Bureau and Advertising Department to promote settlement of the West. The U.P. needed to know the resources throughout the west in order to decide where and how to extend their railroads to commercial advantage. Strahorn was perfect for the job, and Carrie accompanied him.

They traveled by horseback and coach as far north as Alaska, and as far south as Mexico. They mingled with Indians, cowboys, miners, saloon keepers, and businessmen. They took part in the social life of many western towns and enjoyed every minute of it. Both were friendly, outgoing, intelligent and prolific writers. Carrie's stories were as eagerly read as Robert's, and were much more down-to-earth and realistic. The railroad

1870 - 1880

barons were happy with the Strahorns, and valued Robert's opinions and the information he provided.

By 1879, attention began to focus on the Magic Circle. The Indians were no longer a threat, Camas Prairie was beautiful and fertile, assorted minerals were showing up in the Wood River area, the government was encouraging everybody to take up land and settle in the West, and the Union Pacific Railroad was ready to transport them.

Robert Strahorn wrote: "Idaho's mountains, ribbed with royal metals, alternating with her sequestered gulches, rich in golden nuggets, cover an area as large as that of a first-class Eastern State." Another time, he wrote: "Idaho's bright warm days are conducive to a cheerful and hopeful feeling which is a great aid in overcoming disease, while the cool nights are productive of a sound, invigorating sleep."

Robert Strahorn was Idaho's first "promoter", and in 1879 the doors began to open into the Magic Circle.

1870 - 1880

THE NEWCOMERS

Warren P. Callahan who found the galena lode in 1864 and filed claims in '73 and '74, came back again in the early spring of 1879 to examine his claims in peace, without having to keep one hand on his gun and the other on his scalp. New and profitable methods had been developed for smelting lead and silver since his original discovery, and his claims, which amounted to little before the Bannock War, were now well worth developing. He worked the area all during the summer, and in the Fall, shipped a batch of ore to test in Salt Lake City with an average recovery of $431.46 in gold and silver per ton - proving that the new mines would pay well, indeed.

All during the summer of 1879 prospectors explored up the gulches and down the ravines. David Ketchum found some promising lead-silver ledges at the head of Wood River, and another belt of ledges was found at the head of Little Smoky, where limited gold discoveries back in 1864 had led to a small amount of mining. Other good assays were gotten from the upper Wood River where the towns of Galena, Sawtooth City and Vienna popped up, all just outside the Magic Circle.

A prospector named Tom Muldoon located a mine about 18 miles northeast of present Bellevue, and it looked good. Tom went away to get help so he could start mining the next year because it was too late in the season of 1879 to accomplish anything before winter set in.

MINING ACTIVITY IN 1879

© Cindy Crow Bitzenburg

1870 - 1880

In 1879 the Joseph Loving family settled on a place later called the Yank Robinson Ranch, built a house there, and were the first settlers on the Big Wood River.

In 1879 Charles M. Black settled on Spring Creek, built a house there, and his family moved in the following Spring. Issac W. Garret also located on Spring Creek and the family moved in the following spring. And, S.E. Stanton and his son, Clark, homesteaded at Stranton's Crossing. Clark had been a scout with Colonel Green during the Bannock Indian war the year before.

In the summer of 1879 Arch Billingsley drove his cattle into the Carey Valley and prepared the land to establish a homestead. His family moved in the following year, and other settlers soon joined them.

It seems that the name of Carey Valley probably should really have been Billingsley Valley, since Arch was the first arrival. However, it was named Carey, after James Carey who was the first postmaster, and the post office and first school house were situated on James Carey's land. That post office was not established until May, 1884.

Ed Bradley settled north of Carey in 1880 and conducted a stage station there for some time. Bradley Hill is named after Ed.

In September of 1879 C.P. Croy discovered some hot springs gushing from the ground which later became known as the "Hailey Hot Springs."

Camas Prairie was deserted by late Fall of 1879. The Indians had all been rounded up and herded onto the reservations and during the summer months there had been mostly just traffic moving through on the trail from Boise to the Wood River Valley.

In the late Fall of 1879, a miner named Frank Jacobs hit pay dirt in his "Queen of the Hills" mine. Frank had one advantage over other lone prospectors - he had someone to

1870 - 1880

share his excitement. A group of folks camped nearby had made up their minds to spend the winter right there in camp, and when Frank rushed in bellowing his good news, they decided on the spot, to name the camp "Jacob's City" in honor of Frank Jacobs and his dandy new mine.

There were twenty-six people in all - and only one was a woman. Mrs. James Loving chose to stay through the winter with her family. They all knew it could be bitter cold, that snow could pile high, and it would be impossible to get out once winter had set in. Their supplies were dangerously low, and they were a bit apprehensive, but felt they could survive. There were no buildings - only tents - some with wood sides. It was a risky situation.

But, luck was with them! At the last minute, when it was still barely possible to reach them, a happy, generous, unexpected Irishman, named Owen Riley, showed up with a load of provisions he had purchased for his own use. He was number twenty-seven and very welcome. His supplies were not enough so that everybody could lead the "life of Riley", of course, but it sure kept them from being too scrawny come springtime. They all survived the winter.

The name "Jacob's City" never really caught on. When others arrived in the Spring, they started to identify the place by the broad, shallow, ford in the river there, and called it "Broad Ford." Later on, it was further confused by some who even called it "Bradford." Today, it is hardly there at all - one mile west of Bellevue.

In its day, it served the needs of the "Queen of the Hills" and "Minnie Moore" mines - both famous, outstanding producers.

"Jacob's City" was the first town in the Magic Circle.

1880 - 1890
1880 - A NEW DECADE - A NEW LAND

Meanwhile, back on the Eastern Seaboard, Jay Gould, the Union Pacific railroad tycoon, decided to build a Union Pacific line from Granger, Wyoming to Huntington, Oregon to connect with the Oregon Railroad and Navigation Co. there. The longest stretch of unbroken track would run through Southern Idaho [434 miles]. So once again, it looked as if Idaho would be only a "land bridge" for the railroad, just as it had been only a "land bridge" for the thousands of wagon trains headed for the fertile fields of Oregon.

Gould's new railroad would be called "The Oregon Short Line" - or "O.S.L." for short.

This might be a good time to take a look at who Jay Gould really was, because his name keeps popping up in Magic Circle history.

Jay Gould was considered a rascal and a scoundrel. But, a very, very rich rascal/scoundrel. He was a powerful railroad tycoon involved in fierce financial struggles with such men as Cornelius Vanderbilt, Leland Stanford, Edward H. Harriman, J.P. Morgan and James J. Hill - all fighting to control huge railroad empires. Not all of these men were "robber barons", but Jay Gould was. He lived in a magnificent castle in Tarryton, New York and made his fortune by swindling naive investors, and plundering companies to add to his own wealth. Remember - it was Jay Gould who bought the Utah Northern railroad from the Mormons for forty cents on the dollar.

He was a financial double-dealer and stock manipulator, and introduced a whole new bag of tricks to the world of high finance. For example, in 1868 Gould, and the equally corrupt James Fisk, got control of the Erie Railroad from Cornelius

1880 - 1890

Vanderbilt by tricking him into buying fake Erie stock. The following year, Gould and Fisk tried to corner the nation's gold market, and in so doing brought about "Black Friday", a financial panic that ruined many other speculators, but made Gould and Fisk even richer. Before he died [in 1892] Gould smugly admitted to being "the most hated man in America", but was reputed to own one out of every ten miles of railroad track in the United States.

Be that as it may, none of the brave twenty-seven at Jacob's City, who were shivering their way through the winter of 1879, ever knew, or cared, about Jay Gould and his doings, nor did any of those who had been there during the summer and fall of '79 but departed for warmer climes to re-group and get ready to go back in the Spring of '80. They were busy blabbing the news all over the country about the mineral finds in the Wood River area, and uncounted hordes were getting ready to swarm into the Magic Circle as soon as possible in the Spring.

The first person to get there was Frank Myers. Frank hitched up a sleigh, loaded it with supplies in Blackfoot, and slid into Jacob's City in late April of 1880. He received a wild, crazy welcome from the "Intrepid 27" who had all survived the winter!

That little camp called Jacob's City was the only settlement of any size for miles and miles around, and it quickly became the hub of the mining activity that followed.

And follow, it did! Hot on the heels of Frank Myers they came! A great flood of humanity surging into the Magic Circle.

The "Rush" was on! Strangers of all nationalities and conditions of life showed up - Irish, Chinese, Mormons Catholics, and assorted whites, blacks, yellows and reds. Many came from adjacent mining areas, like Atlanta, Rocky Bar, or the Boise Basin. But, there were also old Comstockers from California and Nevada of the '50's and '60's, and many of the

1880 - 1890

workers on the Transcontinental Railroad were still hanging around, so they came, too.

This would mostly be hard-rock mining which meant penetrating deep under the surface of the earth. It would take men, money, horses and machines to develop a good paying mine. Some would locate profitable mines, get financial backing and hire hundreds of men to bring out the ore. Others would sell their finds at a good price, and then go on to search for more.

Hard-rock mining transformed men into moles, but those tough, underground workers produced a strain of men whose strength and endurance are still unmatched today.

Hard rock mining was a rough, tough business.

It created wealth and jobs.

It created towns and opportunity.

It ravaged the land and the men who worked the mines. And, it brought white settlement into The Magic Circle - fast!

1880 - 1890

CLAIMING AND NAMING

Hundreds of mining claims were filed during the '80's. When you claimed it - you named it - and the mighty music of those names lilted and thundered through the hills and valleys. Each name revealed a bit about the claimer. Some were boundlessly enthusiastic and optimistic and gave their mines' upbeat names, like: Acme - Back Pay - Blue Ribbon - Bonanza - Big Mint - Climax - Contact - E. Pluribus Unum - Compensation - Era - Eureka - 4th of July - Garden - Gilt Edge - Gold Bar - Golden Glow - Hidden Treasure - High Ore - Hope - La Grande - Les Despencer [no doubt a Frenchman who was certain his mine would dispense wealth] - Liberty Gem - Lucky Boy - Lucky Shot - Lucky Strike - New Year - O.K. - Pork [Pork?] - Prize Taker - Revenue - Square Deal - Surprise - Tip Top - Treasure Vault - Triumph - Trump - Western Home - Wonder - Wood River Pride.

Some were not quite so hopeful, and gave skeptical, solemn or satiric names: Bromide - Burning Moscow - Carboniferous [means containing carbon or coal] - Chloride - C.O.D. - Dead Wood - Greenhorn - Hardscrabble - Hard Times - Last Chance - Maybe - Monday.

Others were named after the sweetheart, wife, mother or whoever: Abbie - Amazon (river? or mother-in-law?) - Anabelle - Anna - Barbara - Carrie Leonard - Con Virginia [how's that again?] - Ellen Stilts - Eunice - Idaho Belle - Isabella - Jennie R. - Kitty - Lee Ann - Lizzie - Luella - Maggie - Maybelle - Minnie Moore - Myrtle - Nellie - Prairie Belle - Ruth - Susie - Venus.

There were nautical miners who remembered the old sailing ships: Argosy - Black Spar - Clipper - Columbia - The Mayflower - Silver Spar.

And, of course, politics were duly represented: The Idaho Democrat - The Idaho Republican - Independence - The Senate - and, no doubt to pay tribute to the voter - The Idahoan.

1880 - 1890

There were dainty flower names: Blue Belle - Butter cup - Daisy - Shamrock. On the other hand, these COULD have been lady friends - Buttercup?

Some claimers looked to the heavens for their names: Blazing Star - Comet - Golden Star - Jupiter - Lone Star - Moonlight - Morning Star - North Star - Red Cloud - Red Rocket - Silver Moon - Silver Star - The Star - and Texas Star.

There were no-nonsense, down-to-earth names, too: Big Camas - Black Cinder - Black Barb - Bullion - Smoky Bullion - Galena - Red Rock - Stockholder.

Some were Royal sounding and quite elegant: Croesus [Croesus was a 6th century B.C. Lydian King noted for his wealth. That was some educated fella who named his mine "Croesus."] The Glendale Queen - Gold King - Imperial - King of the West - Lead King - Majestic - Princess - Queen Bee - Queen Bess - Queen of the Hills - Queen Victoria - Silver King.

Then, there were the famous, or the infamous, or maybe it was the miner himself - or his financial backer: Jack Dempsey - Jay Gould - John A. Logan - Morton Davit - Peter Snider - Wolfe Tone. Some were just surnames: Bidwell - Bismark [the German Chancellor] - Dewey - Dollarhide - Doniphan - Honsdale - Leinster - Muldoon - O'Neil-Clark - Parker - Penobscot - Rogers - Sullivan - Sutherland - Walcott - Washington.

And then there were the informal names: BBB - Battling Jack - Double J. - Edris - Elmo - Emery - Felix - Guy - Jacob's - Johnnie - Lawrence - Little Bob - Lone Jack - Parnell - Woodrow.

Occupations were represented: Bull-Whacker - Gladiator - Mascot - Paymaster - Pilgrim - Regulator - Rustler - Smuggler - Trapper.

Only a few were named nationalities: Bavarian - French - Hispanotia - Oriental - Porto Rico [yes, it was registered that way].

Indian-type names: Arrow - Bannack - Cheyenne Chief -

1880 - 1890

Highland Chief - Idaho Chief - Oswego - Red Warrior - Sitting Bull - War Dance.

And of course, there were "other place" names: Alabama - Alaska - Alturas - Bay State - Baltimore - Belmont - Bellevue - Boston - California - Champlain - Chicago - Gate City - Idaho - Michigan - Montana - New York - Ohio North - Ohio South - Ohio Placer - Ontario - Portland - Richmond - Scotia - U.S. - Utah.

Some just named their mines after the immediate surroundings, or some special place they wanted to remember: Bear Creek - Cottonwood - Deer Creek - Five Points - Garfield Gulch - Hill Side - Junction - Lone Pine - Lone Pine Tree - Mt. View - Point Lookout - Red Leaf - Red Rock - Riverside - River View - Roadside - Rockcricker - Sunnyside - Smoky Junction - State - Town View - West Fork - Wood River.

Surprisingly, there did not seem to be too many "creature" names: Beaver - Big Ox - Black Horse - Blue Kitten - Bob Tail - Buckhorn - Elk Horn - Jumbo - Mammoth - Mountain Lion - Rattler - Red Elephant - Scorpion - Tiger - Tom Cat - Whale.

Or birds: American Eagle - Bald Eagle - Bluebird - Eagle - Eagle Bird - Lark - Oriole - Red Bird.

But there were some "miscellaneous things" names: Cablegram - Cannonball - Flag Staff - Green Mt. Boy - Hidden Hand - Horn Silver - Keno - Little Dorrit [whatever or whoever that was] - Narrow-Gauge - Ornament - The Overland - Pacific Tunnel - Radio - Silver Knob - Silver Pick - Snoose - Snow Shoe - Torpedo - Troy.

One mine was named "Ajax" - the Greek hero in the Trojan Wars.

And I found two Saints' names: Saint Joseph and Saint Idloes [was there really a St. Idloes or did he make that up?]

And, get this, one mine was named "McFarland & Mahoney's Abbey." Two holy Irishmen, no doubt.

1880 - 1890

One claimer went to the Bible for his name: "The Ophir." this was a land rich in gold from which Solomon obtained his wealth.

Some names were mysteries to me: Axalorr - Bazouk - Nay Aug - Pasupsic - Tungad. Could have been of foreign origin or simply a combination of names. Who knows?

Undoubtedly, there were many Irish names that have been lost, because there were many mines in Dublin Gulch, and at one time about half the miners in the Wood River area were Irish. But then maybe they only worked the mines for someone else...

At any rate, these are all the names I came across, I'm sure there were many, many more. Some of these were outside the Magic Circle, and some claims were filed much later than the 1890's, but this collection of names of mines gives an idea of the riches underground, the hurricane of activity to get it out, and the unbelievable number of mines in the area! Some estimate that more than a thousand claims have been filed in or near the Magic Circle.

Mines were not the only things given names by those early arrivals. They named every town, street, mountain, butte, river, stream, creek, spring, gulch, hill, valley and flat. To name something was to honor the namer as well as the named. It sorted things out. It identified. It indicated ownership, individuality, and familiarity. It was home...

1880 - 1890

HOW TO FILE A MINING CLAIM

According to Idaho Territorial law, here is what you needed to know to file that claim:

"All claims may extend three hundred feet on each side of the middle of the vein or lode; stakes and monuments to be taken to mark correct the line thereof. A stake or post not less than four inches square or in diameter and four feet high above the surface to be placed at each end of the ground claimed, and as near as practicable along the course of the ledge, and at each corner of the location. The notice to be posted on a center stake or at the point of discovery or prospecting work. When stakes or posts cannot conveniently be had, well built monuments of stone of like height may be used. The number of feet along the vein, width from the middle of the vein, and description of locality, by such reference to natural landmarks or fixed objects and contiguous claims, if any, as to render the situation reasonably certain from the letter of the notice. Every claim to be recorded, within fifteen days from posting of the notice, in the district where it is situated or at the nearest office to the claim. The county recorders are required to appoint a deputy at any place deemed necessary, and at any place more than ten miles distant from an existing office, upon the petition of ten or more interested locators. Upon failure to appoint such deputy within ten days from receipt of such petition the resident miners may appoint one of their number to act until the county recorder shall appoint such deputy.

Within five days after presenting the notice for record, one of the locators named therein must make affidavit in proper form before the deputy that he is acquainted with the ground described, and that the same has not heretofore been legally located, or if so located has been abandoned or forfeited. The notice recorded is a copy, or substantially a copy, of the notice placed upon the claim, and shall be recorded upon payment of $3.00 which shall be full compensation for administering the oath, and all service connected with the recording. Wilful or malicious destruction of any notice on a claim, or destruction or removal of any stake or monument indicating a claim, is a misdemeanor.

Any mine owner or proprietor may have the right of way for ingress or egress over the claims of others, and shall be entitled to right of way, entry and possession to and across other lands or claims for all the uses and privileges for a road, railroad, tramway, ditch, canal, flume, cut shaft or tunnel necessary to the convenient or better working of a claim. Such right to be granted after petition to commissioners to appraise the damages, all appeal lying to the District Court from the assessment of damages by the commissioners."

Can't you just picture some grizzly, frustrated, grubby claimer trying to figure it all out? Particularly when we must realize that the literacy rate in Idaho at that time was 5%.

But, they did it -

Of course, there was considerable claim jumping. . .

And legal snarls - and yelling. . .

And some shooting. . .

And some pretty serious fighting. . .

And a million, billion Prince Albert tobacco cans buried in the hills and valleys jammed full of claim papers.

KETCHUM

1880 - 1890

While the miners were prowling around claiming and naming, towns were springing up along the Big Wood River inside the Magic Circle. The very first town was, of course, Jacob's City in 1879, but it was followed by Ketchum in early May, Bullion in late May, and Bellevue in June of 1880.

Isaac Ives Lewis was one of the early arrivals and kept a detailed journal of his trip. He recalls that his party arrived where Ketchum now stands, on May 2, 1880 and set up camp for the night. The next morning at about eleven o'clock they pitched a tent, "the first tent on the site of later Ketchum", and then marked out on a piece of brown paper a kind of town plat with blocks and lots, and stuck a few stakes in the snow to represent where the main street would be. They held a little meeting - about half a dozen men - and called the spot "Leadville." A man named Sterling was appointed secretary and town recorder with the power to record one lot for each resident for the sum of $2. The party took four lots, and paid Mr. Sterling $8. This was the first expenditure of money on the present site of Ketchum.

Lewis said he then commenced to burn a pit of charcoal to be ready for assaying as soon as his outfit came in. Another member of the party set up a saloon, and another went to get logs to build a store. Almost immediately, hundreds of men flocked in and had to shovel snow for places to start building.

Their goods all came in on pack animals from Blackfoot, and soon stores, livery stables, boarding houses and saloons began to take shape. A mule in a pack train could carry as much as 450 lbs. separated into two packs - one on each side, and a pack train could have forty, fifty, or more animals. Soon, they would be packing huge pieces of mining machinery into high mountain country.

The first ore was shipped out of Ketchum by Isaac I.

1880 - 1890

Lewis on August 2, 1880 via wagon freight to Kelton, Utah. Exactly three months from the day he arrived in the snow. Freight wagons could carry five tons, but could go only twelve to fifteen miles a day. A "mule skinner" drove the mule teams, and a "bull whacker" drove the ox teams.

The discovery of lead-silver mines in the Wood River Country inspired Starr's Ferry on the Snake River some distance below the present town of Burley.

When the name "Leadville" got back to the U.S. Postal Department, it was rejected. They said there were already too many Leadvilles in the country and it would have to be changed. Those present agreed to rename it "Ketchum" after David Ketchum, a well-known guide and packer who had built a cabin seven miles north and had been around there for as long as anyone could remember.

Some folks claim that David Ketchum's cabin was located on the townsite of Ketchum, but that's hard to accept, because as detailed as I.I. Lewis' journal was, he surely would have mentioned a cabin if there had been one.

Leadville [Ketchum] was the second town to be established inside the Magic Circle.

That same year - 1880 - a promoter from Ketchum went back to Philadelphia to get major capital investments for a smelter that was desperately needed. On October 8, 1881, production commenced at the Philadelphia Mining and Smelter Co. in Ketchum and they were firing charcoal in 21 large kilns. That same plant generated the first electricity in the Territory of Idaho - they installed an electric light system "geared to a water wheel", and power from the turbine also "turned the furnace blowers, the crusher and rolls." The bi-polar generator rated at 20 kilowatts, 125 volts, and 60 amperes, was manufactured by the Edison General Electric Co. in 1858. According to Mr. Irvine E. Rockwell, there were only two Edison-built dynamos in 1880 - one was installed to light a

1880 - 1890

ship, and the other was at the smelter in Ketchum. A remarkable achievement for a pioneer mining town when one considers that it was only two years previously, in the fall of 1879, that Thomas A. Edison accomplished the first practical electric light bulb.

The first child born in Ketchum was Maud Gooding, the eldest daughter of Mr. and Mrs. Frank Gooding. Frank was later elected Governor of Idaho, served two terms, and was then elected U.S. Senator. The town of Gooding was named after Frank.

1880 - 1890
BULLION

About seven miles up Croy's Gulch [west of where Hailey now stands], the mining town of Bullion sprang to life. C.P. Croy and George W. Edgington located the "Jay Gould", and other rich mines there.

Bullion was a "company town" established on May 28, 1880, a little more than three weeks after Ketchum. Bullion was an instant success and contributed a great deal to the growth and prosperity of the area. It quickly mushroomed into a good-sized town. Many of the mine workers had their families with them, so company houses popped up, and even a school house!

Early on they had the usual general store, drug store, butcher shop, livery stable, etc. Two assay offices were kept busy, and there were several boarding houses for single men. Saloons were plentiful.

Bullion was an Irish Town. Most of the workers came either from Northern Ireland [Protestant Orangemen, loyal to England] or Southern Ireland [your regular basic Irish Catholic], so Bullion was also a "fightin' town" with much animosity between these two ancient enemies. There were continual altercations - both verbal and physical - but there was also plenty of the Irish wit, lively "discussions", dainty Irish jigs, a lot of "Blarney", and the soft, lilting sounds of the sentimental ballads about their beloved Emerald Isle and their Mothers.

Bullion was never dull.

By 1882 they had built the Miners' Union Hall, and a pipe line with fire plugs and hydrants. The post office was very busy, and a daily stage was operating to bring people in and out of Bullion on business or pleasure.

Bullion came into being in May, 1880, and by Fall of that same year, had freighted out $17,000 worth of ore!

The mines adjacent to Bullion produced more ore in the

1880 - 1890

early days than any other mining camp in the Magic Circle, and Bullion developed and grew faster than any town in the Magic Circle.

Bullion folks were social and progressive. In August, 1881, they held a GRAND BALL - formal, no less - and invited the towns of Bellevue and Hailey. There were "lots of women", according to the newspaper report, and 40 couples marched in the Grand March at Steward's Hall.

Bullion was a First Rate, Top Notch town.

Today, there is no sign that Bullion ever was. . .

1880 - 1890
BELLEVUE

Three weeks after Bullion came Bellevue. On June 23, 1880, four men - John Walker, Bill Seaman, A.Y. Hash and Ashley York, laid out the new settlement. The stakes marking the boundaries were driven into the ground, and John Walker christened it "Bellevue", a French word meaning "beautiful view." It has also at various times been called "Belleville", "Bettsieville", and "Biddyville", but they are all the same place.

News of the fabulous wealth contained in the nearby hills brought thousands into and through this "gate city", and many of them stopped and stayed. The nearby Queen of the Hills and Minnie Moore mines opened a veritable treasure chest around that area.

Bellevue was recognized as an acceptable name by the Post Office Department, and the post office was quickly established. The first postmaster of Bellevue was none other than our old friend, Owen Riley, the same dandy Irishman who showed up with last-minute supplies for the "Intrepid 27" who spent the winter at nearby Jacob's City.

Almost immediately, Bellevue had a small, four-column newspaper called "The Bellevue News", and the people even managed to get a church built by the Fall of 1880 - Methodist.

Practically everything used in or around a mine passed through a blacksmith's forge, and the tremendous strain to which stage coaches and freight wagons were subject, made the blacksmith shop imperative. Bellevue had one early in the summer of 1880, and business boomed - like the town.

By Fall of 1880 Bellevue claims to have had a population of approximately 2,000 - all housed either in tents, or those hybrid shelters with willow sides and canvas roof.

The first herd of stock reached Bellevue in 1880 when Gobels imported 25 or 30 head of Shorthorn Durhams.

That territorial city of Bellevue, established by the

Territorial Legislature on February 8, 1883, is the only remaining "territorial city" existing in the State of Idaho today. The territorial charters of the cities of Lewiston and Boise were repealed while Pete T. Cenarrusa was serving in the Idaho State Legislature, and Bellevue's territorial charter would also have been repealed at that time. However, Pete, who was raised in Bellevue, and educated in the old Territorial Bellevue School, had a special love for the town, and recommended that the Legislature not repeal the territorial charter of the city of Bellevue because of its historical significance. He felt strongly that it should be preserved, and talked the Legislature into preserving it.

Bellevue was the "gate city" to the Wood River country in those early days - and still is today.

1880 - 1890
HAILEY

John Hailey was an intelligent, energetic man who dabbled in a variety of occupations. At one time he operated a ferry, ran a pack train into the Boise Basin mines, did some farming, stock raising, and mining. He was also active in politics.

In 1879 John was 44 years old and successfully operating stage lines all over the northwest with his partners. He was well aware of the mining excitement on the Wood River, and decided to run a stage line from Rattlesnake Station to Bellevue, through Camas Prairie. Rattlesnake Station was situated in the foothills several miles north of present Mt. Home. In fact, Mt. Home took its name from that stage station which was later changed from "Rattlesnake" to "Mt. Home" by Mrs. John Lemmons, whose husband was a division agent on the stage road.

Stage station intervals were from 10 to 18 miles, according to the distance between streams and springs. These were called "relay" or "swing" stations, and were built to house twelve head of standing horses and provide living quarters for a stock tender and herder.

At intervals of 50 or 55 miles, a "home station" was built to accommodate the same number of horses as the relay station, but larger quarters were provided, and so were meals and sleeping quarters for the passengers. These stations were the homes for the drivers.

John Hailey put up a building on Corral Creek on Camas Prairie, and on June 15, 1880 Charlie Babbington and his family officially opened the station. Charlie Babbington and his family have always been considered the first white settlers on Camas Prairie.

Later that year, in December of 1880, John Hailey filed on 440 acres of land on the main road between Bellevue and

1880 - 1890

Ketchum, with the intention of setting up a "Trade Center" in addition to the usual corrals, stables and feed storage needed for his stage line. However, it was too late in the season to get

Charlie Babbington's Stage Station

anything done on it, so the "Hailey Trade Center" land was barren until the following spring of 1881.

But John Hailey's plan to set up the Trade Center never did materialize.

In early April of 1881 folks started moving in and settling at this centrally located spot, and the town grew quickly and flourished like the wildflowers in the nearby hills.

Resident lots were for sale one block from Main St. at $5 each, with $1 going to the Recorder, and the other $4 to the town fund from which the cost of digging wells, platting, surveying and procuring a U.S. Patent for the townsite, was to be paid. Locators were required to fence their lots within 30 days, and to build within 90 days.

Two months after the first person stopped at Hailey, the following "Letter from Wood River" was published in the Idaho Tri-Weekly Statesman in Boise. It clearly and colorfully describes the new town, and tells how things really were at that time.

The letter is reproduced here exactly as it was written by the Statesman's "Traveling Correspondent."

1880 - 1890

LETTER FROM WOOD RIVER
Hailey, a City that Grows Like Mushrooms

(From Our Traveling Correspondent)

HAILEY, Idaho, June 7, 1881, EDITOR STATESMAN: It is only proper that I should begin my description of the towns on Wood River by first portraying the most promising candidate for the honors of a city, a city charter and municipal government. The infant town of Hailey is two months old today, and is already a bouncer. Situated on the bank of Big Wood river, directly opposite Croy's gulch, it has numerous natural advantages over its competitors. The town is regularly laid out in blocks with a frontage of 300 feet and a depth of 266 feet. An alleyway 26 feet wide runs through each block. The business blocks are divided into lots 30 feet wide and 120 feet deep, and the residence lots have a frontage of 50 feet. The principal thoroughfares are Main and River streets, First, Second and Third avenues. These are crossed by Croy, Bullion, Carbonate, Silver, Galena and a dozen other streets.

Among the business houses already here are the following dealers in general merchandise: C.B. Fox, George L. Hurley & Co., W. B. Noble, G.W. Cranston, Willman & Walker, Louis Eckhart, May & Kriegs, J.O. Swift & Co., S.J. Friedman, J.C. Fox and Henry Swanholm & Co.

Mr. David Falk returned from California last Sunday, and will at once engage in the grain and flour business. Ad Sielaff and Cliff & McCay are dealers in hardware, stoves and similar articles. Joseph Rupert and Riley & Tracy deal in drugs and medicines. L. Woodin, R. Bledsoe and Hall & Co. own the lumber yards and therefore control the situation to a certain extent. Two breweries have been started, one by George Kohlep and one by H. Vorberg. The weary traveler can be accommodated at either Oscar Bache's L. Wines' or Mrs. Graham's lodging houses, while the following well known caterers will supply the inner man "with all that the market affords": J.F. Smith of the Palace restaurant, E. Cramer of the

Pioneer house, H. Russell, Menas & Spencer, Mrs. Miller, J.W. Crampton, Mrs. Abbott, and Love & Dwyer.

Charles Nelson, Dryde McClintock, L. Dorsey and J.M. Banfield own the horse restaurants, where your dumb brute may be fed or starved to order, just as you desire, and where carriages, buggies, phaetons and conveyances of any kind may be had for moonlight rides through the winding canyons.

H.Z. Burkhart & Co. and Rogers & Parsons deal in stationery and reading material. They are agents for the Statesman and receive subscriptions to any paper published in America. E.A. White keeps a fine stock of furniture and can furnish your house from the cellar to the garret, in antique, Queen Anne or modern frontier style, just as your purse may permit and your taste require.

S.F. Lee & Son own the leading blacksmith and wagon shop, while A.S. Warren and Smith & Fox cut porterhouse steaks for those who have tired of grouse and mountain trout.

John A. Hillstead and J.H. Bacon have well fitted assaying establishments. T.M. Rogers is the tonsorial artist, and E.J. Stevens devotes his attention to decayed and aching teeth. Doctors Miller, Crowell and Brown represent the medical profession, while H.H. Rockwell, F. M. Ish, John S. Gray, N. M. Ruick, Frank E. Ensign and J.L. Strickland are the only disciples of Blackstone who have so far rented offices in the town.

I have hesitated about enumerating the saloon and drinking places, for fear that a complete list of all the cocktail artists might shock the temperance people and be the cause of a local option movement such as no other state or territory has witnessed; but as it would not do to omit so important a branch of trade, I shall alleviate the pain it will cause the crusaders by mentioning just 12, and no more, of the leading houses. They are: Joseph Oldham & Co., Barnes & Gusler, John Allen, Perkins & Co., E. Cramer, John S. Ramey, Nelson & Randolph, G.W. Failor, Millican & Wilmer, M. Haines, C.H. Steel and G. De Lancey.

The stage liners are represented here - the Blackfoot by C.B. Fox, who is also agent for the Union Pacific Express company: and the Kelton and Boise City lines by William T. Riley, who has Wells, Fargo & Company's agency.

1880 - 1890

Hon. Geroge M. Parsons occupies the same position here that Petroleum V. Nasby did at Confedrit X Roads, and is also justice of the peace, hence he is styled Judge Parson, in polite parlance.

Hon. George W. Richards, deputy internal revenue collector for the counties of Alturas, Custer, Lemhi, Bear Lake and Oneida, also has his office here and makes the town his headquarters. The Harding Brothers publish the Wood River Miner, and T.E. Picotte, formerly editor of the Lyon County Times, Nevada, expects to issue the first number of the Wood River Times at this place during the next week.

F.W. Drober is here, making preparations to open a branch of the First National Bank of Idaho, and Hugh McCormick, the Salt Lake banker, is also looking around for a location.

Cy Jacobs will open a branch of his Boise City establishment just as soon as his lumber arrives, and a gentleman named Childs is erecting a store for an exclusively wholesale merchandise business.

Now, I doubt if any other mining town on the Pacific coast ever made such a showing in two months time, and I certainly do not know of one that has a brighter future. To be sure, many of the firms in this place do business in canvas tents and nearly all the houses are as yet primitive in their construction, but that is owing to the great scarcity of lumber and material rather than to a disinclination on the part of the people to erect substantial buildings. It is one of the hardships all new mining towns have had to encounter, and which it takes time and perseverance to conquer. Hailey would have five hundred instead of two hundred houses today if the mills could saw all the lumber required.

A. L. M.

1880 - 1890
OTHER MAGIC CIRCLE TOWNS

During the 1880's small towns sprouted wherever there was a big mine, or group of productive mines. They boomed and receded like the tides.

There was a town called "Glencoe" situated at the crossing of Goodale's cut-off about six miles south of Bellevue, near Stanton's Crossing. Stanton's Crossing is still a land-mark today, but "Glencoe" has disappeared completely.

The town of "Doniphan" thrived for about 20 years, but it, too, is now a ghost town, along with "East Fork City", "Gilman", "Gold Belt", "Deer Creek", "Smoky", "Woodbine", "Humphries", "Fisher", and "Elizabeth."

"Bolton's Hot Springs" are now known as "Clarendon Hot Springs."

"Gimlet" was an ore-loading station with a few houses, and in later years was connected to the Triumph Mine by a tramway.

"Carrietown" was located in the Little Smoky Mining district, a rich mining locality which once had a population of 300 - 400 people. Situated at the head of Carrie Leonard Creek, Carrietown wasn't very famous in life, but in death she gave up the bodies of four Chinamen who had gone to work the mine after the white miners had left. Their bodies were discovered by prospectors months after they had been killed. Today, Carrietown is a pile of rocks and rotting logs.

There was a town called "Era." In the spring of 1885, after Frank Martin discovered the Horn Silver mine, a great rush was made for the new riches. A huge dry crusher was built, but after $1,000,000 worth of ore had been taken out of the Horn Silver, and other mines in the district, the ore began to dwindle. The mill was closed in the fall of 1887 and the 3,000 townspeople of "Era" departed.

"Leduc" was the first name given to "Picabo" when the

1880 - 1890

post office was established in May, 1886 - after Peter Leduc, the postmaster. However, that office was discontinued in March, 1887, and re-established two miles to the south in May of the same year. The name "Leduc" was changed to "Picabo" on November 8, 1900. Why "Picabo"? Because the Blackfoot Indians, coming over Bradley Pass looked down upon the clear waters of Silver Creek, which runs at Picabo's back door, and it was they who identified the scene as "Picabo", which means "shining waters" in their language. It is pronounced "peek-a-boo."

Note: Picabo was laid out by the Kilpatrick Bros. of Beatrice, Nebraska who had a construction crew working on the Oregon Short Line in 1882-1883. Four streets in the town were named for Wm. Kilpatrick's sons - Joseph, Robert, William and David. For many years ice was put up and shipped from Picabo for use by the Union Pacific railroad.

On July 31, 1983, Bud and Ruth Purdy celebrated the 100th anniversary of the founding of what is known as the Picabo Livestock Ranch, and which has been in the Kilpatrick family for a century. Bud Purdy who is related to the founder on his mother's side, is the third generation of the Kilpatrick family to own and operate the ranch - and the Purdy's have one son and three grandchildren who just might carry on the Kilpatrick tradition.

"Muldoon" was another major location. Remember when Tom Muldoon located a mine in 1879 but it was too late in the season to develop it? Well, Tom came back in the spring of 1880 and the area was soon swarming with miners and prospectors. Word had gotten out about Tom's find, and as if by magic, the town of Muldoon was born. It was located about 18 miles northeast of Bellevue in a narrow valley. A smelter and sawmill were situated so that everybody coming and going had to pass through the town, which was about a mile wide! There were four main thoroughfares. Twenty-three giant beehive

1880 - 1890

coke ovens were built close to where the lead and silver were smeltered, and in its heyday about 700 men were employed in just cutting logs and feeding those ovens. Each oven was 15 feet in diameter and 15 feet high. The dome was made of brick which was manufactured nearby, and the base was made of rock. About 10 feet from the ground a square, window-like opening permitted the smoke and steam to escape.

At one time, about 1,500 people lived and worked at Muldoon. Food and supplies were brought all the way from Kelton, Utah by ox teams. It was a painful, difficult trip, and very expensive.

Food was a big problem everywhere inside the Magic Circle in those early years. Too many people came into the raw, undeveloped land too quickly. Many of the mining companies had to hire full-time hunters to bring in game to feed the miners. Other early arrivals started to plant crops to help feed man and beast, but it took time.

The town of "Muldoon" lasted about six years. In 1887 the smelter was sold at a Sheriff's sale, but remnants of those magnificent ovens can still be seen today.

Meanwhile, the Territorial Legislature commissioned Robert E. Strahorn to write a "Descriptive History of Idaho", and he wrote a lovely and informative book with the idea of enticing people to come to settle in Idaho. It contained detailed information and was probably the first real advertising promotion in print. It was used often as the basis for numerous brochures, pamphlets, letters, flyers and sales pitches.

Robert E. Strahorn's pen did more for Idaho than many historians seem to recognize.

1880 - 1890
THE ALTURAS COUNTY SEAT

The towns along the Wood River became much like a big family. They all faced the same problems, lived in the same area, and depended upon each other. They traded and competed, loved and hated, lived and died together - and they had some swell fights!

They all agreed that the Alturas County Seat should be moved into the Wood River District because there were so many more people there, and Rocky Bar was just too far to travel to do county business. They petitioned for a special election, it was granted, and the date set for September 11, 1881.

Remember now, the baby town of Hailey was only five months old at that time, but tough - and growing fast. There was already a powerful "clique" in Hailey, determined to control the county, known as the "Hailey Ring." The Ring became notorious for their craftiness in political affairs, and the agitation for the new county seat developed into a lively political war. Everybody took sides. Rocky Bar, Ketchum, Hailey and Bellevue were all in the fight to get the County Seat.

Election Day! Ballot boxes were collected from all over the county. But wait! Indian Creek and Cannon Creek were missing! Too bad. They counted the ballots anyway, and the vote lined up like this: Bellevue - 1071; Hailey - 1070; (one vote difference) Ketchum - 356 and Rocky Bar - 236.

Formal announcement was made that Bellevue was the winner and Bellevue folks cheered and clapped hands while Hailey folks muttered and grumbled and stamped their feet. They objected loudly crying "foul", and flat-out refused to accept the results of the election.

Legend has it that Francis Fox, one of the first settlers of Hailey, suggested a horse race to determine the winner. She said that in the South this was done to decide important issues, and the idea appealed to all.

1880 - 1890

A large crowd gathered on the day of the race. Two "impartial" men drove the horses. The matched team from Hailey won easily. Hailey was then declared the County Seat.

Bellevue cried "foul", "foul"!

Nasty words were bandied about. Bellevue was accused of taking complete lists of hotel registrations from Salt Lake City and using them in a list of local voters! Hailey was accused of having more votes than there were people in the county! The case headed for the courts. . .

But wait! A few days before the trial date, the missing ballot box from Indian Creek was discovered in Mountain Home - still locked! And those Indian Creek voters had given Hailey twenty more votes than Bellevue.

Hailey was officially and formally and finally declared the new County Seat of the Mighty Alturas Empire.

What about the ballot box from Cannon Creek?

"Twas never found, and it was decided that no one in Cannon Creek had voted - probably.

1880 - 1890
HAILEY - SOLD!

John Hailey never did actually reside very long in the town of Hailey. After a couple of months, he and his family moved to the Spring Creek area south of Bellevue where they homesteaded. Later on, in 1884, when he was elected to his second term as Idaho Territorial Representative, they returned to Boise.

Guess you could say John abandoned the infant town when it was only a little over a year old, because that was when the town of Hailey, County Seat of Alturas County was sold, lock, stock, and barrel, to the Idaho-Oregon Land Improvement Co., for $100,000!

The Idaho-Oregon Land Improvement Co. was a subsidiary of the Union Pacific Railroad owned by Jay Gould, and had been organized "to purchase and improve lands along the Oregon Short line Railway and its branches; to establish colonies and towns; construct irrigating canals; waterworks; steam heating works; engage in the manufacture of lumber, brick, flour and similar enterprises, and has a capital of $500,000."

This same company was also getting ready to establish the towns of Caldwell, Mountain Home and Shoshone. All would be developed with the coming of the Oregon Short Line Railroad.

And who was in charge of this new company, The Idaho-Oregon Land Improvement Co.? None other than our old writer friend, Robert Strahorn, who arrived in Hailey on May 28, 1882 and completed the sale of the town on June 24, 1882. He chose to retain the name "Hailey", and was assisted by a young man named Andrew W. Mellon who would be the new town Treasurer. Mellon picked up a hatful of experience in Hailey, and later became the United States Secretary of the Treasurer, and got to sign all the money.

1880 - 1890

Less than two months after Robert Strahorn and company bought the town of Hailey, the right-of-way for the "Wood River Branch" of the Oregon Short Line was secured. This meant that the railroad would shoot right up into the new Wood River mining country. The new railroad would affect everybody and now the town of Hailey would be developed by "professionals", and big money and important people would take an interest.

The residents were over-joyed!

All they could talk about was the coming of the railroad and what it would do for the mines; what it would do for the cattle and sheep industry; what it would do for the farmers; and what it would do for just everybody! Manufactured goods could be brought in large quantities, at comparatively small cost - furniture, tools, equipment, food, cloth, and on and on. Everything the people could produce could easily be railroaded out and sold at high prices in far away marketplaces - minerals, lumber, farm goods, cattle, sheep, and wool.

The new Wood River Branch of the Oregon Short Line would bring the market to the Magic Circle - and the Magic Circle to the market.

1880 - 1890
GROWING PAINS

Three years! Three tough, mean years from the time the first prospector started mining in the Magic Circle in 1880, until the arrival of the railroad in 1883. Three years of growing pains - but, they were amazingly productive years, and many changes took place.

The mines were profitable, but the freight costs were exorbitant, and the extremely high cost of meat and food in the mining camps turned many disillusioned miners to farming and stock raising.

At the same time, rumors of big profits in mining were drifting back to the capitalists on the East Coast, and they began to turn their attention to the Magic Circle. There was big money to be made here - money from the mines, money from the railroads, and money from the land!

The government desperately needed the products of our mines, and our people worked diligently to dig out the metals and get them back to their mills and mints. In order to be more efficient at the task, that same government subsidized Jay Gould and the Union Pacific to get the roads through so as to entice people to settle along the routes to grow crops and raise livestock to ship to the markets in the heavily populated Eastern cities. The government offered plenty of ways to own a farm for anyone willing to settle down and work the land.

But, for those first three years, our friends in the Magic Circle struggled along without much help from that government - and without a railroad. The giant, creaking, lumbering freight wagons hauled the ore out, and brought everything else in - at a snail's pace. The nearest railroads were at Blackfoot - about 135 difficult miles over Bradley Hill, or at Kelton, Utah about 175 difficult miles away. Sometimes they had as many as three wagons trailer-hitched together pulled by as many as twenty mule or horse teams, or sixteen yoke of oxen. Slow, painful, hazardous trips through mud and mire, over bumpy, rocky mountain trails and through streams and rivers.

But they did it!

Everybody who had a wagon of any size was in the freighting business. Endless supplies were needed and business was brisk. Prices were sky-high. Some of the mines were so isolated it was impossible to reach them with any kind of wagon at all, so everything was carried in by pack trains, and the ore came out the same way.

Mail and passengers came in on John Hailey's stage coach from Blackfoot and the Boise Basin; others came on horseback, or walked, carrying their bedrolls and other possessions on their backs, sleeping on the ground and fixing their meals as best they could. John Hailey's stage stations gave the walkers a place to get an occasional meal and a warm place to sleep.

The mines were being developed at a rapid pace. Most of the ore was galena (lead and silver) and had to be smelted to separate the metals from the ore using heat, air and fluxes, so the first need was to build smelters. Soon, there were four giant smelters in operation inside the Magic Circle, and uncounted kilns for making charcoal to fuel them. The smelters made it possible to ship "bullion" instead of the raw ore that had to be shipped to Salt Lake City or Denver to be smelted. The over-all freight costs lessened a great deal after the smelters were in operation, and the mine owners netted a much better return.

Meanwhile, the "camp followers" were busy running boarding houses, saloons, livery stables, and every other imaginable business to serve the scores of people milling about. One observant Irishman named Buckley took note of the large mouse population in Bellevue - left for parts unknown, and returned with 150 cats which he promptly ransomed for $5 each!

1880 - 1890

Buckley was the first cat burgler in the Magic Circle.

Hundreds of prospectors were scouring the hills in search of new mines, and hundreds more were settling in the camps and towns to work for the mining companies. Many had their families with them, and the presence of women softened the rough edges of the raw, new communities. Schools, churches and social clubs were formed and men were cleaner, neater, and better behaved, and stopped cussin' an' spittin' on the floor "when a lady was present."

Mining was a hazardous occupation in many ways, but one of the most common problems was lead poisoning from the lead mines and smelter works. On August 24, 1881 a Miners' Hospital was built and ready to receive patients. This was the first hospital in Idaho Territory - a frame building near Hailey Hot Springs about two-and-a-half miles west of Hailey. Each person who worked at the mines was assessed one dollar a month for board, room, and medical and surgical treatment. In connection with the Miners' Hospital was a ward for the care of the sick and dependent poor of the county. The hospital could accommodate 50 patients, was provided with hot and cold bathing facilities, and a good sewage system. (It was completely destroyed by fire in 1896, having served many during those fifteen years.)

Newspapers were circulating, daily stage coaches came and went, freight and mail were every day occurrences, and Hailey started a tradition that is still going strong today - "A STUPENDOUS, COLOSSAL JULY 4TH CELEBRATION!" People came from miles around to celebrate the 4th at Hailey. That first celebration, in 1881, featured a Grand Parade with a Goddess of Liberty float; a literary and musical program including an "orator"; twelve little girl Maypole dancers; the Hailey Band plus several vocalists; baseball games; horse races; fireworks and a "Grand Ball" in the evening to top it all off!

1880 - 1890

By 1883 a brick plant was working in Hailey turning out bricks for the intended County Courthouse and the lavish Alturas Hotel across the street. Business houses were carrying a fairly good stock of necessary items, and even some frivolous ones - like ribbons and laces.

There were educational facilities, churches and good residences in all of the Wood River towns. And Hailey - the Alturas County Seat - had 20 lawyers! Twenty! Bellevue and Ketchum had one or two - but Hailey had 20!

The United States Land Office opened for business in July of 1883, with Homer L. Pound (yes, Ezra's father) as the first Register.

All in all, the Wood River district had pretty well grown up by 1883. Things were moving right along, and everything and everybody seemed to be working..........except for the transportation.

Heavy freight wagons still creaked back and forth loaded with ore, bullion and supplies, and stage coaches were still jouncing along the roads with courageous tight-lipped drivers and sharp-eyed men "riding shotgun" beside them.

However - the railroad was on the way.

1880 - 1890
CAMAS PRAIRIE

While all of the frenzied development was going on in the Big Wood River area, Camas Prairie was still "just a passage way" from Boise to Bellevue.

There were no real settlers on the Prairie until 1880. Many travelers still passed through on the Goodale Cut-Off, but nobody stayed around very long because the Indians were still a threat. The Goodale Cut-Off, by the way, picked up a few other names - like "The Old Emigrant Road", "The New Emigrant Road", and it was called the "Road to Montana" by the miners moving from the Boise Basin to the Montana mines. In those days people drew their own maps and identified things as they knew them.

So, when the mining rush came to the Wood River Valley, the Goodale-Cut-Off became a major road from the Boise Basin. As soon as the Indians were cleared off the prairie, more and more ranchers brought their livestock in for the summer to get fat on the abundant grasses. Big ranchers from Oregon often trailed livestock through, headed for market. Jared Peck, one of the early pioneers kept a record of that great livestock migration, and recorded 32,000 head of cattle driven over Camas Prairie in one season - 1880!

It took two years to drive those cattle from Oregon to Omaha.

So, there was a lot of traffic through Camas Prairie, but few stayers.....

The record shows that the very first "stayer" was an honest industrious, blacksmith named William H. Spencer. He came to Alturas County back in '63 when he did some mining. He served as Alturas County Assessor at one time and also Deputy Sheriff. Spencer built a cabin on Willow Creek, about 15 miles west of the Big Wood River, and plied his trade as blacksmith for travelers on the Prairie.

1880 - 1890

On March 31, 1880 he was found dead on the floor of that cabin, apparently from natural causes. They reckoned he had been dead about six weeks when they found him. He was given "a decent and respectable burial near his cabin."

And, of course, there was Charlie Babbington and his family running the stage station. Actually, Charlie was the first settler on record to settle down and start farming the land.

But how about Spencer the Blacksmith? Was he really the first white "settler"?

Or were the "mystery people" really the first?

When the first settlers began arriving on Camas Prairie in 1880 they found a number of well-constructed fireplaces with rock chimneys, spaced at regular intervals and strung out along a creek and across the prairie for about ten miles! They named it "Chimney Creek", but could find no clues as to who had built the structures, or what happened to the builders. It was obvious that a large group of people had been hard at work at one time. They must have lived in temporary shelters such as tents or wagons, while they were building the fireplaces, cutting grass and hay and preparing to spend the winter.

But - the cabins were never built - only the fireplaces. And the people disappeared!

Why? Did the Indians attack and wipe them out? Or run them off? Or capture them? Was the winter too severe, forcing them to leave? Were they ravaged by disease? Animals? Did they starve?

We will never know for sure. The only evidence remaining of those industrious souls ever having been there is the name -"Chimney Creek." The chimneys are all gone now - like those who so carefully constructed them.

Some of the folks thought the settlement on Chimney Creek may have been one of the early Mormon settlements which were sent out of Salt Lake City, even before 1860. A similar settlement was laid out on the Lemhi River about 1856,

1880 - 1890

and another on Toronce Creek in southeast Idaho named "Chimneys." There was also one in Oneida County named "Stringtown", and still later - in 1888, a similar settlement of LDS people was located along the river north and west of where the Twin Lakes Reservoir (also called Mormon Reservoir) was later built. It was about three-quarters of a mile long, and was also named "Stringtown."

The only hitch in establishing the fact that the chimneys on Camas Prairie were built by Mormons is that the head office in Salt Lake City had no record of such a settlement on Camas Prairie, but did have records of all the others. . .

Some speculate that the Mormons on Camas Prairie might have been "Josephite Mormons." . .

One of the first families on Camas Prairie in 1880 started a sawmill in the hills to the north, so the early houses there were built of native timber. The hills provided a good supply of lumber for the buildings on the prairie, and a good supply was always available to help fill the demand for timbers for the nearby mines.

The first dance held on Camas Prairie was in the summer of 1881 (not counting all the Indian dances held there for centuries). It lasted all night long. Kids slept on floors and benches while the folks danced the night away. There were "40 gentlemen and 11 ladies", so those "ladies" got a whale of a work-out and danced every dance. They had to be strong and sturdy and accommodating to swing around all night long. The extra gentlemen were probably some of the cowboys tending cattle there.

During those first couple of years, the Camas Prairie white folks welcomed travelers and news of the outside world during the summer months, but when winter came, the whole prairie shut down and the settlers saw only their close neighbors. They got together for quilting bees and rug bees and celebrated holidays together - weather permitting. They

1880 - 1890

organized a Literary Society where they scarfed down hearty, home-made food by the ton, every Friday night, and debated the questions of the day. And they sang! Often! Songs like "Beautiful Dreamer", "Little Brown Jug", and "Buffalo Gals."

One organization deserves special mention because of its uniqueness: Lucy M. Nelson tells about it in her "History of Camas Prairie." It was called the "McGuffey Club", and was composed of older women who had learned to read from the old "McGuffey Reader." There were six members, and they met at each others' homes to put on a little program, and discuss the new and old methods of teaching reading. They took their lessons from one old "McGuffey Reader" one of them still had.

Up until 1882, there were probably no more than a dozen families on Camas Prairie - but in '83 and '84, after the railroad started running, the first wave of settlers rolled in.

1880 - 1890
SHOSHONE - THE RAILROAD TOWN

The giant steel railroad net, falling over the United States, pulling in large and small communities alike, would soon be steeling its way into the Magic Circle in the form of the Oregon Short Line.

Shoshone had been selected as the stopping place to build the shops, and it was the first spot, since leaving Granger, Wyoming, that the Oregon Short Line would be building permanent railroad shops. Work started in 1882 on a large water tank for the steam engines, a round house, machine shops, blacksmith shops and everything else needed for the railroad.

The Shoshone business district erupted on both sides of the new railroad right-of-way, and the town popped up around and about.

They came from all directions - good guys, bad guys, railroaders, gamblers, rascals, ruffians, rapscallions and lawyers - all milling around in the mud or dust, prattling and glabbering, drinking, carousing, making friends, enemies and deals.

The hub-bub never stopped. Lot jumpers were numerous, bad whisky unlimited, saloons on every corner, guns fired at all hours, 10 to 15 arrests a day - and they just "threw the crooks into jail" - literally. The jail was a hole in the ground with a shotgun up top.

A two-page weekly newspaper called "The Rustler" was soon circulating news and ads. Crude boarding tents and rooming houses appeared out of nowhere. Endless lines of heavily laden wagons filled with all kinds of building material inched their way through the streets, fired along by scorching blasts of hair-raising profanity from the teamsters.

As the railroad grading and construction camps moved closer to the town, big payrolls came with them, and plenty of money changed hands. Every nationality was present among those itinerate railroad laborers, called "boomers", and the contractors had to keep tight control with "pick handle authority."

Working on the railroad was hard manual labor demanding great muscle and stamina, and those who stayed with it were so tough that even after a ten-hour work day they were still wound up enough to "rassle" and wrangle, punch, box, hit and be mean. Scores of men, who were given passage to the job, would work one day, pull the pin, and keep right on going. It was just too rugged for most of them.

It was often said by those who knew, that of all the mining towns, cow camps, boom towns and railroad camps in the West, Shoshone was the toughest of them all. Stabbings and shootings were common. Not one "respectable" woman in town. Wild carryings-on round-the-clock, and the gambling dens threw away the keys. Twenty-two saloons served customers day and night.

Out in the sagebrush on the outskirts of town, lay a crude, lumpy, unkempt cemetery, and it was told far and wide that every man in it died a violent death - except one - who got drunk and fell in the river and drowned!

The main man in Shoshone at that time, was a slick dude named "Pinkston", owner and operator of a two-story saloon appropriately named "Pink's Place." It had a bar, Wheel-of-Fortune, Faro, and Stud Poker tables, fallen women upstairs, and men fallin' downstairs. Pink was the Godfather of the local Mafia in charge of vice, villany, foul play, double dealing and corruption. He was a natty dresser, always outfitted to the nines, and his looks were indeed startling - he had white, white skin, and black, black hair, and with a name like "Pink", he was literally the most colorful character around. But nobody made fun of Pink - he was the top dog, and he was IN CHARGE.

Mention is made of "Pink's Woman", but no clarification

1880 - 1890

as to their legal relationship. Some thought she was his wife, while others.....? Nobody dared ask. She was just "Pink's Woman."

Shoshone was not all bad, however. There were representatives of the United States Department of Justice and Interior on hand, and also a goodly number of Secret Service men employed by the Union Pacific railroad. They all kept a low profile though, and nobody bothered them much.

1880 - 1890

WHAT'S IN A NAME?

The name "Shoshone" has a little history all its own.

Back in the early trapper days when those first French-Canadian trappers met up with the local indians, they had a little trouble communicating. When the French speaking trapper was asking the Indian "who are you", the Indian made a weaving motion with his finger, indicating they were "weaver people." The trapper decided the motion meant "snake" (or the French, Les Serpent) so indicated such on his map, and then named the big river after them. Which was a nice thing to do, but it was all a mistake because the sign never meant "snake" at all! So the trappers went on down the river, came across the mighty falls, and promptly named them "Canadian Falls" to honor their own country.

The Indians, of course, never called it the "Snake River." They called in "Yam-pa-pah", meaning "the stream where yampa grows." Yampa was abundant along the river, and its roots produced bulbs about the size of pigeon eggs which furnished food for the Indians, much like the Camas. Later on, the Indians also called the river "Po-og-way", which means "road river", alluding to the Oregon Trail which followed the course of the river.

The Indians called the great falls "Pah-chu-taka", which means "hurling waters leaping" in their tongue.

The word "Shoshone" came from the Indian words "shawnt" meaning abundant, and "shaw-nip", meaning grass. Grasses were very important to those weaver people, and they used a great deal of it. When some of the later French trappers heard the Indians pointing excitedly at a nice area abundant in grasses, calling "shawnt shaw-nip", they started to call the Indians by that name. However, the words and sounds underwent some changes after dancing through the nasal passages of the French language, and came out sounding

1880 - 1890

something like "Shown-sho-neep." By the time it got to the English people, it began to sound more like "Sho-sho-nee", and finally, down through the years, it evolved to "Shoshone." It has been spelled many different ways.

By 1868 maps were showing "Shoshonee or Snake River", and "The Great Falls", instead of "Canadian Falls." However, three years later, maps were showing "Shoshone Falls", clear as day.

So, the word "Shoshone" underwent a number of changes, but has its roots in the Indian Language - "shawnt shaw-nip."

Some historians say the falls were named way back in 1849 by Major Osborne Cross, who was leading a regiment on a military scouting expedition from Ft. Leavenworth to Ft. Vancouver. He wished to erase the name "Canadian Falls" given by the trappers, and showed it on his map as "Shoshonee Falls" after the Indians. Could be....At any rate, "Shoshone Falls", was named before the town of "Shoshone."

And the town of "Shoshone" was not always called "Shoshone." At first, it was only a camping spot frequented by cowboys who drove their stock through the area and used it as a watering hole. Frequently, in the Spring, a heavy snowfall in the mountains would cause the Little Wood River to overflow, leaving a soggy bog, so to the cowboys, it was "Bog Bottoms."

Later on, when the railroad people decided to make it the junction point of the O.S.L. and the Wood River Branch, they named it "Junction City." Still later, in October of 1882, the U.S. Post Office came along and officially christened it "Naples", because some of the Italian folks thereabouts were boasting about the "mild Italian climate." (The first school in Shoshone was called the "Naples School.")

Which brings us to the question, how did it come to be named "Shoshone"? Two possibilities - one, the railroad builders established "construction camps" along the line as they

1880 - 1890

progressed, and frequently it was the engineer who named the camps. If this was the case on the O.S.L. the engineer was obviously smitten with Indian names, because the camps leading from American Falls to Naples were - "Napati", "Wapi", "Minidoka", "Kimama", "Owinza", "Wacanza" and "Naples" - "Naples"?? Somehow it just didn't fit - so it may have been the engineer who changed the name to "Shoshone."

The other possibility - as the railroad grading crews and tracklayers moved closer to the spot, landsharks hustled in and applied for a patent on the townsite, and some say it was they who named the place "Shoshone City."

Along the way "Shoshone Falls" also picked up another name. Some white traveler saw the magnificent falls, compared them to Niagara, and proclaimed them "The Niagara of the West." He spread the word about the spectacular falls on the Snake River in Idaho, and eventually, people became curious to see them first hand.

One of those curious souls was a young lad named Charlie Walgamott who first visited the falls in 1878 - the year the Bannocks were on the warpath. Charlie was on a stage coach out of Oregon with two "elderly women passengers" who had made arrangements to take a side trip to see the "Niagara of the West" they had heard about. Charlie decided to go along with them. They spent several days exploring around the falls, and Charlie fell in love with the place. Five years later, he returned with his bride, Lettie, and they home-steaded on the south side of the falls.

In the summer of 1881, they went up to the new town of Hailey, and in August, their first child, a son, was born there. Tragically, this son, the first child ever born in Hailey, died only a few days after birth. Later that summer, Charlie and Lettie moved back to their homestead by the falls.

Charlie had a small boat to cross the river above the falls, and that small boat was the ONLY way to cross the river there.

1880 - 1890

Soon after Charlie and Lettie got home from Hailey, Robert Strahorn, Carrie, and a party of friends made a trip to the falls from Hailey. Among that "party of friends" was W. A. Mellon, so it was a pretty classy party. There was no sign of a road at that time and they were all on horseback. Carrie strahorn later wrote about that trip.

It had been a long, rough ride and Carrie tells how they got there at dusk, and were most anxious to cross the river and have a place to sleep for the night. But, they were unable to get the attention of the "party" (Charlie) on the south side to come and take them across. They yoo-hooed and called and shouted, but were completely ignored. They were forced to spend a miserable night trying to rest on the rocks worrying about rattlesnakes and varmints. Next morning, bright and early, here comes Charlie in the boat, and very pleasantly rowed them across. They were so happy to see him that nobody complained or even mentioned the bad night, and never did get an explanation as to why he had ignored them the night before.

The only really good view of the falls was from the south side of the river, and Carrie wrote a colorful and exciting story about the magnificent "Niagara of the West", and the wonderful time they had exploring.

Coming and going on that trip took them through the place called "Bog Bottoms." It was 1881.

Early in '82 Charlie Walgamott took on a partner named Joe Sullaway. Joe was a veteran stage coach driver, and the two of them planned to develop the falls as a tourist attraction. They heard the O.S.L. would soon be rolling into "Junction City", and some of the folks might be interested in making the 25-mile trip to the falls, if there were transportation available.

They gathered together a used 11-passenger stage coach, a good team, an old heavy wagon, and rounded up 10 or 15 wild mustangs. They were ready to build a road to the falls.

They hitched the team to the old heavy wagon, tied the mustangs strung out behind, and jolted and slam-banged over the sagebrush and rock piles to break a trail. Never did even bother to pick a rock nor grub a sage out of the way - just kind of flattened a path they figured they could get the stage coach over.

They called it the "Walgamott-Sullaway Road", and it was the first North-South "highway" in Idaho!

To say that business was "slow" at first, would be to lie. There was no business - at first. Charlie and Joe would come roaring hell-bent into town on that stage coach, loudly announcing "stage leaving for the falls in ten minutes", "stage leaving for the falls in ten minutes." Then they would come to a screeching halt at the "stage station", walk up and down the streets yelling that the stage would leave in ten minutes, and then - even though nary a soul got on the stage, they would both spring to the driver's seat and take off, hell-for-leather down their new road headed for the falls.

But - as soon as they were out of sight, they would pull over, unhitch the team, and while away the hours in the sagebrush, playing cards, or talking, until it was time to roar into town again announcing another trip to the falls.

It worked! Slowly, slowly, business picked up, and soon they were carving another road out of the rock wall of the canyon wide enough to take the stage right down to the falls. The earlier Indian trail into the site had provided single file passage only.

Next, they established a ferry which served as a means of access between the settlements north of the river, and those on the south - like the stage station at Rock Creek, and they put up a tent hotel against the north canyon walls overlooking the falls. By that time, Charlie and Joe knew every rock and bush in the area, and started to conduct sightseeing boat trips on the river.

1880 - 1890

This whole tourist business took quite a long while to develop, and somewhere along the line, the falls definitely became "Shoshone Falls", and Naples became "Shoshone City." The only positive information I could find is that the Naples post office was officially changed to Shoshone City in March of 1883.

Charlie and Joe tied Shoshone Falls and Shoshone City together with their crazy road. The round trip took three days on the stage, one going, one sightseeing at the falls, and one back to Shoshone. This was after they got some customers, of course.

The tourist business, after such a slow start, was good for Charlie and Joe. They were lively, colorful characters who knew everything about the falls, and were well-known and respected. Charlie wrote several books about his years at Shoshone Falls, and Lettie was postmistress at the Shoshone Falls Post Office when the new, big, two-story hotel was built a few years later.

In his book "Six Decades Back", Charlie tells a story about a young man who knocked on his door one dark night in the fall of 1884. Charlie guessed him to be about 20 or 21 years old. He was very polite, and told Mr. Walgamott that he had 25 cows with him that he had driven down from the Wood River country, and was looking for a place to winter them. Charlie's name had been given to him as someone who knew the area and might direct him to a good spot.

Charlie made him welcome, and helped him bed down the cows while Mrs. Walgamott fixed supper. The young fellow told them he was from Indiana and had heard about the wonderful mineral riches in the Wood River Mines. Lured by the promise of wealth, and the romance of the West, he landed in the mining camp of Bullion. He was unable to get work in the mines because of his slight build, but he did find another job, saved his money, bought a few cows in Blackfoot, and sold

1880 - 1890

the milk to the miners in lieu of whisky. He worked and saved and bought more cows, and was now looking for a place, perhaps in the Snake River canyon, where he could winter them without constant attention.

Charlie told him about a nice place down in the canyon where there were some beautiful blue, blue lakes. He followed Charlie's directions, settled down by the blue lakes, planted trees and produce, and hauled it up and sold it to the miners on the Wood River. Where it was impossible for him to go with wagons, he used pack horses. He also opened a small store in Shoshone in a little room in front of the newspaper office where he sold his produce.

He was a congenial young man, a hard worker, bright, energetic, and imaginative.

His name was Ira Burton Perrine, and he was destined for greatness in Idaho.

1880 - 1890
THE OREGON SHORTLINE RAILROAD

The O.S.L. was built by independent contractors - graders, bridge builders and track layers who set up their own camps, hired their own crews and furnished their own supplies. The railroad provided free transportation to the railhead, which was a big help to the track layers, but not much for the graders and bridge builders working ten to a hundred miles ahead in the wilderness. Supplies had to be freighted ahead to them, and the contractors had a problem finding enough local teamsters willing to take their wagons over the treacherous lava rock, waterless desert and giant sagebrush. It could wreck a wagon fast - and the horses didn't like it either. So, getting supplies to those crews was a major problem.

Another big problem for the contractors was the traveling saloon. Anyone with a license, and a supply of whisky, could legally go into business on government land. And business was brisk! Those "boomers" were rough, tough, hard-drinking men with money (the pay was good), and a gigantic thirst. They would get "drunker'n ol' Billy Hell" every chance they got, and it was up to the contractor to use "pick handle authority" in dealing with them.

Two O.S.L. contractors named Carlyle and Corrigan nabbed a couple of renegades named Tex and Johnson and ordered them out of the country. Tex and Johnson refused to move, so the company clerk arrested them on the spot, and they were hanged forthwith from the new railroad bridge at American Falls. Carlyle and Corrigan then closed all the saloons for miles around.

That was "pick handle authority."

Further down the line, between American Falls and Shoshone, one fellow robbed and killed a man. The killer was caught, but there was no tree or tall place around from which to hang him, so they just tied two wagon tongues together and stood them upright with the culprit hanging between. They left him dangling there in the desert as a warning to others.

That was "pick handle authority."

The laborers were paid in cash, and it was up to the contractor to go to some town that had a bank, pick up the payroll, and then sweat out the return trip carrying the money. He was fair game for every outlaw in the territory, and payrolls bound for isolated camps were repeatedly robbed. Usually, there was an informer right in the camp who would alert the boys on the outside when the boss was leaving to get the cash. Some of the robbers even worked out an easy, efficient system to relieve him of his burden - five men would move in as a team and lift the payroll in a matter of minutes. With the help of guns, of course.

Even when he got the payroll through intact, the contractor had another problem - the minute the crew got paid most of them would sneak off to the nearest saloon or town to drink, gamble, fool around and spend their money. Then, the beleaguered contractor would have to go after them, or else round up another bunch who had already spent theirs.

Working on the O.S.L. through the Idaho desert was not your most attractive occupation. Rattlesnakes, horned toads, tarantulas, scorpions and ticks were all over the place, and even the roughest of men sometimes got squeamish about sleeping on the ground. They could cope during the day when they could see and kill the critters, but knowing they were crawling around all over at night could put a guy's nerves on edge. Nobody wanted to sleep with a rattlesnake, and many carried thick, rough ropes in their blankets to circle themselves at night for protection.

It was mighty difficult - any way you looked at it.

1880 - 1890
THE WOOD RIVER BRANCH OF THE O.S.L.

James H. Kymer got the grading contract for an eight-mile stretch on the Wood River Branch, that ended about five miles down Wood River out of Shoshone. On the first pay-day, his camp was filled with swaggering, staggering, fighting drunks. Next pay-day, same thing. He couldn't figure out where the whisky was coming from way out in the middle of nowhere. After checking every tent and wagon, he finally located the "saloon" in an inconspicuous tent just outside the camp. He approached the man and politely asked him to leave. The fellow smugly shook his head and pointed to the liquor license tacked to the tent pole, saying he was on government land and legal.

Kymer said nothing, strolled back to where his dynamite was stored, cut a stick in two, picked up a cap and fuse, and bored a hole in the dynamite with a pencil. As he walked back to the whisky tent, he calmly lit a cigarette, stood again in front of the whisky man, fuzzed out the fuse, lit it with the cigarette, and informed the peddler that when the fuse got down to where he wouldn't dare pick it up, he would toss it into the tent. "I'll go! I'll go!" screamed the frenzied fellow, and started to scramble frantically about. When the fuse got short, Kymer tossed it away - not too far from the tent, where it exploded in a thunderous roar. The tent shook and started to fall down, the man's horses broke loose and scattered, and Kymer calmly told him he was on his way back to get another stick.

Well, the saloon keeper took off like a shot, and from that moment on Jim Kymer enjoyed an admirable reputation, and never again did he have to cope with "legal saloons on government land" anywhere near any of his camps.

That was "pick handle authority."

1880 - 1890

When Mr. Kymer bid that contract for the branch line, it appeared to be a fairly easy area to grade - on paper. Not so. Most of it was over lava rock, and it was impossible to lay track over such an unyielding surface. It would jostle a locomotive to pieces in no time. He was forced to cut into the lava a foot or so below grade, then fill with earth. Except - there was no "earth" for miles around. The wind, down through the ages, had swept that area clean as a whistle, and he had to haul dirt and fill for miles over those incredible lava beds. So, in addition to having to find teamsters to haul his supplies into camp, he had to find even more to haul in the fill.

And that was not all of his problems - there was much difficulty in gouging out the lava rocks. Blasting with black power did little more than heave up huge pieces of lava too big to handle, and then he would have to blast those pieces apart. Even at that, they would still "cleave together" making them extremely difficult to load and haul away. Sometimes the big blasts barely cracked the surface of the lava, blowing down instead, into large ancient bubbles and tubes in the lava itself.

The work was extremely hard, and frustrating, and every pay day his men deserted in droves.

His freight costs were monumental. For every dollar spent purchasing case goods, it took more than two dollars to get it hauled to his camp. By the time he finished his eight mile stretch, he had done a good job, but was deeply in debt. The O.S.L. bosses, however, were aware of his unforeseeable problems, and gave him a 30-mile grading contract between Mt. Home and Boise which put him back on his feet financially. That stretch was so easy he had to blast only one time, and said that Boise was paradise compared to wild and wooly Shoshone.

He did mention one advantage on the Wood River Branch - the river was teeming with trout, and could be dynamited out by the wagon load. Deer, too, were plentiful, and during the season many were taken to feed the population.

1880 - 1890

In one season alone, a man named Frank Coran supplied 250 hind quarters to one outfit for 3 cents a pound.

It is estimated that it took a crew of a thousand men, mostly Irish, Chinese and Italian, to build the Wood River Branch of the Oregon Short Line. The telegraph lines, which were vital to the running of the railroad, were strung at the same time. An Idaho Statesman reporter watching the digging of the holes for the telegraph poles was impressed by the long, looong, handled shovels and "spoons" calling them the "queerest looking utensils imaginable."

The railroad brought into the Magic Circle still another dimension of the population - surveyors, section men, telegraphers, conductors, engineers, brakemen, boomers, porters and firemen - to add to the "mix" already there - the prospectors, mine workers, farmers, cattlemen, sheepmen, freighters, teamsters, merchants, saloon keepers, doctors, lawyers, land speculators, government workers, construction workers and assorted craftsmen and con artists.

The Magic Circle in the early 1880's was a representative capsule of Idaho Territory. It was the brightest, busiest, most exciting spot in the entire territory.

The first railroad construction train pulled into Shoshone on February 17, 1883, laid track one mile past the town to the West, then turned back and went to work on the Wood River Branch. The last spike of that branch line was driven at Hailey at 10:30 a.m. on May 7, 1883, and the following year it was extended to Ketchum.

The first telephone in Idaho Territory came into service in Hailey on October 1, 1883, was extended to Bellevue and Bullion by October 7th, and to Ketchum on November 1st.

Hailey, Ketchum, Bellevue and Bullion were all becoming more and more prosperous, along with numerous mining camps in the area. The estimated yield of the mines in 1883 was three-and-a-half million dollars, and the following

1880 - 1890

year the estimated returns from the mines was five million!

Our old friend Robert Strahorn, publicity man for the Union Pacific and Manager of the Oregon-Idaho Land Improvement Co., predicted that Hailey would soon be the "Denver of Idaho"!

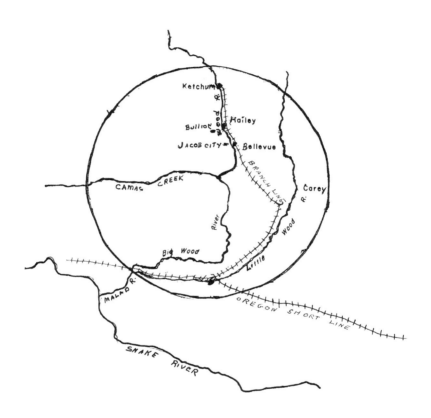

1880 - 1890
THE CONSTITUENCY

By 1886, the mines in the Wood River Valley were being worked to full capacity.

Hailey quickly became the commercial, financial, political center of the area and was also considered the "Social City of the Mountains." There were beautiful wide streets, lovely homes, fine hotels and business establishments; dancing schools and drama classes, quartets, self-improvement activities and lectures on womens' rights. Lots of parties, roller-skating, bicycling, horseback riding, sleigh rides and hay rides, skiing, and dozens of "bees" (quilting, rug and honey), to help each other, as well as to socialize.

Yes, the other towns on the Big Wood were "social", too, but none so much as Hailey. Hailey had the "Silk Stocking Element" - formal, polite and very proper. No lady's wardrobe was complete without a "black silk." The dresses were of grosgrain, long enough to touch the ground, and full enough to allow for the bustle then in vogue. To the women of the area, the coming of the railroad meant contact with the outside world. It stood for progress, new neighbors, more social activities, and visits from prominent people "outside." It meant that dress goods would be cheaper and easier to get, and the telegraph would bring the latest news of the world. For more than four years, Hailey had the distinction of having THREE DAILY NEWSPAPERS, which was more than any other town in the entire territory.

Another "element" in Hailey furnished entertainment for the free-spending types who wanted to play Faro, poker, roulette and other games of chance. Dozens of establishments were open round-the-clock. Horse races were held on a regular basis and were very well attended by all of the "elements." Hailey, Ketchum and Bellevue all had fine race tracks.

Baseball was by far the favorite game, and singing

around a piano, the most popular social pastime. Seems like everybody sang in those days. Many a tracklaying foreman was hired chiefly for his singing ability because his singing seemed to make the work go smoother, kept the men in better spirits, and they would often all join in. Popular songs of the day were "I've been workin' on the railroad", "There is a Tavern in the Town", "While Strolling Through the Park", "Clementine", and "Just a Song at Twilight."

In 1884 the W. W. Cole Circus pulled into Hailey and 6,000 people attended! The railroad made traveling entertainment possible, and there were circuses, road shows, tent shows, and "Chataquas." A Chataqua was a traveling lecture and entertainment group and was very popular all over America at that time. They appeared wherever the railroads reached. The name "Chataqua" came from the headquarters town of Chataqua, New York where the concept originated.

The Wood River Mining District had its share of prominent and famous people - some of whom reached very high places in life. Some were native born, others were frequent visitors. Ezra Pound, the famous and controversial poet, was born in Hailey during the time his father, Homer Pound was the first register of the United States Land Office there. And, of course, Robert Strahorn, Vice-President and Manager of the Idaho and Oregon Land Improvement Co., was a well-known writer who later became famous and sought after in railroad circles and ended up being a millionaire. He named "Della Mountain", just west of Hailey, to honor his writer wife, Carrie Adell. (He called her "Della" and she called him "Pard.")

And there was Hugh Wallace, who was once Secretary of the Idaho and Oregon Land Improvement Co., in Hailey. Hugh married the daughter of Melville W. Fuller, then Chief Justice of the the Supreme Court of the United States. Later Hugh Wallace was appointed Ambassador to France by Woodrow Wilson.

William Hyndman was an early resident of Ketchum,

and practiced law there. He was a Major in the Civil War and a prominent mining man. Hyndman Peak was named after William Hyndman.

Another Ketchum resident, Frank R. Gooding, served two terms as Governor of the State of Idaho, and also as United States Senator. His daughter, Maud, was the first child born in Ketchum, and the town of Gooding was named after Frank.

And, we must not forget the famous Jay Gould, "the richest and most hated man in America", who was no small potatoes either. He would arrive in his own private train, accompanied by his family, friends, and guests from everywhere from New York to Omaha. Gould's entourage would consist of a number of private secretaries, cooks, porters, and other attendants, and his private train was complete with locomotive and tender, baggage car, commissary car, and two private drawing coaches - or more. The Gould parties came to enjoy the beautiful scenery, fish in Silver Creek and the Wood Rivers, explore the towns, visit the mines and were absolutely delighted with their stay in the magnificent Wood River Valley.

Along in the mid-1880's British and California capital began to flow into the Magic Circle. London interests purchased the largest of the Wood River mines and such prominent California investors as George Hearst acquired Wood River property.

Hailey had several hotels. The "Merchant's Hotel" and the "Grand Central" were not so hot, but the "Alturas" and the "Hailey Hot Springs" hotels were very grand.

Construction on the Alturas began on March 22, 1883 but was delayed for lack of funds until Thomas Mellon, father of Andrew Mellon, advanced $15,000 and took a mortgage on the Alturas. It was opened to the public with a "Grand Ball" on May 25, 1886. That was the first Mellon Ball in the Magic Circle.

Thomas Mellon was a wealthy banker and financier in

1880 - 1890

Pittsburgh, and his son, Andrew, was the young man working with Robert Strahorn in the Idaho and Oregon Land Improvement Co. Andrew lived in Hailey, and his father, Thomas, had financial interests in the Wood River Valley. Andrew later became a partner and President of the Mellon National Bank in Pittsburgh. He was active in many industries and director of several financial and industrial corporations. He founded the town of Donora, Pennsylvania where he established a large steel plant. He engaged in many philanthropies, and aided in establishing the Mellon Institute in Pittsburgh. He was Secretary of the Treasury of the United States under three successive Presidents - Harding, Coolidge, and Hoover. He was U.S. Ambassador to Great Britain, and left his important collections of works of art, and a gallery building in Washington D. C., to the American people. Congress, in accepting this gift, named the gallery the "National Gallery of Art."

Any town in the world would have been proud to have had a resident like Andrew Mellon. Hailey did, and was.

When the Alturas Hotel opened in 1886, the Wood River Times wrote, "It is admitted to be the finest hotel between Denver and the Pacific Ocean."

It had several unique features: a pipe was run from a hot water spring two miles west of Hailey to heat the hotel and fill a large swimming pool. Such famous people as Jay Gould made annual trips to visit the hotel and soak in the beneficial mineral waters. The rooms were beautifully furnished and there was a bar connected with a billiard hall. It cost $35,000 plus $8,000 for furniture and $5,000 for the bar.

The Alturas was the ultimate - but not for long.

Two years later, Robert Strahorn and Co. purchased the Hailey Hot Springs property and the Lamb ranch, plus a controlling interest in the Electric Light Works. He built the fabulous "Hailey Hot Springs Hotel", bath houses and other

1880 - 1890

extensive improvements. Located about two miles west of Hailey, the hotel was formally opened to the public on June 20, 1889 with a "Grand Ball." Guests came from far and near and it instantly became the social center of Hailey. The building was valued at $100,000 with the property at $20,000 more. The Grand Opening was attended by the elite of Hailey, Bellevue, and Bullion, plus their Elite guests, in glorious evening dress - the Silk Stocking Element.

Ten years later, on July 27, 1899, the Hailey Hot Springs Hotel was completely destroyed when a fire broke out on the second floor above the kitchen. The guests were organized quickly into a water-bearing brigade by one of the guests of the hotel, and although there were only minor injuries, everyone's possessions were lost.

There were three ladies in the plunge bath when the fire broke out, who refused to come out of the bath house until someone brought them some "proper clothes." There were tense moments, but someone got "proper clothes" to them and they emerged at a gallop, unscathed.

The loss of that beautiful hotel was devastating to the community. The people who lived in the area had regularly enjoyed the mineral hot springs , and visitors from far and near cherished the time they spent enjoying the luxuries of that famous hotel, and sloshing about in the wonderful, effervescent hot springs.

THE DAMPHOOLS

An organization called the "Damphools" was active in the Magic Circle in 1883. A letter to the editor of the Wood River Times brought the Damphools into prominence. Following is a reproduction of that letter dated June 13, 1883:

HAILEY AND BELLEVUE
THE BELLEVUE DAMPHOOLS
They Propose to Come
To Hailey on the
Fourth of July,
to Bury the Hatchet

TO THE EDITOR OF THE TIMES: - At a meeting of the Damphools in Bellevue, last night, it was resolved to turn out on the Fourth of July and go to Hailey. The line of march from Bellevue to Hailey, going and coming, to be on the railroad tracks, each member to count the ties both ways, under penalty of expulsion from the order. If any of the members are indisposed at night, they will be sheltered in the Hotel de Furey, and the start postponed until they are let out. We expect to be cordially received by the Order of Cranks.

The hatchet will be duly buried by the two organizations in a gallon of buttermilk, and we expect a number of Hailey ladies to stand by us.

In the afternoon, there will be a grand ceremony, during which the 10 degrees of the Order of Damphools will be conferred upon a number of deserving citizens. All the lawyers and doctors will get the 10 degrees: the editor of the TIMES will also get the 10 degrees, and be the first initiated. This out of regard for his lying abilities and he may also have

1880 - 1890

the extraordinary degree of Eminent Grand conferred upon him.

Yours respectfully,
THE EMINENT GRAND
THE WOOD RIVER TIMES
June 13, 1883

Obviously this "event" was an inside joke circulating between Hailey and Bellevue. I could find no further information on this "Damphool" thing, didn't know what they did or what caused the "hatchet" business. I was interested in it because of the name.

A hundred years later "Dam Fools" will again show up in the MagicCircle.

Stand by. . .

THE CHINESE

1880 - 1890

There were quite a few "elements" of society in the Wood River Valley in those days, but the low man on the totem pole was the Chinaman. Many of them came into Idaho after finishing work on the Central Pacific Railroad in 1869. They settled in the mining towns, set up laundries, cooked at the mines, or were shifted from camp to camp by the contractors.

The Chinese did the back-breaking, degrading work that no one else would do. Miners frequently sold their worthless, worked-out claims to the Chinese, laughing all the way to the bank about their cruel joke. However, the Chinese often had the last laugh because they worked the claim harder, and longer, and more diligently, and in most cases returned the mine to production. But, even then, they were forced to pay a special "Chinese Miners Tax" of $4 a month to work in the mines.

They endured much suffering at the hands of others, and everyone well knew the meaning of "he hasn't a Chinaman's chance." They were robbed, beaten and murdered, and no one came to their aid. Chinese massacres (blamed on the Indians) where as many as a hundred were killed at one time, were ignored. They were not permitted to testify in court, so had no recourse whatever. They were considered inferior to all others in every way, and the only people regarded as "foreigners."

"Anti-Chinese Societies" flourished all over the West.

The Chinese population in the Wood River Valley amounted to several hundred, with about 200 living in Hailey along upper River Street adjacent to the Red Light District, where they often found work as servants, woodcutters or cooks. They were industrious gardeners, and raised vegetables to sell to the townspeople. And, they did everybody's laundry.

Sometimes, Hailey folk were embarrassed to meet their own "unmentionables" flying down the street on a windy day. The Chinese would carefully lay out the freshly laundered

1880 - 1890

garments on the roof-tops to dry, but if a sudden gust of wind came up, the laundry would take off like it had a mind of its own, leading a parade of harried Chinamen scurrying down the street after it.

In spite of the fact that they played an important part in the development of the West, the Chinese were cruelly discriminated against. They were easy to identify and still clung to their old traditions. They wore long pigtails trailing down their backs, and smoked opium in "dens." Their house of worship, called a "Joss House" was decorated with strange creatures and odd things.

People were suspicious of them. Like the time in Hailey when someone noticed that the dog population seemed to be dwindling, and at about the same time, a couple of Chinese started to peddle "novel-shaped sausages at extremely low prices." The Wood River Times put two-and-two together, questioned them about where they got the meat, and one finally confessed.

Yes, it was.

The Times editorially denounced the sausage and put the restaurant keepers on guard, and further commented that the Chinese were no doubt wintering largely on domestic animals.

There was a smaller Chinese settlement along the river at Bellevue, and they also operated a laundry. Bellevue's Charter still contains an anti-pollution law forbidding them from discarding their soapy waters, or anything else, into the river.

The Chinese believed their soul could not rest in the hereafter until the body was interred in China, and it was the sacred responsibility of those still living to see that the body (or at least the bones) were returned to China for burial. So, on top of all their other problems the living Chinese were obligated to carry out this gruesome task. And they conscientiously did so.

1880 - 1890

Don't know how many other folks actually knew about this practice, but they found out in a hurry when the Wood River News-Miner published a story about several Chinamen who, in accordance with their custom, were caught digging up the remains of their countrymen buried near Bellevue, and carefully cleaning and scraping the bones preparatory to sending them back to China. Only problem - the "remains" were still not quite done, and they were dumping the dried and partially decayed flesh into a ditch in the lower part of town. "Pieces of decayed flesh large as a man's hand were found on the edge of the water, and other portions of the refuse matters were in the water."

Needless to say, the townsfolk were horrified! That water was used by those living in the lower part of town for domestic purposes!

The cry went up - THE CHINESE MUST GO!

On January 20, 1886, a committee was formed to notify all Chinese that the people wanted them to wind up their affairs and be out of town no later than May 1st.

But, on February 10th, Hop Chung and Sam Wing of Hailey, Quong Lee of Ketchum, and Ye Lee of Bellevue, called at the office of the Wood River Times and put in an advertisement to run for one month, stating that the Chinese WOULD NOT leave Wood River. They claimed they could neither sell nor dispose of their property, and by leaving, they would lose about $35,000 in the three towns.

Even though the anti-Chinese movement was in full swing, and the committee was demanding that they get out, some of the local folks were apprehensive about losing all that cheap labor. Who would do their laundry and other dirty work if the Chinese were forced to leave? They talked about it a lot, and before long, resentment against the Chinese eased, and began building against the anti-Chinese forces! If they wanted to get rid of the Chinese, they should think of a way to replace them with good help!

1880 - 1890

On June 2nd, 1886, an editorial appeared in the Times saying that the people of Hailey were wrong to boycott the Mongolians, and that it was un-American to do so. "Even though the Wood River Times has always been anti-Chinese, it will not uphold a conspiracy to injure any man's business," the editorial said.

The Chinese were not forced to go. But the bone business was.

They remained for almost 64 years, until the early 1950's when the last Chinese-operated restaurant in Hailey closed down.

There is very little left in the Wood River Valley to indicate the once large Chinese population.

1880 - 1890

GIRLS! GIRLS! GIRLS!

When the flap about getting rid of the Chinese was in full swing, two gents, Rice and Foster, came up with an idea to replace the cheap labor. They were "Immigration Agents" who traveled the East and Mid-West promoting the territory and enticing people to "Go West!." The railroad made their work easy and possible by giving them special rates, and supplying thousands of pamphlets, flyers, and brochures describing the territory in glowing terms.

Dr. Rice, as he was called, never missed a chance to make a buck, and figured it would be an easy matter for them to bring out young, strong "girls" to be servants to replace the Chinese - or wives if anybody wanted one.

The following item appeared in the Wood River Times on March 31, 1886:

Dr. Rice says: "For every 20 men in Idaho there is not more than one woman. This is certainly embarrassing and will continue so until there is an effort made to secure female help. If my advice is followed, in less than 4 months, the maidens of the East will be found in abundance all over the territory. First, let each bachelor wanting a wife, put into a pool $5 and each person wanting a servant, also add $5 to the pool. This will pay the expenses of these girls, and those sent out will be such as any bachelor in the territory would be pleased to select from. By following this advice, the families get their servants, society is benefitted, the bachelor is made happy by securing himself a loving wife, and the girls sent out will write back East to their friends to come out so before the first installment is married off, there will be abundant help to take their places as servants and each bachelor will be certain of a wife. Anyone who cannot afford to pay $5

1880 - 1890

for such a luxury would not treat a wife with as much consideration as his mules and one who would not pay $5 to get a good servant girl would not pay her wages after she had earned them. You have responsible people that you can trust this business to, and not until you have done this can you rid the country of the heathen Chinese."

Dr. Rice was also busy recruiting potential settlers, and reported from Omaha as follows:

"One party of 50 or more colonists will come from Novo Scotia to join the colony that will leave here either April 20 or May 4. I will also send out quite a number from Keokuck, Iowa. Everything looks favorable for a colony of from 200 to 500 but I cannot, of course, say just how many will go. The first colony will leave here April 20, 1886."

On April 24, 1886 the Wood River Times reported:

"Dr. Rice informs the Times that plenty of good Scandanavian girls are willing to come to Idaho and work for $5 per week but that there are very few who have money enough to pay their passage although it is only $25. The fare must therefore be paid at this end. Now all who want girls must deposit $25 for each girl in McCormick's bank in Hailey, then they must see Dr. Rice and arrange with him. Dr. Rice will probably charge a fee of $5 per girl."

I was never able to find out exactly how many girls came to the Wood River Valley and Camas Prairie under Dr. Rice's "program." Maybe the deal was not so attractive after the price went up. Do know that his promotion to entice settlers worked

1880 - 1890

pretty well, and was definitely part of the first "wave" of settler immigration into the Magic Circle.

Of course, shortly after Dr. Rice's announcement about bringing "girls" out, the folks decided that the Chinese didn't have to leave after all, so the market for servant girls might have just petered out.

Wonder if there were ever any takers on the "wife" offer.

1880 - 1890
CAMAS PRAIRIE SETTLERS

Settlers began coming into the Magic Circle in droves in the Spring of 1884 on the new railroad. Robert Strahorn and the Union Pacific had been circulating thousands of tempting, colorful brochures all over the country, promoting the area in glowing terms, and Immigration Agents like Rice and Foster were working hard on their "colonization schemes." The railroad offered special rates to anyone willing to make the trip.

The first carload recruited by Rice and Foster, arrived in early '84. There were 150 people, nearly all able-bodied men, and about a dozen women. 147 stopped at Bellevue where all of the vacant houses had been secured for them. They came mostly from Iowa and Wisconsin, but some came from as far away as Maryland. The following day another carload arrived from Nebraska. All were headed for Camas Prairie to take up homesteads as soon as the snow was off the ground.

They arrived full of hope and the dream of a farm of their own, but no one had told them anything about what kinds of crops would mature in the short growing period that exists on Camas Prairie, nor any of the other disadvantages they might encounter, such as: the high altitude of the prairie; lack of proper air drainage which could cause unexpected frosts when crop damage was possible; uncertain rainfall causing possible drought; grasshoppers and crickets that sometimes swarmed over the prairie, and the hard, cold winters with deep snow.

Horse and cattle camps still dotted the prairie but were mostly on streams along the foothills and they stayed for only a season or so. There were also some sheep camps which brought about a constant struggle between the two, to see who could get the most range. Many of the larger cattle barons had sold out by that time, and some of them were going into the sheep business. There was a saying among the settlers –

"cattlemen and sheepmen are very much alike. The only difference is the cattleman would let his stock eat you out if they wanted to, but the sheepman would herd them there until he knows they had."

When those optimistic new arrivals came to Camas Prairie they filed claims on the land, even though many did not have a single piece of machinery or horses with which to cultivate and plant grain. Some managed to build shelters and fences, and somehow stay alive with the hope of developing the area.

The towns of Soldier, Critchton (pronounced Cri-ton), and Corral were established.

Things really started to come apart about 1886 when the grasshoppers blackened the sky and ate everything in sight. For five years in a row they came, followed by two years of Army crickets. The hapless settlers fought them desperately, driving wagons, pulling rollers, herding sheep and horses over the prairie trying to stamp them out, but nothing worked, and the grasshoppers still came in great black clouds. It was impossible to eke out even a bare existence under such circumstances, and the weary, heartsick first wave of immigrants to Camas Prairie gradually gathered their few belongings and fled in despair. Only a few survived the pestilence. Lonely buildings and fences were left to the elements. Posts rotted and fences fell down and became a menace to horse owners. Wire-cut horses were common for those crossing the prairie.

And very few travelers crossed now - everybody traveled on the train.

The winter of 1889 - '90, known as the "hard winter" deposited 21 feet of snow on Camas Prairie. That's right. W.A. Sifers, the United States Weatherman for a number of years, kept a record of the snowfall.

The bad winters continued. . .

1880 - 1890
OTHER HOMESTEADERS

The pioneer families who settled the choice meadowland south of Bellevue were by 1884, settled and producing, when that first wave of Camas Prairie immigrants arrived by train. The Timmermans, Stantons, Blacks, Browns, Dittoes et al, were developing their homesteads into fine farms and ranches. Most of the land around them had been taken up, and farms and ranches were blossoming.

Way back in 1877 a man named N.R. Woodworth filed on a tract where the town of Gooding now stands. He built the first house there - a rock building - put in the first dam, and dug the first ditch that ever took water out of the Little Wood River.

On up the Little Wood, Sam and John Hunter diverted water to their land in 1882, and from 1883 to 1887, new farms were taken up and water brought upon them. At that time, farms were necessarily limited to good tracts along the rivers.

In 1885, David C. Calhoun filed on 160 acres on the east shore of the Big Wood River about four miles south of where it joins Camas Creek. He was granted a patent on November 2, 1885, and soon built a large, 4-bedroom, two-story home, a barn, sheds, planted trees and settled down with his family.

Four years later, on October 5, 1889, a patent was granted to William H. Carpenter for 160 acres adjoining Calhoun on the south, and he settled down with his family.

One year later, on December 15, 1890, Thomas Brew moved onto 160 acres just west of Carpenter.

Calhoun, Carpenter and Brew were all on the Eastside of the Big Wood River.

One month after Brew was granted his patent, J.H. Decker, on January 15, 1900, took 640 acres (40 of which were assigned to J.A. Green). Decker's large grant was located north of Calhoun and on the west side of Big Wood.

Two-and-a-half years later, Owen Riley - the same Owen

1880 - 1890

Riley who was the first postmaster of Bellevue, and who brought supplies to the "Intrepid 27" and who spent the winter at Jacob's City in 1879 - was granted a patent on the 160 acres just north of Decker.

On February 6, 1904 Christopher P. Rice was granted a patent on 80 acres north of Riley.

All six of these farms - Calhoun, Carpenter, Brew, Decker, Riley and Rice - were later completely submerged in the Magic Reservoir.

1880 - 1890
THE MORMONS

One-fourth of the population of Idaho Territory were Mormons settled in southeastern Idaho. And they practiced polygamy.

During the first twenty years of Idaho's growth, people minded their own business, and left the Mormons alone. However, news of the Mormons and their "plural wives", was seeping out into the nation at large where the prevailing code of morals was at odds with the Mormon belief. Anti-Mormon prejudice grew to full-blown indignation. As a result, in 1884 Congress passed the Edmunds-Tucker Act which made polygamy a penal offense, and the Idaho Territorial Legislature passed the famous "test oath" which provided that no one could register to vote, or hold office, without first swearing that they renounced polygamy, "and all other crimes defined by law."

Of course, no member of the Mormon Church could take such an oath, and consequently the southeastern counties were ruled by the few non-Mormons who could. In some of those counties it was impossible to find even 12 people who could take the oath, which made it impossible to get a jury together. So in reality, there was no "law" at all because it was impossible for anyone to have his day in court.

Many Mormons were indicted, tried, and sentenced under Federal law, and typically, as in most disputes based on moral and religious issues, all sorts of absurd charges and countercharges were made. There was much bitterness on both sides.

In 1886 the Republicans held their State Convention in Hailey, and nominated Fred Dubois, a hard-core anti-Mormon, as Territorial Representative to Congress. The Democrats convened in Bellevue and named John Hailey to run for that office.

1880 - 1890

Dubois won.

The "Mormon Question" was a political football, and the Mormons were relentlessly persecuted, and prosecuted, until October 6, 1890 when the head of the church forbade the further teaching of polygamy as Mormon Doctrine.

The Magic Circle in those days was no more a "melting pot" than any other place in America. More like an assortment of hard, jagged rocks tumbling about in a cement mixer, grinding, grating and wearing away at each other.

The Indians were still roaming sadly about; the Chinese were washing clothes and smoking opium, shunned by just about every other human; the Mormons were being convicted for polygamy and unlawful cohabitation; the cattle and sheep men were fighting over the grazing land, and the grasshoppers were winning the battle on Camas Prairie.

There was a powerful "movement" underway to get the state capital moved to Hailey, and the politicians were busily trying to rearrange the counties to each one's own best interest.

The "movement" never moved far, but they did succeed in cutting up the counties.

Alturas County had been created by the Idaho Territorial Legislature at its first session in Lewiston in 1864. It encompassed all of the present Blaine, Camas, Elmore, Gooding, Lincoln, Jerome and Minidoka counties, plus the better part of Butte, parts of Custer, Bingham and Power.

In 1881, a portion of Alturas and Lemhi counties became Custer, at the same time Hailey became the county seat of Alturas.

On February 7, 1889, a "rump legislature" - one that meets after the regular session has adjourned - met the day after adjournment and split Alturas into three parts by creating Logan and Elmore out of part of Alturas. Then, that sneaky rump legislature falsified the records by back-dating them by one day.

1880 - 1890

The people did not want the change - but they had no say.

The politicians did it.

And the mighty Alturas Empire began to crumble.

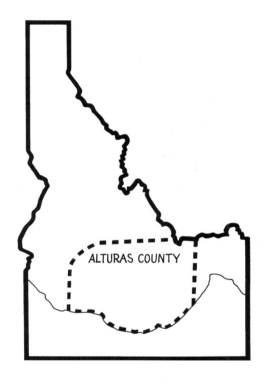

1880 - 1890

THE ICE CAVES

The "Ice Caves" were "discovered" during the 1880's. They have also been called "Mystery Caves." Probably because there are so many stories and legends about them the mystery is which ones are true.

Alpha Kinsey, a young lad tending sheep (or goats?) in the area, is credited with "discovering" the caves in 1884. Seems he came upon his sheep/goats drinking water from a pool of melted ice in the barren desolate lava waste. He followed the ice-pool and entered the main cave with a lantern and long cord to guide him. He climbed through narrow crevices until he came to a solid wall of ice.

Word of Alpha's discovery quickly reached the alert ears of the saloon-keepers in Shoshone, and they high-tailed it up there to chip away at all that nice ice. For six glorious years they advertised and sold "THE ONLY COLD BEER IN THE WEST!." When they finally had to stop chiseling in 1900, they had carved out a room 60 feet wide by 14 feet high by 60 feet long!

Nearby Kinsey Butte was named to honor the pioneer family of Henry H. Kinsey who homesteaded there. There were 14 in the family - twelve children and the parents. Alpha was somewhere in the middle. . .

However, long before Alpha "discovered" them, the ice caves had been found and lost quite a few times. Stories abound. For example, this one is supposed to be absolutely, so-help-me, true: During the Placer days of the Boise Basin (early 1860's) two hoodlums had been systematically robbing lone miners of their gold. But, it was beginning to get too hot for them around the Basin, so they decided to get out while the gittin' was good. They saddled up, headed east, and got as far as the old Cottonwoods Road that passed near the ice caves, when they spotted a posse on their tail! They whipped their horses faster and faster and turned off the road into the lava

1880 - 1890

fields toward the ice caves. It was mighty rough going for the poor, abused horses and they soon collapsed. The two stinkers were forced to make their way on foot, stumbling and scrambling through the lava. Exhausted, they finally took refuge behind a pile of lava to try to make a stand. But, the posse was in hot pursuit, quickly surrounded the culprits before they knew what was happening, and shot 'em both dead. The loot - estimated to be at least $75,000 in gold - was not on them. The posse looked around and turned over rocks, but never found the gold. They decided the crooks must have stashed it somewhere between the road and the caves before they caught up with them. It was impossible to thoroughly search such an expansive field of lava so the posse went home empty-handed. The gold is still there.

Here's another account that's supposed to be gospel: Two gun-men held up a Wells-Fargo Stage and made off with more than $80,000 in raw gold. Later on, the two got into a big fight and one killed the other and took off with the gold. The posse was hot on his trail, so he turned off the Cottonwoods Road into the lava rocks, picked his way carefully in the direction of the Ice Caves, and finally hid the gold under some lava rocks. He marked the spot in his own secret way and quickly made his get-away, planning to pick up the loot after the trail had cooled. But, it didn't work out that way - his picture had been out on "Wanted" signs for some of his other crimes, and he was picked up and chucked into a Montana prison. When he finally got out, years later, he went back to where he thought he had buried his gold and searched and searched and never could find the spot. He's still out there looking. . .

There are lots of other stories about the Ice Caves being used as robbers' roosts and places for hiding ill-gotten gains. The robbers all seemed to know about the caves. Next time you're out there poking around among the rattlesnakes, keep an eye out for all that lost loot.

1880 - 1890

Now, a word about all that lava - Idaho has the largest unbroken field of lava on the North American continent. Great out-pourings of lava have covered 23,000 square miles - or one-third of the State's area, reaching a depth of 5,000 feet to as little as a few feet. Geologists figure that numerous volcanos were active along the northern half of the Snake River Plain about four million years ago, and have continued off and on up to within 150 to 600 years ago. The molten material - called basalt magma - oozes and shoots up through cracks in the Earth's crust. This material was so forceful and so fluid that some flows ran as far as 100 miles. No one knows how many caves there are in these vast lava fields. A cave is formed when the outer surface of the lava flow cools and hardens while the inner part stays hot and continues to flow, forming a hollow cylinder with lava-rock walls. Down through the centuries flow after flow piled up in layers to form the Snake River Plain so some of the caves are deep, deep, while others are fairly shallow and near the surface, such as the Ice Caves, which are part of the most recent flow of eruptions from nearby Black Butte.

A small portion of the cave roof fell in, the hollow tube filled with ice, and people started dropping in and leaving their loot-gold out in the yard somewhere.

So, the Snake River Plain is a vast region of twisted and woven lava, fallen-in tunnels, arched bridges, potholes and pits. In winter, the ice in some of the caves will actually melt. In summer, it freezes rock hard. Even on the hottest days, when the temperature of the surface lava has been raised by the sun to a blistering heat, only a few feet down the ice stands firm and solid. In some places both hot and cold water may run side by side out of a fissure.

The startling subterranean nature of the area was further revealed when the city of Shoshone was only an infant. A hotel owner started to drill for water, and about 20 feet down discovered that his drilling tools had vanished! Investigation

1880 - 1890

showed there is an enormous chamber under the town - apparently bottomless - because stones dropped into the hole that had been drilled, were heard striking the walls from side to side on their way down, until they reached such depth that the echoing reverberations could no longer be heard. The cavern thereupon was used for the hotel's sewage. Nobody knew or cared where the waste water ultimately ended up.

One of the fallen-in tunnels.

1880 - 1890

S. D. BOONE

In 1886, when the Wood River mining district was in its hey-dey, Samuel D. Boone stepped off the train in Hailey. Soft-spoken and courteous, he was 28 years old, and fascinated with the sights and sounds of this magnificent, rugged new country.

He came from Bloomsburg, Pennsylvania where his family were successful farmers, stock raisers, and prominent in educational work. The old homestead, which had been in his family for 150 years, was originally purchased from William Penn.

Soon after arriving in Hailey he entered into a partnership with Judge E. B. Lemmon in the real estate and insurance business. The firm was called "Boone and John."

He lost no time in getting acquainted with Southern Idaho and its people. The business required that he must know the area well, but it was his own insatiable curiosity that drove him to examine it through a microscope. He studied maps of streams and rivers, trails and roads, and then rode out to inspect everything first-hand. He examined the soil every time it changed from mountain to meadow to sagebrush desert, and knew every landmark between the Sawtooth Mountains and the Snake River.

And he met the people. Made at least ten new friends a day. He wandered among the affluent and the struggling dirt farmers, gathering knowledge about their problems and accomplishments. There was always something new around the next corner for Mr. Boone, and his interest in people was genuine. He listened, and learned and "pondered."

He became very "taken" with irrigation and spent long

1880 - 1890

hours talking with and watching the irrigators. New farms were steadily appearing along the streams and rivers and he visited them often. He studied everything he could get his hands on regarding irrigation, and investigated several "community canal companies" around Boise and Franklin.

His farming background assured him that much of the sage brush desert land to the south, along the Snake River, could be magically transformed into excellent crop land -- if it had water.

In 1888 Boone talked Judge Lemmon, and several others, into going in with him to develop the first irrigation "system" in Southern Idaho. He had all the necessary facts and figures, and had chosen the perfect place on the Snake River. Altogether, he managed to amass $10,000 and went ahead with the preliminary work. But, before long, more money was needed, and although he tried desperately to interest others in the plan, he was unable to raise the necessary funds.

Unfortunately, the end of the money was the end of the project, and his first attempt to construct an "irrigation system" to get water to large tracts of land away from the river, had to be abandoned.

However, time proved that he was right on target. He was just ahead of his time -- by about twenty years. The "Minidoka Project" was later developed in exactly the same place, by the U.S. Reclamation Service. It was the first Reclamation Project in Idaho. And even then, "costs far exceeded estimates."

S. D. Boone (in 1888) was the first in Southern Idaho to attempt a large scale irrigation project taking water out of the Snake River to irrigate the desert.

1880 - 1890

THE STATE OF IDAHO

The extraordinary eighties inside the Magic Circle represented America in a nutshell. All kinds, shapes, sizes, colors, types, races, creeds and nationalities were on hand. The population boomed from zero to thousands, and mining developed from zero to millions in those ten years. Miners, farmers, ranchers, sheepmen, cattlemen, cowboys, merchants, investors, lawyers, gamblers, freighters, railroaders, rich and poor all interacted in a chaotic kind of turbulent harmony. About half of Idaho's cities resulted from that boom, and the territory gained enough adultwhitemales to become eligible for Statehood.

It really hadn't been all that great being a "Territory." For example, people in a Territory could not vote for the President of the United States, even though he was the one who appointed their governor, chief judges, and other administrators, most of whom had practically been standing in line waiting for a political plum. The people called them "carpet bag rulers" and Idaho had a long list of them.

Sure, the people in the Territory could elect their own men as "delegates to Congress", but those delegates could never VOTE in Congress. All they could do was sit in and listen, and do their best to influence some real member of Congress.

True, the people had the right to elect their own Territorial Legislature, but if they went ahead and passed some law or made some rule that Congress didn't like - it was no deal. Actually, the Territory had taxation without representation, and the local politicians hammered away at that point until finally, in 1889, they called for a Constitutional Convention, and on the first Monday in June, 1889, the people of Idaho Territory elected delegates from each county (72 in all) to attend that convention in Boise on the following July 4th. In twenty-eight days they came up with a Constitution for Idaho,

1880 - 1890

which was, for the most part, modeled after the Constitutions of older states.

It was ratified on November 5, 1889 by an overwhelming majority. The final count showed that 12,398 votes had been cast in favor of adoption, and only 1,775 against.

Of course, there were some folks living in the Territory who were not permitted to vote -- Mormons - Chinese - Indians - Blacks - Women. . .

The Statehood Admission Bill Passed the United States House of Representatives on April 3, 1890, the bill was signed by President Benjamin Harrison, and Idaho officially became a State of the Union. Fred Dubois, Idaho's Territorial Delegate to Congress, handed the pen to the President, and Idaho became the forty-third State. Territorial Governor George L. Shoup automatically became Governor of the new State of Idaho.

Within a period of two-years, six states joined the Union; Washington, Montana, North Dakota and South Dakota in 1889, and Idaho and Wyoming in 1890.

The great United States of America was busily gathering its chickens under its wing.

When Idaho passed from a Territory to a State, it was in pretty good financial shape, and not too bad population-wise. The 1890 census reports 84,385 people, with 315 schools in operation and 25,741 children of school age.

In the act of admitting Idaho into the Union, Congress gave the new state the following gifts:

    100,000 acres of land for scientific schools

    100,000 acres of land for State Normal schools

    100,000 acres of land for the support and maintenance of an insane asylum

    100,000 acres of land for charitable, educational and reformatory institutions

    50,000 acres of land for the State University

1880 - 1890

50,000 acres of land for the support and maintenance of the penitentiary

90,000 acres of land for an agricultural college

32,000 acres of land for the Capital building

46,080 acres of land for University purposes act of 1881

They also gave to the State of Idaho, for public school purposes, two sections of land in each township of 36 sections, which amounted to about 3,000,000 acres. In addition, Congress gave to Idaho the United States Penitentiary with its equipment and 160 acres of land connected with it.

These lands were under control of the State Land Board. Some would be sold off, and some would be leased, but before any could be sold, it had to be appraised, and the appraisal could not be less than ten dollars per acre. Often, it was much more. The land had to be advertised and sold to the highest bidder. Purchasers usually had nine years to pay for it, one-tenth in cash, and one-tenth each year, with interest at 6% per annum to be paid yearly on all deferred payments. Leases were usually charged according to the value of the use of the land, and not made for a term longer than 5 years.

Most of the mountainous country in Idaho was marked out as forest reserves which were managed and controlled by the United States Forestry Bureau through local agents appointed for that purpose. Livestock was allowed to run on these reserves by paying a small grazing fee.

In 1890 the stage was set for the State politicians to strike up the band and start playing musical chairs for POWER!

In 1890 the United States government considered the "Frontier" officially closed.

"No more wild and wooly West. You guys settle down out there now."

1890 - 1900
A TIME OF CHANGE

There was a great surge of activity in the political arena when Idaho became a State. Departments, boards, commissions and councils were created, as well as committees, administrators, new counties, and districts necessary to handle State business.

The Great Seal of the State of Idaho was adopted. Designed by Miss Emma Edwards, it is the only seal in the entire United States to have been designed by a woman. So there.

The new state caught the Magic Circle in a state of change. It was rapidly developing from a mining region to a farming and stock raising community.

The Wood River District had been the richest mining area in the Northwest. Labor problems threatened the mining boom in the mid 80's, but it was not until the early 90's, when the price of silver dropped way, way down, that the good times were over for the mines.

The big smelter at Ketchum was the first to close, and others quickly followed. Hundreds of men were thrown out of work, and by 1892 silver mining had fallen into a severe decline.

The Exodus followed as homes, camps, mines and towns were abandoned even more quickly than they were built.

The bad news was nation wide. The "Panic of 1893" was the worst depression known in the U.S. up to that time. Prices for farm produce sank to rock bottom. Banks, saloons, stores, mining companies and railroads closed down. The first railroad went bankrupt in February, 1893, and within four months, 74 railroads and more than 15,000 companies failed. 574 banks closed their doors, and from one end of the country

1890 - 1900

to the other, unemployed men walked the streets, and Coxey's Army marched on Washington D.C.

The Wood River mining region was deader than a door nail.

"When the going gets tough -- everybody leaves."

It wasn't just the poor economy that caused trouble in the Magic Circle - it was the weather, too! There had been several successive years of drought and grasshopper infestations, and long, cold winters. But the winter of 1890 had been particularly long and hard. The snow came early, piled high, and stayed late. The mercury dropped far below zero and stayed there. Wind blew and snow swirled for days on end. All of Southern Idaho suffered terribly.

When Spring came, the land was covered with bloated carcasses of cattle and sheep that had perished in the storms. Thousands were lost, and the livestock industry was devastated.

Nevertheless, it has been said that the winds of that terrible winter blew open the door to agriculture in Southern Idaho. Before the destruction of their livestock, the ranchers who ran cattle and sheep on what are now irrigated farms, would have objected strenuously to anyone taking over their grazing domain. But that winter sounded the death knell to the open range livestock industry in the area.

Those early cattle had been driven up from Texas, and were generally a tough, poor breed. Some were so wild no one could catch them, and many lived and died in the mountains and canyons. After the "terrible winter", instead of cowhands riding hell-for-leather after the wild-eyed critters, the ranchers who were lucky enough to still be in business, got busy and improved the breed, and ordered their cowboys to move these "slow and easy" into the corrals so as not to run the fat off them. Fat was money, and they got a lot fatter standing around being fed in the feed lots during the winter. So did the cattlemen.

1890 - 1900

But, it wasn't just cattle. That miserable, bitter winter, combined with the lack of feed, killed stock by the thousands. Fred Gooding, camped south and west of Shoshone with 2,500 sheep, lost a thousand when they piled up around the camp wagon. Another band of 2,000 sheep south and west of Notch Butte suffered a loss of 1,300, and S. J. Friedman of Hailey had 10,000 sheep on the Marley Burn - after the storm he had 1,500.

So those two great pioneer industries - mining and open range stock raising - were dying, and folks began to realize that the real wealth might just be in the land itself. The new style of fattening stock in feed lots would create a lasting demand for fodder that could only be met by bringing water in quantity upon the arid lands.

It was time to start thinking seriously about irrigation. BIG storage dams. BIG diversion dams. BIG, LONG, DEEP canals. And, BIG money!

1890 - 1900
IRRIGATION AND THE GOVERNMENT

The Mormons started irrigating way back in 1860 when some of them migrated north from Salt Lake City and established the town of Franklin - the first "town" in Idaho. About that same time, gold was discovered in the Clearwater country and soon after that the miners had moved into the Boise Basin also. The Mormons were living quietly in wagon boxes, clearing their land to start farming, and the wild and wooly miners were dancing and prancing around about their gold discoveries while frantic "camp followers" were trying to provide food for them.

So, despite the pronounced differences in their beginnings, the two great irrigation empires of eastern Idaho and southwestern Idaho, were started at almost the same time. Mormon settlements spread northward along the Snake River, and the discovery of gold in the Boise Basin led to farming in the Boise Valley. By 1863, lands immediately adjacent to the Boise River were being farmed, and one year later, canal companies were being formed.

Irrigation did not begin inside the Magic Circle until April 1, 1877 when Nathan Woodworth made the first diversion of water from the Little Wood River where Gooding now stands. However, by 1890, when Idaho became a State, most of the lands adjacent to the Little Wood, Big Wood and Camas Creek were taken up.

During the thirty years from 1860 to 1890, irrigation could be found in many "stages" throughout the Territory. You could find one-man-digging-his-own-ditch to irrigate his land right next to the river, and you could find places where several neighbors joined together to build community ditches, which they would then own in common, to deliver water to their farms farther away from the river.

1890 - 1900

In some places there were "corporations" that would hire the construction of deep, long canals, but the corporation would then own the canals and charge the farmer for a water right, plus a yearly sum for keeping the canals in repair. This was not too popular with the farmer because he would be forever beholden to the corporation for water. Farmers, being the independent, self-sufficient folks they are, hated having to be dependent on anyone else for anything, but at that time, they would have done just about anything to get water onto their land. Most of them were getting that land either through the Homestead Act of 1862 which was 160 acres free, if you could live on it for five years without starving to death, or the Desert Lands Act of 1877, where the government would give a man and his wife 640 acres IF THEY COULD GET WATER TO IT.

So, they did what they had to do.

As soon as Idaho became a State, the new senators and representatives began to pressure Congress for help. They were not alone - other arid western states were also pressuring, and in 1894, the first step was taken when Congress passed the Carey Act.

Introduced by Senator Joseph M. Carey of Wyoming, it said Congress would donate a million acres of land to each arid state on the condition that the State would cause the land to be irrigated and reclaimed. Each state was given the authority to make contracts with corporations, or farmers, to construct "irrigation systems" and as soon as the state could show that the works had been built, the U.S. would issue patents to the state, and the state would then convey the land to the settlers. Also, "the land must be reclaimed within ten years after the Carey Act was passed!" This meant that everything had to be COMPLETED by 1904! Now, who on earth would take on building a large irrigation system without any security for their money, and then be forced to finish it by 1904?

1890 - 1900

Nobody.

Back to the drawing-board. In 1896, Congress amended the Carey Act to protect "whoever advanced the money for construction." It said the state could permit a lien against the land for the expenses incurred in reclaiming it, plus reasonable interest. In this way, whoever advanced the money would be protected and encouraged to increase their investments.

Still no takers. The money men were not interested because the requirement that it had to be finished by 1904 was still in there.

Finally, in 1901, the Carey Act was again amended to provide a ten-year period from the TIME THE PROJECT WAS STARTED. That fixed it, and by this time the whole country was talking about irrigation and reclaiming the West.

One more stroke - the following year Congress Passed the "Reclamation Act", also known as the "National Irrigation Law" and the "Newland Act of 1902", where Congress decided to deposit monies received from the sale of the public lands into a "Reclamation Fund" which would be used to build and maintain irrigation works. So, the Federal government began developing its projects right along with the private companies.

The first federal project in Idaho was the Minidoka Project started in 1904 and completed in 1909. The Minidoka Dam generated the first Federal electric power in the Pacific Northwest - 16,000 kilowatts. This power was used to operate pumps to irrigate land at a higher level, with the surplus being assigned to nearby communities.

So this put old Uncle Sugar himself in the irrigation business.

Meanwhile, back at the ranch, the Idaho Legislature was doing its homework to qualify for its million acres. "Irrigation Districts", similar to "School Districts" were set up, plus a State Board of Land Commissioners, a Reclamation Engineer to supervise the works, and all of the other red tape required to

1890 - 1900

supervise, regulate, control, and inspect the upcoming irrigation systems.

The time had come...

1900 - 1910

GO WEST! GO WEST!

LAND! LAND! IRRIGATED LAND! TAKE THE GAMBLE OUT OF FARMING! GO WEST! GO WEST!

Orators, politicians, railroads, land salesmen, farmers' organizations, Boards of Trade, Commercial Clubs, and government agencies were all promising and promoting! Countless speeches were made about the opening of the big irrigation projects in the West. Pamphlets, booklets, leaflets, and brochures offered the great American Dream - A FARM OF YOUR OWN! A new beginning in the fabulous, fertile, far-off West! Inspirational literature was included in immigrant handbooks, railroad guides, gazetteers, almanacs, government reports and thousands of "flyers" were circulating in stores and saloons, all painting this vast, unknown country in the rosy glow of a heavenly garden of Eden.

Irrigation was being promoted in all of the areas of the main Western rivers and their tributaries, including the basins of such rivers as the Colorado, Sacramento, San Joaquin, Rio Grande and Columbia. <u>Their</u> water arrived in 1901, along with a flood of opportunity-seeking settlers. The world watched, and the most optimistic hopes of the promoters were realized. The Imperial Valley ultimately became one of the garden spots of the nation.

So, the invitations were out, and the West boomed again. This time it wasn't gold - it was water!

Hundreds of enthusiastic souls headed West, "where the hand clasp's a little stronger, the smile a little longer, the skies a little bluer and friendships a little truer", and of course, where good land was cheap. Many were European immigrants fresh off the boat. From 1901 to 1910 America experienced the peak period for immigrants admitted into the United States.

Ragtime music was just becoming popular, and Scott Joplin's "Maple Leaf Rag" was all the rage. Gang singing and

1900 - 1910

Barbershop Quartets could be heard throughout the land. Player pianos encouraged them with the printed words rolling right along beside music. The whole country seemed to be engaged in a melodious sing-a-long. America was breaking out of the strict Victorian influence and becoming a happier people. Songs were written about everything that was going on - telephones, telegraphs, steamships, bicycles, railroads, trolley cars, airplanes and automobiles.

Carrie Nation, The Temperance Terror, and her hatchet, were chopping up saloons all around Medicine Lodge, Kansas, and the average man in America worked ten hours a day, six days a week. In Chicago, the horse population of 83,330 generated over 900 tons of manure every day. New York City had just opened its first subway, and completed its first skyscraper - the Flat Iron Building, 22 stories high!

In 1903 Orville and Wilbur finally got their motorized bicycle contraption off the ground for twelve seconds, and Teddy Roosevelt finally got the French government off the ground in Panama. America took over the canal.

Hailey, Idaho was busy extending telephone lines to Boise, Shoshone and Blackfoot and the lady telephone operators in Hailey were very unhappy about their pay, and complained. They wanted a $5 a month raise because their room and board cost $30 a month and they were paid only $25. Those uppity women. . .

Nevertheless, the real highlight of 1903 in Idaho, was the first land opening in Idaho. It was held in Shoshone in July, and the promoter was I. B. Perrine, that same young lad with the cows who Charlie Walgamott had directed to the Blue Lakes back in 1884. Perrine had settled there, living for four years in a dugout while he cleared his land, and raised abundant crops of hay and grain - by irrigation. He planted berry bushes and orchards, carefully toting each special bush and fruit tree down into the canyon on horseback, (the only way to get there), over

1900 - 1910

a narrow treacherous trail. The produce from his Blue Lakes farm was astonishing! He exhibited fruit as far away as Paris, France and won numerous awards for excellence. The Smithsonian Institute even made wax copies of the Blue Lakes fruit as the most perfect specimens of the time.

Now, Mr. I. B. Perrine was promoting the first Idaho land opening under the Carey Act. A good-sized crowd attended, but not much land was sold - only a few thousand acres. People were spooky at that first sale. Cautious folks afraid to be the first. Besides, it was such a new concept--this irrigating out of canal systems. Nobody was quite sure just how it would all turn out. So they held back and looked at the ground and shook their heads. Perrine was disappointed with the small sale, but it didn't stop him. He immediately organized the Twin Falls Investment company to handle the sales, and by the end of the first year had sold 117,000 acres! Perrine was incredibly far-sighted, and energetic, and he well knew what this land could produce.

Who could buy the land?

Anyone 21 years old, and a citizen of the United States. All you had to do was go to the office of the agent, register, look over the maps he had there, and make several choices of land if you wished. Some of the buyers would carefully go out and inspect the tracts, while others would give their Power of Attorney to an agent to select for them. It was a great opportunity for speculators. When you registered, you paid a deposit of $3 per acre for water, and 25 cents per acre for the land. Then, you put your name in the drawing box and when your ticket was drawn at the opening, you could choose your land. Everything was fair and square and all handled right there in front of the public. Usually, a keg on the back of a wagon with the drawing done by a local child. All openings were conducted by the Idaho State Land Board. If someone else's name was drawn before you, and took the piece of land

1900 - 1910

you wanted, you would then have your second or third choice when your name came up.

After you were drawn and you made your choice, you were required to sign a ten-year contract with the irrigation company for the balance due on the water right. You had three years to "prove up", and would have to pay the additional 25 cents per acre for the land at that time.

The first payment to the company for the water was due when they got the water to your land.

The cost of the land was always 50 cents per acre, which was the price Uncle Sam put on all of the Carey Act Lands.

The price of getting water to it varied from place to place, depending upon how much it would cost the company to build the works.

1900 - 1910

THE WOOD RIVER VALLEY IRRIGATION ASSOCIATION

S.D. Boone was an intelligent, capable, many-faceted man. His real estate and insurance business was thriving, he was active in politics and served on the Republican State Central Committee. He was a member of the Board of Trade, and Founding President of the Hailey Commercial Club. He was an active "Booster" who spent a great deal of his time and money promoting Idaho and the Wood River Country.

Soon after he landed in Hailey, an attractive new school teacher arrived, and they were married in 1889. Mary Ann Burke, was a native of Massachusettes, and Irish to the core. Her quick wit and sense of humor matched his own, and they were a very popular couple indeed. They had one child, a son, Frank.

Mr. Boone's complete faith in large-scale irrigation had never wavered, and now that the Carey Act was finally workable, he was more enthusiastic than ever. Best of all for his confidence, was the news that the first government reclamation project in Idaho was to be the Minidoka Project, where he had spent the $10,000, five years before on preliminary plans and surveys. It confirmed that he had been right all along.

The fact that there were already many successful farms in the area irrigating from the streams and rivers proved that the soil was rich and fertile. All he had to do was get the "magic" to it. He had long ago fallen into the habit of referring to irrigation water as "magic." He was a popular and colorful after-dinner speaker much in demand, and his talks were most often about the "magic of irrigation."

He attended the land opening in Shoshone, and was well-acquainted with I.B. Perrine and his plans. Six months after that opening, on January 6, 1904, Boone called a public meeting in Hailey for anyone interested in irrigation. More than a hundred people turned out.

1900 - 1910

He told them there was $16,000,000 in the Reclamation Fund, and only $2,000,000 had been appropriated to Idaho. He said there were 17 streams capable of irrigating hundreds of thousands of acres from sources within Blaine County. He rattled off dozens of facts and figures about irrigation possibilities right here. The crowd was ecstatic, and with him all the way. They elected him delegate to meet with the chief of the Irrigation Bureau at Pocatello to further the cause, and voted to organize the "Wood River Valley Irrigation Association." S.D. Boone was elected Chairman, with instructions to draw up the constitution and by-laws.

All over Southern Idaho people were excited about the irrigation projects, and now the people of Blaine County were actually planning their own! More meetings. More information. Optismism! Encouragement! We can do it! Hailey will regain its "old-time importance"! Lincoln County was invited to join Blaine, and the talk continued about water rights, locations, where would the dams be built? The canals? How much would it cost to ready the land? When could a farmer expect to show a profit? On and on.

Mr. Boone tried to answer all of the questions, and visited frequently with I.B. Perrine and his people in Twin Falls. Perrine had set up two companies - the Twin Falls Land and Water Co. to build the irrigation system, and the Twin Falls Investment Co. to handle the land sales and set up the townsites. Twin Falls was the "model city" and growing by leaps and bounds. All of the material to build it came right through Shoshone. A $35,000 hotel was being built there, and on the drawing board were such industrial features as flour mills, oatmeal mills and sugar factories. They were reaching for settlers from farmers in Illinois, Minnesota, and other midwestern states.

Some of the men involved in the Perrine operation were Buhl, Milner, Kimberly, Filer, Gooding, Heyburn, Murtaugh,

1900 - 1910

Hansen, Dubois, and John Hailey. They all turned into towns. Mr. Perrine turned into a hotel, a bridge, a coulee, and an elementary school. There were those who insisted the town should be called "Perrine City" instead of Twin Falls. It never was - except by "those."

By the end of 1904, Mr. Boone had covered every possible location for irrigation works in Blaine County.

The next step was - MONEY!

1900 - 1910
MEN, MONEY AND HARRY WILSON

1905 got off to a nice start for the Boone family: Mrs. Boone was appointed to the Board of Trustees at Albion Normal, and Mr. Boone's "Wood River Irrigation Association" was coming along. Boone and Art Smith of Hailey, and Guy C. Barnum and I. Hill of Shoshone, were involved financially with the association, and Presley Horn in the Land Office at Hailey was active. Plans were to build dams on Fish Creek, Willow Creek, Little Wood River and Big Wood River. Four dams in the future of the Association.

Meanwhile, the Milner Dam on the Snake River was nearing completion and people were coming from all directions to witness the closing of the gates. One young visitor became the talk of Idaho when on March 2, 1905 he jumped off the cliff at Shoshone Falls, landing in a pool below, and escaped unharmed. His name was Harry Wilson, whose mother was a Cherokee Indian and his father a Frenchman. Harry had arrived in Shoshone a few weeks before the big event and with several companions, went to the falls. The Shoshone Journal reports:

> "They were intoxicated, and Wilson declared his intention of leaping from the brink to the pool 235 feet below. In the presence of a large number of persons, he walked out on the rock and began preparations for the jump. His friends and others present realizing the danger that he was risking his life in a leap, tried to dissuade him from the reckless act. He was stubborn and refused to listen to their advice. They were afraid to go near him because of the danger of falling from the rock into the deep chasm. They tried to coax him, but to no purpose. Wilson looked over the dizzying height, turned to the crowd gathered there, waved his hand and leaped out into the air.

1900 - 1910

He turned a complete somersault, and his body shot down into the big pool. A moment later he appeared at the surface uninjured except for a slight flesh wound on his leg caused by striking a rock."

Harry made quite a splash that day, and gave the tourists something to write home about.

On May 1, 1905, the gates at Milner Dam were closed, and water flowed triumphantly along the 65-mile Twin Falls South Side Canal. S.D. Boone was among the 2,000 jubilant people on hand to celebrate the great occasion. The works would reclaim about 200,000 acres at a cost in excess of $3,500,000. Construction had begun on March 1, 1903, two years and two months before this great day, and it was a resounding success!

All of this was tremendously encouraging to Mr. Boone and his associates. They returned to Hailey full of fire and enthusiasm to push their own projects through with vigor.

But, they needed money - a lot more money.

Every so often some Easterner would roll into Hailey to visit the Wood River Mines with an eye to buying a claim or two, and at the same time do a little fishing, hunting and vacationing in the lovely "Heavenly Heights." One such person, Charles Hernsheim of New York rolled in on June 8, 1905 to look over some mining claims on Stanley Creek, check out the Red Elephant group and just "vacation" for a while. Hernsheim came from a wealthy New York family. His forebearers had made lots of money in their day, and Charles was one of the lucky, wealthy family members who automatically came into the fortune.Shortly after his arrival, he met S.D. Boone - and shortly after that, he was getting an earful about the plans for large-scale irrigation in Blaine County. Boone showed him around, told him all about the "Wood River Irrigation Association", outlined the preliminary work already

1900 - 1910

and proudly pointed to the tremendous success of Perrine's Twin Falls tract.

Would Mr. Hernsheim be interested in joining the local investors?

He would, indeed! And had some ideas of his own to throw in.

On September 15, 1905, Boone and Hernsheim publically announced proposed construction on Fish Creek, and Hernsheim jumped on the train back to New York "to interest a few friends in the enterprise."

November 3, 1905: S.D. Boone, Guy C. Barnum, I. Hill and "Eastern Capitalists" announce proposed construction on Willow Creek. "Surveyers working on the site now. Willow Creek reservoir will irrigate 40,000 acres", they stated.

November 17, 1905 announcement: "Two big reservoirs will be built - one on Little Wood and one on Big Wood. The site of the proposed dam on Little Wood is three miles above Carey, and on Big wood, opposite Tikura, a loading station on the OSL. The company has already purchased about 1,000 acres of land to be submerged by the Big wood reservoir, and several thousand dollars have been expended in preliminary work."

It was further announced that a NEW COMPANY has been organized in New York by Charles Hernsheim, and the project has been financed. The enterprise was started by the "Wood River Irrigation Association" whch has been sold to the new company, and Mr. S. D. Boone will be the Western Manager. Charles Hernsheim will be General Manager.

Eureka! The needed money had arrived! Boone's "magic" was beginning to work!

On November 25, 1905 Mr. F.P King, Engineer, was completing his large survey map covering the land to be submerged by the backwaters of the dam on the Big Wood River. As requested earlier by Mr. Boone, he carefully and

1900 - 1910

neatly printed the name of that dam in large, black letters on the bottom of the map:

"MAGIC DAM."

1900 - 1910
THE IDAHO IRRIGATION CO., LTD.

The new company was named "The Idaho Irrigation Co., Ltd." with Articles of Incorporation filed January 3, 1906 showing Hailey as the principal place of business. "It is to acquire, construct and operate water works for irrigation and power; to acquire and dispose of water, electric and gas companies, gas plants, hotels, townsites, and to conduct a general industrial enterprise." Capital $450,000.

The incorporators: W.P O'Connor, Banker, President, New York; Charles J. Hernsheim, New York, Vice-President and General Manager; S.D. Boone, Hailey, Western Manager and Sales Agent; Theodore L. Peters, New York, Secretary-Treasurer.

In April, 1906, Hernsheim again showed up in Hailey, this time with several "Eastern Capitalists." They were wined and dined and taken out to see the sites of proposed dams on Fish Creek, Little Wood River and Big Wood River (no mention of Willow Creek). The surveys were well underway, and the total cost would run around two million - or more. 3,000 families were expected to settle on the lands, which would otherwise be worthless without water.

The "Eastern Capitalists" were impressed.

Then, they all went down to the Snake River to see the Milner Dam, and on to see the new City of Twin Falls. They also looked over the work going on by the Twin Falls North Side Land and Power Co.

The "Eastern Capitalists" were impressed.

Then back up to Camas Prairie to check out what was going on there. For many years, Camas, Wildhorse, Cow, Three Mile, Deer, Soldier and Corral Creeks had been farmed with waters from those streams. Now, a Mr. Parkinson of Illinois was in the process of constructing a reservoir on Cow Creek, and expected the dam to be completed by October, 1906.

1900 - 1910

The Twin Lake Reservoir was underway, with an eye to completion by Fall of 1907. That system would water 11,000 acres and Fred Jenkins of Soldier was the prime mover. Work on Wildhorse Creek Reservoir was planned to begin September, 1906 to water 11,000 acres, and also on Malad Reservoir, which was expected to irrigate 5,000 to 6,000 acres on the west end of the Prairie. Also, by December, 1906, the Carey Irrigation Co. planned to supply water to 12,500 acres.

The "Eastern Capitalists" were by this time very impressed with all this activity, and agreed to consider buying into the "Idaho Irrigation Co., Ltd."

Almost immediately, the names of the new stockholders were published. All strong financiers. All friends of the Hernsheim family. T.W. Carpenter and Richard W. Comstock of Providence, Rhode Island, and all of the others were retired New York financiers - J.M. Loomis, Robert H. Guet, J.W. Murphy, E. Burton Hart, Jr., Wm. K. Everdell, Oscar T. Sewell and Edward P. Slevin.

The company was now capitalized at one million dollars - all fully paid up!

When the good news hit Hailey, everyone was estatic! Mr. Boone and his family had always been well-liked and respected, and the Commercial Club felt it was time to put together an evening of appreciation and tribute to: "S.D. Boone, whose every effort, every word, every moment seems to be devoted to the betterment of the region."

Folks came from far and near to take part in the salute to: "Mr. S.D. Boone, and his 'Magic'."

It was a grand evening indeed.

1900 - 1910
ARVADA–ALBERTA

Hailey was listed as the company headquarters because Mr. Boone was located there, and it was certainly an attractive vacationland for anyone who showed up to inspect the project. However, from a practical standpoint, the supplies and materials coming in on the railroad would have to be unloaded at a point closer to the construction sites. Mr. Boone decided on a little jumping-off spot on the Hailey Branch named "Alberta", in honor of the first child born in the little scatter of houses there. When the railroad first went through, the engineer named it "Arvada", but when Alberta Strunk was born, the folks there insisted upon calling it "Alberta." They won.

The first canal to be built from the diversion dam would lead directly to Alberta, and another advantage was that Alberta was situated smack in the middle of the "Marley Burn." Several years previously, a rancher named Marley, wishing to make a clearing, decided to burn off the heavy growth of sagebrush. The fire got away from him and ended up burning about 50,000 acres. This "fortunate accident" made the area particularly attractive for potential settlers because it would save about $5 an acre, and a lot of hard work having to clear the land. Besides, the sagebrush had been very thick there, and everybody knew "where the sagebrush grows, the soil is unsurpassed."

Given all this, Alberta seemed destined to become a good-sized town, even though materials were freighted from a spot on Silver Creek at first.

One of the first needs for the new town of Alberta was a good hotel, and Mr. Boone asked a long-time Hailey friend of his, Mrs. John Thomas, if she would like to move to Alberta to operate a new "Alberta Hotel." Two years earlier, her 8-year-old grandson, Frank Pope, had moved to Hailey to live with her, and they were both enthusiastic about the move.

1900 - 1910

    In the fall of 1906, Alberta began to come alive. Men, horses, supplies, machinery and other goods began arriving daily on the railroad, and the air was filled with the jangle of harnesses, and the shouts of men at work. By December, work was started on the main canal, and the diversion dam located three miles below the proposed site of the big Magic Dam. The general contractors were the Slick Bros. of Boise, and J.S. Long, a sub-contractor for the stone work. On December 21st. Charles A. King, Chief Engineer for the Idaho Irrigation Co. reported about 75 men and teams at work at the Slick Bros. Camp, and 47 men and 10 teams at Long's camp. Long's contract called for 65,000 yds. of rock work which would take about a year to complete, and the entire project should take about three years. Work was being rushed to complete the diversion dam before the high water in the Spring.

    The Idaho Irrigation Company's grand and glorious irrigation system was underway, and the year 1906 came to an end.

1900 - 1910
ALBERTA

1907 began on a happy note all across the nation. Times were good. America was building. The first radio broadcast had just been made on Christmas Eve, 1906. The Panama Canal was under construction, and the automobile was quite a fancy, new gadget. The expression "get a horse!" was popular, and automobile sales were unpopular. America was singing the newest tunes - "In My Merry Oldsmobile," "Wait Til the Sun Shines, Nellie," "You're a Grand Old Flag," and "I Love You Truly." Hobble skirts were just coming into vogue, and men wore celluloid collars and high-button shoes. Oklahoma was getting ready to become the 46th State of the Union.

The Alberta Land Opening was set out for June 24, 1907.

How could there be a "land opening" when the company was just getting started building the system? To give the buyer time to prepare his land before the water was turned in, and it also gave the company time to sell whatever land was not sold at the opening. The Idaho Irrigation Co., Ltd. expected to have the first water available on the Alberta Tract the following year as it would be delivered from the diversion dam currently under construction, and the canals to Alberta should also be ready by then.

The opening date was approved by the State Land Commission and flyers and pamphlets were sent out to the Mid-West, Oregon and Washington. Local newspapers kept readers informed of the progress on the works, and large-sized buttons were distributed stating:

"Get Wise and Come to Alberta, Idaho for Big Carey Act Land Sale June 24, 1907."

The Shoshone Journal was the most active local newspaper to sing the praises of the irrigation developments, because Shoshone itself figured to be the big beneficiary of all the activity going on around it.

There were three large projects being developed during

1900 - 1910

1907, and Shoshone was right in the middle of all the action: The Twin Falls Land and Water Co. was building the North Side Canal; the government was developing the Minidoka Project; and the Idaho Irrigation was working to the North.

The Twin Falls Land and Water Co. started work on the North Side Canal from Milner to Jerome on April 1, 1907. The fantastic success of their project south of the Snake River made them doubly optimistic about the North Side. Kuhn Bros. were their financiers, and had big ideas about developing the area, including an electric railway they were planning. The openings of their lands were set up on a series basis as the project developed. The first was the Eden-Hazelton Opening on April 23, 1907 - 30,000 acres priced at $30.50 per acre ($5 more than the South Side lands).

Next, the Jerome-Wendell segregation scheduled for October 1, 1907, and finally, the Bliss-King Hill Opening which would not take place until January 2, 1909. However, all of the company's time was currently spent in devloping the townsite of Jerome, which was patterned after Twin Falls. Jerome would be a "company town" with streets all neatly laid out. Townsite lots would be sold at the Land Opening. The company provided streets, water, lights, office buildings, a hotel and strongly encouraged businesses to move in.

Early in May, publicity about the Alberta Land Opening began to show up in the local newspapers, along with stories about the activities there: "Surveyors have completed platting the townsite of Alberta," and, "Alberta will be an all-brick city," followed by the story of how Messrs. Boone and Hernsheim were in Alberta one day several months ago and discovered that the clay in and around the townsite was perfect for good-quality bricks. They decided to make Alberta an all-brick city, and to furnish the bricks at a nominal cost. "A brick plant is underway with all kinds of modern brick-making machinery."

1900 - 1910

There were stories about the Alberta Hotel that would soon be started and would cost $18,000 to build; about the millionaire sugar merchants who planned to put in a big sugar factory; and others planning a flour mill. It was announced that Dan Beaton's corrals would occupy six blocks; that the Alberta Lumber Co. was moving in and would take up a full block; that there would be storehouses, two restaurants, Frank Mitchell's brickyard, and Wes. B. George's cement block manufacturing plant. An implement firm, warehouse and other structures were planned. Deneke & Reeves would soon open the Alberta Mercantile and Reeves had made application to be the new postmaster. A bank would open soon, they said, and a grocery store would be moved in, complete, from Boise. Alberta already had the railroad depot, a telegraph and telphone system, a townsite area covering 320 acres of land with plenty of cheap water power, and good domestic water.

And there was also an editorial praising Mr. S. D. Boone, "the man who conceived the idea."

> *"There must always be great moving spirits behind such vast enterprises. Men possessed of the ability to grasp great opportunities, to conceive the idea, and to interest capital in the idea, as well as the ability to execute the plans after these conditions have been met. On this project these honors belong to S.D. Boone of Hailey, and Charles Hernsheim of New York. Mr. Boone is the man who conceived the idea and to whose organization is due largely to his efforts and faith in the project. It requires no small ability to transmit one's faith in a scheme involving the expenditure of millions of dollars, but Mr. Boone has that ability. He also had the ability to inspire Mr. Hernsheim to such an extent as to cause that gentleman to lay aside his many large business enterprises and give a large portion of his personal attention to develpment of the*

project. Men who take thousands of acres of sagebrush absolutely without value, and by the magic powers of irrigation transform it to thousands of valuable homes, dot the landscape with cities, and add to the general happiness of the race, are worthy of places in the Halls of Fame. The people of Idaho recognize that fact, so that in local circles they almost invariably speak of this as the 'Boone-Hernsheim Project'."

On June 14, 1907, the following story appeared in the Shoshone Journal, and says it all:

"Alberta, Lincoln county is to be the scene of a notable land opening on June 24th, when the first 40,000 acres of Idaho Irrigation Company's great reclamation project is open for settlement. There have been some big openings of Carey Act Lands in Idaho, openings where millions of dollars worth of land was sold or contracted for in a single day, but now with the eyes of the whole country on Idaho for a chance to invest in her fertile soil, the publicity given the formal opening has only served to whet the appetite of the hungry and ravenous land-buying public for irrigated lands. More and more and yet more, is the constant cry and each opening of such land only interests a larger number of buyers. The demand is increasing faster than the supply, and the irrigable land, necessarily limited in the area, is going so fast that every thinking man knows that it will soon be gone, so every opening advertised has a cumulative effect for the next. The thousands who have read of the Twin Falls land openings and then learned of the later marvelous development of resources there, are only too anxious to try a sure thing at what they at first neglected."

"If the Alberta opening is not the most successful of all,

1900 - 1910

there is nothing in argument - there are physical advantages that will make the Alberta section particularly desirable. Except for proximity to market, there is almost no choice in the land, soil, elevation, drainage, slopes are so uniform as to make the last chance in the drawing almost as good as the first. This is a wonderful advantage in the development of any country, especially where conditions are so favorable for a great industry like the building and operating of a sugar fatory which is in prospect here. One of the most important factors of any irrigation project - the one thing that makes it possible for any such project to exist, is a permanent water supply. This is assured the Idaho Irragation Co. by the building of one of the greatest storage dams and reservoirs in the United States. The dam will be 125 feet in the clear and the reservoir will have a shore line of 25 miles - it will contain 200,000 acre feet of water, enough to make an abundant supply for the tract for a year without taking any of the summer flow. The reservoir will take up the winter flow of the spring flood waters of the Big Wood and Malad rivers, the dam being built just below the confluence of the two streams. The streams having their source largely on the north slopes of the Sawtooth Mountains, the highest and snowiest in the state. The water supply comes more slowly and has a permanency that makes it ideal for the purpose. Some idea of the magnitude of the dam may be gained from the fact that it is to cost a million dollars or more, that the work will require more than a year with all the force that can be employed, and that the payroll will be about $25,000 a month in labor alone. Work is proceeding on the canal diversion dam two miles below the reservoir dam."

"*A train of at least four pullmans is to come from Salt Lake City to attend the opening representing a part of the*

1900 - 1910

far east delegation. One car of land-seekers will come from Boise. These, of course, do not include the many applicants that will drive in singly and in small parties. The company is making expensive preparations to care for the people who will attend the opening. A building 95 feet long has been put up to serve as a temporary hotel while two others are to be put to the same service. It will be possible to serve 1,000 people as the Pullman cars are to remain on the tracks at Alberta and will give accommodations to many of the visitors. The train service is such as to allow the visitors to obtain hotel service at Shoshone and Hailey."

"The electric plant to develop 350 horse power and one of the most complete in the West is being installed on the Little Wood River at Alberta. This will be available for manufacturing very shortly. As the soil and climate are well adapted for the growing of sugar beets it is expected that beet culture will be one of the principal industries. Mr. Post of New York, one of the financiers of the company is prominent in the sugar business of the country and perceives an immense sugar factory there to handle the beet crop."

"Interested parties have already investigated the possibilities of a vegetable canning factory at Alberta, finding conditions just to their liking. They have decided to install a plant at once and install a pea-huller. Wild peas grow in riotous profusion on the tract, showing the soil is right for the culture of peas, which will be the staple product from the first. There is only one pea-hulling machine made, and it is never owned, only leased to the canner who by the terms of his lease has exclusive control of the use of the machine for a radius of 100 miles. The Payette cannery is at present the only one in the state using one of these machines."

1900 - 1910

Other industries are to be encouraged by the company. The land is to be put on the market at a price of $35.50 an acre, including the state fee of 50 cents an acre. Of this, the first payment is $3.00 to the company and 25 cents to the state. The other payments are extended over a period of the remaining 9 years."

There is nothing better in all the West than the gold-irrigated lands of Lincoln county which are to be opened at Alberta on June 24th!"

Amen.

ALBERTA LAND OPENING

1900 - 1910

The great day arrived at last! The Alberta Land Opening! The sun was shining, the weather was beautiful, and the air crackled with excitement. People came from all directions - families in horse-drawn buggies and wagons, single riders, walkers and many on special railroad cars. The crowd was in a friendly, festive mood.

There were "agents" present. Men acting for speculators hoping to draw one of the first ten or twelve numbers which would entitle them to choice lands adjacent to Alberta, which they figured would soon be worth thousands. These agents carried Powers-of-Attorney, and took care of all the details for their clients.

Everyone registered had already selected the acres he wanted, and many were registered for second and third choices. Most had gone over the land, then identified it on the maps drawn up by the company. For example, if Mr. Jones registered for Plot 20, which consisted of 40 acres, he had a good chance of getting it if his name was drawn early. However, if his name was not drawn until later, someone else might have already taken Plot 20, and he would have to take second or third choice.

Price of Alberta land was set by the State Land Board at $35.50 an acre. The price was based on the cost of getting the water to the land - that is, to within 1.2 mile of every quarter section - the landowner had to take it from there. That $35.50 covered $35 for the water right, and went to the company. The 50 cents went to the State for the land. When registering, each person had to deposit a certified check for $3.25 per acre. $3 to the company, 25 cents to the State. For example, if one registered for 40 acres, the deposit would be $130; 80 acres, $260 etc. up to 160 acres, which was the limit under the Carey Act.

$1,400,000 was in possession of the company before the

1900 - 1910

drawing! Title to the lands would be granted after 30 days residence on them, and residence had to be established within six months after having been notified that the water was ready to be delivered.

The proceedings began at high noon. There was a little opening ceremony with Mr. Boone welcoming the folks on behalf of the Idaho Irrigation Co. He also mentioned that work would soon commence on the big Magic Dam, and assured the folks that the diversion dam, which would deliver the water to the Alberta tract, would soon be finished and settlers could expect water next year, as soon as the canals were through. The crowd cheered! He spoke of the bright future for Alberta, announced that the company had donated 1/2 block of property in the Alberta townsite for a school, and pointed out the many other advantages in the area. He introduced Miss Geneva Wilson, a pretty 10-year-old lass from Hailey, who would draw the tickets, and finally, he introduced the State Land board representative who would conduct the drawing. All Carey Act Land Openings were conducted by the State Land Board.

The rules and regulations were announced, questions answered, and the drawing began, with the townsite lots drawn first. All contracts were sold with the requirement to build only brick, stone or concrete buildings.

One hundred and fifty names were in the townsite box. Mr. C.D. Lemukull, bookkeeper for the company, got two lots right off the bat, and announced that he planned to have them cleared immediately for a tennis court. Seems he and Charles Hernsheim considered themselves tennis experts and were looking forward to having the courts.

More than 100 Alberta town lots were sold that day.

Next came the drawings for the farm land. 320 persons were registered, and Mr. A.M. McClenahan of Greeley, Colorado had the largest number of registrations - 22 in all. Most were by Power-of-Attorney.

1900 - 1910

Before the first name was drawn, Col. M.J. Sharp, former registrar of the Hailey Land Office got up on the platform and announced that he would pay $5,000 for the first number drawn, which would give him first choice of the land. The crowd gasped! $5,000 was a fortune in those days (the laborers on the project were getting $3 a day for ten hours work). There was much oohing and aahing, and hurried discussions about whether one would be wise to take him up on it if they got the lucky first number.

Col. Sharp, himself, had about 20 tickets in the box representing cash deposits of $7,500 for himself and those he represented.

Little Geneva Wilson stepped forward to draw the first precious number. A hush fell over the crowd and every eye was riveted on the little girl. For a seemingly interminable time, her little hand fumbled and stirred and turned the tickets over and over in the keg. Finally, she selected one, and slowly, slowly she minced across the platform and handed it to the State Land Board Representative.

He took the ticket, studied it long and carefully, smiled, raised his head and let his eyes roll leisurely over the crowd - and back again. No one even breathed. You could hear a pin drop. At last, in a loud, clear voice, he announced the name on that first lucky ticket - "Colonel M.J. Sharp!"

Everyone was stunned! There was dead silence!

Then - one man burst out laughing. . .

And the whole crowd suddenly dissolved into gales of laughter. . .

The tense moment was over. The deal-of-the-day had fizzled out, and that SHARP son-of-a-gun got the first ticket without having to pay anyone the $5,000.

They ended up giving Col. Sharp a lusty round of applause.

And they all told the story again and again, forever more.

1900 - 1910

The newspapers reported that the Alberta Land Opening was a "conspicuous success!"

It was.

Except that a great majority of the deposits were withdrawn afterward. The speculators who had hoped to get in on the first ten or twelve numbers - and didn't - took their money and left - perhaps to try their luck again at another land opening.

1900 - 1910
THE SUMMER OF 1907

All summer long the Idaho Irrigation Co. pressed hard to sell land not taken up at the Alberta Opening. Agents scoured the country for potential buyers. S.D. Boone spent several days in the Spokane area and returned with contracts for 1,500 acres. But it soon became imperative for him to give his full attention to the construction work going on; the settling of Alberta; and the advertising and promoting for the upcoming Gooding Opening on September 24th. This was a mere seven days BEFORE the scheduled Jerome-Wendell opening now being heavily promoted by the Twin Falls North Side Land and Water Co. They were moving full-steam ahead on that north side development, and had already set up an office in Jerome to advertise and sell the Jerome-Wendell tract. Very stiff competition indeed for the Idaho Irrigation Co.

As of the summer of 1907, the Idaho Irrigation co. had 110,000 acres segregated to them - 40,000 on the Alberta tract, and 70,000 at Gooding. The State of Idaho agreed that when Magic Dam and the proposed canals were completed, there would be more than enough water available to efficiently irrigate these tracts, and Mr. Boone moved forward vigorously and confidently, in spite of some serious problems that cropped up.

There was an embargo on lumber, coal, and wood which slowed things down to a screeching halt. Two large traction engines - an Advance Tandem Compound and a Reeves Cross-Compound with elevating graders - had been shipped into Alberta ready to build the road to the construction sites, and they just sat there, gathering dust, for lack of coal to make them go. The Alberta Bank stood half-finished and silent, waiting for lumber, and the brick-making kilns were cold, waiting for wood to start burning. The Spring of 1907 had had a high run-off and the contractors were held up waiting for the water to go

1900 - 1910

down sufficiently to begin work again on the canals and dams.

All told, until the middle of July, it seemed that everything that could go wrong - did.

But, there were some bright spots - the Alberta Mercantile Co., which carried a complete stock of general merchandise, was far enough along to be open for business, and that helped. Many of those who had already bought land on the Alberta tract were arriving with their families and starting to build prove-up shacks and prepare the land for the arrival of water. The well-drilling outfit from Boise was putting down the first well at the company office.

Over at the Magic damsite, the farms that had once been on the river had all been vacated - Calhoun, Carpenter and Brew on the east side of the Big Wood, and Decker, Riley and Rice on the west bank. C.P. Rice and his family were the last to leave. The company had bought all of that land, and the settlers had the privilege of disposing of their buildings and livestock. The backwaters of Magic Dam would soon cover those farms under twenty feet of water - or more.

It should be mentioned that still another company was building an irrigation ditch inside the Magic Circle, out of the upper Big Wood River. The "Big Wood River Reservoir and Canal Co." had claim to 300 inches of Big Wood water, enough to irrigate 3,000 acres. G.B. Bovinger and Ben Darrah had about 1,000 acres under this ditch, and others in the company were Fred W. Gooding, Frank Glenn, G.B. Gerring, and John Lierman. In the summer of 1907 work was completed on their main ditch with water already running in the upper end of the ditch.

A bird's-eye-view of the Southern Idaho sage brush desert that summer would have been startling, to say the least. Practically every area was swarming with horses, machines, and people. Hundreds of tents at construction camps, great blasts of dynamite constantly booming like heavy cannon fire,

1900 - 1910

hurling tons of lava rock into the air; canal cutters; ditch diggers; dam builders, and new settlers grubbing sage brush by hand, optimistically looking forward to the arrival of the irrigation water.

On August 9th, Messrs. Brush and Micklewait arrived in Alberta to take charge of the new Alberta State bank. The two-story building was nearing completion and promised to be one of the best banks in the State. All white brick, a manganese safe, no less, safety deposit boxes, a vault, and the finest of counters. The top floor would contain seven finely decorated office rooms.

Alberta was beginning to shape up. Land sales were being made daily "to practical farmers coming in to make homes, the most desirable class of citizenry."

There were enough families in the area by late August to warrant the happy announcement that SCHOOL would begin this fall!

The fall of 1907?

Yes.

1900 - 1910
THE FALL OF 1907

Mr. Boone had been spreading himself so thin he barely stopped long enough to eat. He worked day and night, as most of the responsibility seemed to rest on his shoulders. He was constantly on the move, solving problems, making decisions and trying at the same time to get everything ready for the Gooding Opening on September 24th. Charles Hernsheim, on the other hand, spent most of his time taking pictures of the canals and construction works and giving interviews to the newspapers.

In mid-September, Charles hopped on the train to New York to confer with the financial backers, and when he returned to Idaho he nagged and badgered Mr. Boone constantly to hurry everything along and "rush the work" because the backers were not happy with the progress.

Mr. Boone finally told him flat out that it was impossible to have everything ready in time for the Gooding Opening on September 24th, and the date would have to be moved back to give him more time. He had barely had enough time to take care of all of the problems at Alberta, without having to deal with Gooding.

He applied to the State Land board for a later opening, and the new date of November 14th was approved. At least he would have time to better prepare.

The change of dates was publically announced and advertised, and they went to work immediately to get the land staked out better for locaters. They then set up a sales office in Gooding, made transportation arrangements for the big day, and began seriously working on the dozens of other details. It was sad to lose the attractive September 24th date because the weather would surely have been favorable, and of course, it would have given them the jump on the Jerome Opening. But - it had to be done.

1900 - 1910

Mr. Boone, who had a flair for slogans, coined a catchy one for the Gooding Opening - "COME TO GOODING - AND YOU'LL COME FOR GOOD!"

And, Gooding did have a lot going for it - both the town and the tract. It was the only tract in Southern Idaho located on the main line of the Oregon Short Line, and would soon also be the junction point for the new electric railway. 20,000 acres around the townsite had been under cultivation for about 20 years and was by this time a very attractive piece of country. Many trees dotted the landscape, and potential buyers could just gaze out over the land to see how beautifully everything flourished there.

The townsite of Gooding was owned by then-Governor Frank Gooding, who had already had it platted and staked, and scheduled to be sold on the same day the Idaho Irrigation Co. opened the tract. Originally, the spot was named "Toponis" (meaning Trading Post) by that Oregon Shortline Engineer who liked Indian names, but when the Gooding family homesteaded a great deal of land around the little railroad siding, it quickly was identified as "Gooding" by the locals.

Frank Gooding was Idaho's first foreign-born governor. He served two terms, and was also the first governor to have a town and county named after him. Frank was a self-made man who amassed a fortune from land and livestock, but his election and terms as governor, were "an accidental violation of the law," because Frank wasn't even a citizen of the United States! When he later campaigned for the U.S. Senate, this little oversight was brought out, and he withdrew. However, he did then become a United States citizen, and was later elected to the U.S. Senate legally.

All of the water destined for the 70,000 acre Gooding tract would be delivered by the Idaho Irrigation Co. right out of Magic Reservoir. The other, older ranches already there, were all irrigating directly out of the rivers.

1900 - 1910

Late in September, Boone and Hernsheim were both called back to New York to meet with the financiers, several of whom returned to Idaho with them to check out the progress for themselves. They were all getting pretty spooky and insisted that the work be speeded up. "Push the work with vigor," they demanded. The Slick Bros. assured them that rock work could be done almost as well in cold weather as warm, agreed to double their work force immediately, and ordered two more giant machines to be delivered as soon as possible.

Public announcements were made, and newspapers carried stories about work now beginning on Magic Dam - the "Million Dollar Dam." "Water will be on the Gooding Tract next year!" they shouted, and all of the wonderful, encouraging news was told and retold in the Idaho Irrigation Co. ads and news stories. The old financiers had really built a fire under Hernsheim and the company.

And, the newspapers continued to report favorable progress. The following article appeared on October 11, 1907 in the Shoshone Journal:

> *"The Slick Bros. moved several hundred men to the dam to commence work. First, they will install three 12" centrifugal pumps, the largest in use, to pump out the water to allow laying the foundation for the dam. The foundation will be concrete and there will be a concrete core clear to the top of the dam. A wing, or coffer dam, will be built to keep the main flow of the river out of the way while foundation work is in progress, then the pumps will be put to work and the excavation can go on without interruption. Two large tunnels - large enough to carry the full flow of the river even in flood season - will be run to take the water away from the dam proper. They will either be laid out in the open river bed and built entirely of concrete, or they will be concrete-lined tunnels through*

the solid flow of lava that form part of the dam. they will be about 500' in length. Gates are being put in to allow the tunnels to be used at any time to drain the reservoir, for power, or for any purpose whatsoever."

"Horses now being used at the dam eat a car of oats every three days. An electric power plant with 400 horse power is being built, and they will be using electric drills to move the whole mountain down to the river bed to make the dam. All of Southern Idaho is being scoured for hay and grain to feed the horses working on the dam."

The very next day - October 12, 1907 - Chas. Hernsheim quit!

Sold his holdings in the Idaho Irrigation Co., abandoned the project, packed it in, flew the coop, resigned as General Manager - and took the first train back to New York!

Why?

Rumors! Rumors and rumblings about troubles in the banking industry!

Hernsheim said he had to get back to save his family estate, and so did all of his old family friends who were financing the Idaho Irrigation Co. They knew about the Panic before it hit and were trying to save their own skins.

They quickly appointed S.D. Boone General Manager of the company, and turned their attention to their personal family fortunes.

1900 - 1910
THE PANIC OF 1907

1907 had been a good and prosperous year all over the country - until October, when the "panic" hit. It is often referred to as "the rich man's panic," but it affected everybody in the United States. It hit hard - and fast - and deep.

A handful of wild speculators were primarily responsible, and the trouble surfaced when they got caught.

October 16: The Mercantile National Bank of New York city requested help from the clearing house. Following their investigation of the condition of the Mercantile, the clearing house announced they would help - only on condition that all of the directors of Mercantile would resign. The President, and some of the directors, had been speculating heavily in copper. Aha!

Well, this scared the daylights out of just about every other banker around, because there had been a lot of wild speculating going on and they all scurried around to protect their own back-sides.

October 21: The National Bank of Commerce announced that it would no longer accept checks of the giant Knickerbocker Trust Co. When Knickerbocker depositors heard this, they stampeded right down there to get their money out, and the run of the banks was on! Knickerbocker opened their doors in the morning - and closed them at noon.

October 24: The Panic hit the New York Stock Exchange. The banks were in their most critical phase, and restriction of credit was so severe that if allowed to continue, would reduce the Exchange itself to general insolvency. But, good old J.P. Morgan stepped in, and with the help of the President of the New York Stock Exchange, managed to prevent a disaster there.

But, the bank troubles got worse, and the monetary system all over the United States seemed headed for collapse. When the depositors withdrew their money, they hoarded it -

sewed it up in the mattress, buried it in the back yard, or just socked it away somewhere else. It is estimated that approximately three-hundred-million-dollars just disappeared from sight.

This caused the banks to put a limit on the amount of cash they would pay out to depositors, which forced banks in cities like Pittsburgh and Chicago, where manufacturers' payrolls created an urgent need for great sums of currency, to issue "emergency currency" commonly called "scrip".

The use of scrip quickly spread throughout the land - clean out to Idaho. . .

Scrip is simply and I.O.U. certificate showing what the holder is entitled to - could be stock, or land, or money. Sometimes it is transferrable and sometimes it is not. Sometimes nobody would honor it. In the case of wages, it merely stated that "the company" owed the bearer a certain amount for services already rendered.

The Idaho Irrigation Co. started to fall apart. All of the old retired investors who were backing the project were deeply involved in money problems in their own New York back yards, and, like Charles Hernsheim, suddenly wanted "out" of the company. Their own fortunes were tied up in the money panic, and the flow of funds to Idaho slowed - then stopped.

The Slick Bros. were still at work on the dam, even though the money crunch was killing them. The local newspapers typically protected their readers from any big, really bad news about the local irrigation projects, even though they were all in trouble because of the Panic. The news always seemed to be encouraging, and optimistic, and all of the wonderful plans and proposals were repeated again and again.

At the same time - the construction companies were forced to pay in scrip.

Suddenly, out of the blue, the Shoshone Journal broke the story:

1900 - 1910

"FRED W. GOODING BUYS LARGE BLOCK OF STOCK IN THE IDAHO IRRIGATION CO.!"

Fred Gooding, Governor Frank's brother, was a well-known, respected and wealthy gentleman. It was announced that Fred would be on the Board of Directors of the company, that he had looked over the works and said the big ditch was the most complete work of its kind he had ever seen, and that the Slick Bros. were excellent contractors and very conscientious in their work. The Big Main Canal was completed to within six miles of Alberta and the last six would be easy digging, compared to the first fourteen which had been mostly through heavy rock.

When Fred Gooding got in, everybody was pleased because they knew Fred would never get involved in a losing deal. Fred was SOLID.

So, they all happily started getting ready for the big Gooding Opening on November 14th.

1900 - 1910

THE GOODING LAND OPENING

November 14, 1907: It was one of the biggest land openings in Southern Idaho - 70,000 acres of Carey Act Lands (actually, it was 68,896 acres, but round numbers are easier). All arrangements had been made to handle the crowd, and there was a good, big crowd! 600 to 700 people! The hotel was fully booked; tents with warm, comfortable bunks were set up; neighboring farm houses offered rooms; and three sleeper cars were left on the railroad tracks. Several restaurants and the hotel, served meals all day long. The new little town of Gooding overflowed with people from near and far - such as Kansas, Yellowstone, Washington, Oregon and Utah. Special local trains were put on to transport the local people. For example, one left Ketchum at 7:00 a.m. stopping at Hailey, Bellevue, Alberta and Shoshone, arriving in Gooding at 10:30 - home at 9:20 in the evening. The round trip fare was $2.95, and the round-trip from Shoshone to Gooding was 65 cents. An exciting, holiday atmosphere prevailed, and picnic baskets were plentiful.

It rained.

'Til noon.

There was a lot of scurrying about, high-spirited puddle-jumping, greeting friends and neighbors, good-natured visiting, laughing, and gossip.

There was good news: Paul S.A. Bickle, Chief Engineer of the Twin Falls Canal System had definitely, definitely decided on the route of the Milner-Gooding North Side electric Railway. Crews would begin at Jerome and work east and west, he said. That electric trolly would soon be running all over Southern Idaho, up through Camas Prairie, over to Boise, and south to Nevada and Utah! Yes, sir!

And, there was bad news: Much talk and concern about the Panic, and how it would affect the Idaho Irrigation Co.

1900 - 1910

project. Charles Hernsheim's sudden departure didn't help, but the fact that Fred Gooding was now "in," did. Those who understood the national situation were deeply concerned, because the strain of the Panic was definitely beginning to show in the Idaho economy. The railroads were stopping all construction, and were accepting freight on a cash basis only. And then, of course, there was the fact that the construction companies were starting to pay in scrip. . .

Messrs. Lisle and Barber, the land agents in charge of selling the Gooding town lots, were running all over the place. A bank, sugar factory, canning factory, cement block factory, hospital, etc., were all being agitated by those wanting to invest. Those two real estate agents worked like beavers that day, and sold $80,000 worth of Gooding town lots. Not bad, for one day's work.

At the official Carey Act Land Drawing, the Idaho Irrigation Co. sold 10,000 acres of farm land, and the first name drawn was Mr. Wm. MacNeill of Placerville, Idaho.

All told, the Gooding Opening was considered a whopping success - in spite of the damp weather and gloomy economy.

As of that day, November 14, 1907, all of the land segregated to the Idaho Irrigation Co., was open for settlement - 110,000 acres total - 40,000 of which were on the Alberta tract and 70,000 on the Gooding Tract. The Slick Bros. were hard at work on the Big Magic Dam, as well as the main canal heading into Alberta; S.D. Boone was in full and complete charge of the enterprise; all of the land was officially open for sale, and SOLID Fred Gooding was on the Board of Directors of the Idaho Irrigation Co.

The day ended on a high note - and everyone went home tired, but happy.

1900 - 1910

SMALL TOWN NEWSPAPERS - 1907

Small town newspapers were the main source of information. The editors and publishers were practically "family" and printed all of the local news. The Shoshone Journal covered the irrigation projects going on all around the town, because they were important to the people there. The Idaho Irrigation project was spread to the west, north and east of Shoshone, and the Twin Falls North Side irrigation project was moving along to the south of Shoshone. The electric railway was planned to cut south of Shoshone from Milner to Gooding.

The Wood River Times, on the other hand, was still concerned primarily with the mining activity in the Upper Wood River area, because the people there were still involved in mining - although not much was happening in that industry. Occasionally an editor would visit another town and come home to write a story about what was going on there - but for the most part, the papers stuck to the local stuff.

The Shoshone Journal came up with a unique and sassy way of collecting its subscription fees. In loud print on the front page would be a threatening notice:

"You will keep right on receiving the Journal UNTIL YOU PAY YOUR BILL! the only way to ever stop the paper from being delivered to you is to PAY THE BILL."

Did it work? Don't know. The notice was right there threatening away every week for most of 1907.

The front page typically carried advertisements, plus the important local news if there was room. Those ads were real attention-getters and got right down to brass tacks asking personal questions like - Do you suffer from blotches, scaly

1900 - 1910

crusted humors of skin and scalp, eczema, rashes, itching, chafings, inflamations, piles, tumors, cysts, warts, vapors, depression, strong perspiration, rough red hands, or any number of specific "womens' problems" too explicit to mention here? If so, they had the answer and the "cure" - ointments, potions, lotions, elixirs, brews, physics, bitters, tinctures, salves, balms, nostrums, liniments or some kind of patent medicine to put you right back in the pink of condition, make you sound as a bell, fresh as a daisy, in fine fettle, fit as a fiddle - and peppy!

Turn the page and you would find a seralized, long-running romantic story which was eagerly awaited and read and discussed by the "ladies." The men never read such giddy stuff, or at least they never admitted to it. Then, too, some folks could not even read.

The local news was always reported in detail - weddings, deaths, births, and every lurid shocking, frightful particular of some gory, bloody, horrifying accident that happened to human or animal during the past week. And finally, there were bits of drollery, wit and humor by the editor - mostly "inside jokes" about the townsfolks, who were flattered by the attention.

The important events in life were properly written so they could be snipped out and kept and treasured by the participants and their heirs.

Such an event was reported on October 18, 1907 in the Shoshone Journal:

"SHOSHONE YOUNG PEOPLE EMBARK ON MATRIMONIAL SEA."

"Jacob E. Rosseler and Miss Barbara Williams were united in marriage at 12:30 p.m. Tuesday, October 15th at the home of the bride, by the Rev. Thomas M. Patterson, Pastor of the Baptist church. The bride is a native of Missouri and has lived in Shoshone for about a year during which time she has become deservedly popular. Mr. Rosseler is a well-known Big Wood River rancher. Miss Donna L. Williams, sister of the bride, acted as bridesmaid and G. Matthias as groomsman. A number of initimate friends were present to enjoy a beautiful and delicious wedding dinner at the close of the ceremony. The Journal extends congratulations."

Remember back when the Idaho Irrigation Co. was first being formed and plans were announced for an irrigation project at fish Creek? Nothing more was mentioned about it until the following item appeared in the Shoshone Journal about the end of October, 1907:

"John E. Hayes of Twin Falls, a civil engineer who laid out more townsites in Southern Idaho than anyone else, came through town and talked about the 'Sooners' who filed ahead of time up on Fish Creek. Hayes had been working on the surveys for the dam there last year, and had been up to look over the Fish Creek reservoir and canal system which work he had charge of before he shut down last year. A lot of 'Sooners' came in and filed on the land before the irrigation was completed, and as they would not sign contracts for the water to be stored in the reservoir system, it took away all the business of the construction and financing companies so the work was stopped. There is a possibility that the matter will be adjusted so as to make it possible to complete the work with profit to all concerned. As it is now, neither the financiers nor the homesteaders can make a cent."

So much for the Fish Creek project.

1900 - 1910
THE 1907 NEWS

Late in 1907 the biggest lawsuit in the history of Idaho (up to that time) was coming to a head, and it was brought by twenty farmers on the lower Big Wood River. against almost 700 defendants farming above them on upper Big Wood. They wanted this water rights thing cleared up in a court of law once and for all.

The older farms on the lower river had been irrigating for many years, and in point of time and right, those first comers should have been first served, but it wasn't working out that way. Each new homesteader settling farther and farther up the river, claimed his full filing of water, and when each one took out all he had claimed during the peak irrigation season, there was not enough of the regular flow to supply everybody, and it was the older farmer downstream who was cut short. No wonder they were mad about it.

They were asking for a court decree to apportion the water, so that a system of gates could be installed, with a ditch rider put on to see that no one would take more than he was righfully entitled to. Why, some of those new upstream clodhoppers would claim more water than they could possible use, and then, by Gawd turn the waste water out so it ran across into the Little Wood, taking it clean out of the channel where it belonged! Those low-down %#!@Z*!!! stealin', thievin' varmits!

So the big water fight was moving into the courts, and lawyers were having a field day. Every attorney/lawyer/shyster/mouthpiece/counselor for miles around, was involved with someone who was involved in that lawsuit. All of the litigants had to show up to defend their rights or be left with dry farms on their hands. More than 2,000 pages of testimony were taken.

Note: this particular water rights case had no affect

1900 - 1910

whatever on the Idaho Irrigation Co. project because theirs was a "storage water" situation. They had the unchallenged right to the water of the river DURING THE SEASON WHEN IRRIGATION WAS NOT BEING CARRIED ON, which covered nine months of the year, as well as the period of flood water, when the greatest volume of water came down.

The hard times brought on by the Panic really hit Southern Idaho by late 1907. Construction companies were forced to lower wages, railroads stopped cconstruction work over the entire country, and all but sealed up the source of capital coming into Idaho from the east coast. Passenger trains through Shoshone fell off 50%, trains were shortened, and the cars that were running, were not full. The O.S.L. dropped two trains completely. Other states also suffered serious derangements because of the Panic, and practically every big construction company outside of Idaho had already been shut down. Dark times, indeed.

* * * * * *

But lo and behold! A bright spot appeared amid all the gloom and doom. It flashed on the scene through a front-page story in the Shoshone Journal on December 13, 1907. Right in the middle of the front page was a big picture of an Indian family - father, mother, and baby all with long black hair - and the Dad was stirring something in a big, black iron pot hanging over the fire. The caption underneath asked, "DID YOU EVER SEE A BALD HEADED INDIAN?" A catchy question! The picture was surrounded by the announcement story of a new industry that was starting up in Shoshone that promised to become of national importance! The manufacturing of Sagebrush Hair Tonic! There had been an Open House at the tonic office in the Stockgrowers' block the Sunday before, and the public was invited. The first item to be manufactured, the

1900 - 1910

article stated, would be the Sagebrush Hair Tonic, made from sagebrush combined with "other ingredients" to make it the most effective hair grower on the market. Indians have successfully been using sage from time immemorial as a hair

Did you ever see a bald headed Indian?

tonic, and now civilized chemists have turned out a product far superior to what the Indians had. Exhaustive tests and opinions of medical men proved this to be a really great preparation and nothing on the market could approach it in excellence. Other preparations will be added as soon as they can be perfected, with shampoo only a little behind the tonic, they said.

The story went on to explain that more than two years ago Frank Whittington and Tom Starrh, the local druggist, began investigating sagebrush for its tonic properties. Starrh spent months of his time since then in chemical research, called in notable outside chemists, and has now so perfected the preparation that it can be absolutely guaranteed! They now have enough of the "sagebrush essence" to introduce the

1900 - 1910

product, and next spring, a fine factory will be built in Shoshone, of either brick or stone, and manufacturing in wholesale quantities will then begin. A "considerable force" will be hired.

"The company has made no effort to sell stock, but one man - a banker from another state - is so impressed with the preparation that he has applied for $8,000 in stock, another banker wants $2,000 and demands are coming in from all sides for a chance to get in at the bottom. The company will provide for its buildings, and then go after the business of the world in such a way that will astonish those who have not known of its possibilities."

"Mr. Ed Holden will be in charge of the office and look after the detail work of the company. F.E. Whittington is President; Frank Millsaps, Vice-President; T.M. Starrh, Secretary-Treasurer, The Board of Directors include F.E. Whittington, Fred W. gooding (SOLID FRED), T. Millsaps, T.M. Starrh, E.W. Walters, and Fred R. Reed."

The story ended up with a big finale: "The company is starting out to put on the market an article superior in appearance, in a package as attractive as the article itself is superior to other preparations, and the market should open wide its arms for a chance to buy such an excellent preparation! Who wouldn't have a good head of hair when it can be grown by the use of the most typical of all hair products? A tress of wavy, hair, long and fine and beautiful, should be incorporated on the Idaho State Seal, and will be, when the product comes into general use!"

So, 1907 ended in the Magic Circle on some low notes - and on one hairy high note.

One more note: They never did get that hair on the Idaho State seal (you knew that).

1900 - 1910
"DID YOU EVER SEE A BALD-HEADED INDIAN?"

The sagebrush hair tonic business was handled out of Tom Starrh's Drug Store for almost a year. Tom had a good reputation around town, and even marketed a few of his own medicines, such as "Starrh's Laxative Cold Tablets," 25 cents a box, and "Starrh's White Pine Cough Syrup" in 25 cent and 50 cent bottles. In March of 1908, Tom went back east to purchase the machinery for the factory - a steam dryer, a filter, bottling apparatus, and everything else needed to manufacture the hair grower on a large scale.

The factory would be located on West Rail Street. "Rail Street" in Shoshone was just that - a "rail" street. The trains went right through the middle of the town's main drag, and there was still plenty of room on both sides of the multiple tracks for other traffic to tool back and forth, and park a horse and buggy at an angle. Rail Street was a very, very w-i-d-e street - about a block. Still is.

The new hair company had been very active from the start, and stirred up a lot of interest with their bald-headed Indian slogan. Other towns soon began to take notice, and Twin Falls, Mt. Home, and Boise, all tried to lure the company to their town. When a block of several thousand shares of tonic stock was put on the market, all three towns tried to get hold of it so they could pull the factory their way, but the Shoshoneans outfoxed them by rushing in and buying up all of the stock. Hardly a single share was sold outside of Shoshone, so the majority of stockholders had an interest in developing the town, as well as a direct financial interest in the company. The stock had been introduced at 50 cents a share, and the second offering sold at $1, so all one had to do was look at the short time it took those first investors to double their money.

By early June, 1908 things really got underway. First, a

1900 - 1910

carload of 75,000 bottles arrived, all sizes up to a gallon (for wholesale druggists). And they were the prettiest bottles! "More like a fine perfume bottle than for a staple medicine," the Journal reported.

Next, the machinery arrived, and crews were put to work unloading and installing. One morning the citizens of Shoshone were startled to hear a new strange "Toot! Toot! Toot!" They had become accustomed to the train tooting signals, but this was a new and different sound. What? What? A steam whistle had been installed at the tonic factory! And it was a happy sound indeed for the Shoshone folks - after all, most of them owned a piece of the business, and it was music to their ears. The Journal triumphantly boasted: "This factory, with a real live steam whistle, will bring more hair for the bald, more money for the poor, more prosperity and fame for the factory!"

It was the first factory in Shoshone.

"Picking gangs" of twenty or more, were soon circulating among the sagebrush with orders to bring in only the tender, this-year's growth tips of the plants. An artist was engaged to beautify the front of the factory with a huge, colorful mural of a giant-sized Indian with thick, heavy hair flowing down his back, and the big question shouting in large print - "DID YOU EVER SEE A BALD-HEADED INDIAN?" It was the first bill-board sized sign in Shoshone, and startled many a railroad traveler as they passed through the town. The sign itself soon became a celebrated landmark, and passengers were often told ahead of time to watch for the Big Indian in Shoshone.

The first big shipment of Sage Brush Hair tonic went out in September, 1908 to "far-off frozen Alaska." The Journal ran the story:

"Four experienced salesmen are now on the road

1900 - 1910

full-time selling the Sagebrush products. The Alaskans of Ketchican want more hair - they want skins growing on their heads and they want them quick, before the calendar and frost overtake them, so they sent a hurry-up order for the great hair grower to protect themselves against the long, frigid nights. The goods will go out at once and the frozen North will rejoice!"

By October, the factory was swamped with orders. F.E. Whittington returned from a trip to Boise with orders sticking out of all his pockets. The tonic was booming, and sales were running from $75 to $100 a day. One dealer alone bought $600 worth of tonic, and others came close to that. The salesmen so far were contacting only the barbers and barber-supply houses, and not even touching the retail or wholesale drug trade or public demand!

Two more carloads of bottles were quickly ordered.

That Bald-headed Indian slogan proved to be one of the cleverest advertising gimmicks of its day. By December of 1908 the company was in the process of expanding. A new steam heating plant was installed, and the factory was soon turning out rivers of tonic AND Sage Brush Shampoo!

"Toot! Toot! Toot!"

1900 - 1910

NIGHTMARES AND DREAMS

January 8, 1908: W.K. Everdell, Vice-President of the Idaho Irrigation Co., and N.M. Burick, company attorney, came out to Idaho from New York to help Mr. Boone audit the books, take inventory, try to put the company on a cash basis, and request extensions of time on the bills. Money was still very scarce. The Slick Bros., who had been forced to pay in scrip, and many of their employees had filed liens against the company. There were also some very large, past due accounts to general creditors around Hailey and Shoshone.

Rumors and gossip ran rampant, and everybody blamed everybody else for the trouble. Fingers were pointed and bad words were bandied about.

January 17, 1908: S.D. Boone resigned! No! Yes! W. K. Everdell stepped in as General Manager of the Idaho Irrigation Co.

Shock waves reverberated through the Magic Circle. "This had been Mr. Boone's project from the start!" "How could this happen?" "Mr. Boone is our friend and neighbor, and we respect him and know him to be an honest man!" "He's a victim of the Panic - that's what!" "We're ALL victims of the Panic!" "What will happen to the Idaho Irrigation Project?" "What will happen to those of us who bought water rights and land from this company?" "Will the canals ever be completed?" "Will Magic Dam be abandoned?"

All of this was disturbing, troubling news for everyone, and there was a great sadness for Mr. Boone and his family. The project had been his dream and he had worked endless, exhausting hours with a dedication rarely seen, only to lose it all now, because of a Money Panic thousands of miles away!

Well, at any rate, the word was out that the company was in deep financial trouble, and it wasn't long before "they" began showing up.

The first was "an enterprising gentleman with an active

1900 - 1910

brain and a trunkful of money" who came with an offer to buy the entire townsite of Alberta. He had a lot of money, "whole lathers and doodles of the real stuff," the newspapers said. But the company was aware of the value of the town and said "no deal." Alberta was doing nicely, thank you. It boasted the largest lumber yard in the country; two excellent general stores; a large, well-equipped livery barn; a saloon; a new bank building; the Irrigation Co. headquarters building; a brand new well 430 feet deep, with 30 feet of the best water in the world; and the Alberta Hotel where Mrs. John Thomas served the "best meals in the West - every bit as good as Delmonicos!"

Along in February, Mr. Everdell reported that the Idaho Irrigation Co. prospects were the best! "Ample new capital is being interested to make the enterprise a complete success." Horsefeathers! What he really meant was that the company was up for grabs and he was trying to make it sound good. The Slick Bros. were moving all of their men, horses, mules and equipment away to a job at Glenns Ferry! The State of Idaho had withdrawn a large unsold part of the Gooding tract from the company's segregation, and those settlers who had already bought land on the Alberta and Gooding tracts were standing around in their fields wondering "what now?" One diversion dam was complete, and there were 14 miles of main canal, with elaborate concrete and steel headgates, winding around out in the middle of nowhere.

The truth was - Magic Dam, and the "project" were in Limbo!

* * * * * * *

Note: Elsewhere in Idaho in 1908 the "crusade" to get rid of that "Idaho Panhandle" was once again underway. When the territories had been made into states, their boundaries were more reflective of politics than of physical geography. Spokane thought

1900 - 1910

the divisions "so unnatural" that in 1908 this hub of the Inland Empire clamored for a new state. The "State of Lincoln" would eliminate Idaho's panhandle and settle the whole matter. The same type of crusade went on in 1881 and now they were at it again.

The panhandle stayed.

* * * * * * *

1908 was an exceptional year for Shoshone. Everything seemed to improve over 1907. In addition to all the flap about the new tonic factory, the old wooden sidewalks in the town were torn up and replaced with cee-ment!

In May, the Shoshone Journal installed a new linotype machine, the latest and best, for $3,750. The Journal was proud and optimistic, and said the new acquisition showed great faith in the town.

A glove manufacturing industry was started about mid-summer. Crothers & Sons, Glovemakers, began making heavy cloth gloves, looking to replace the expensive leather work gloves on the market. If the cloth gloves caught on, Crothers planned to increase the line to carpenter's aprons, jackets, and other heavy cotton cloth goods. They started out with three "foot-powered" sewing machines, and stated that a good sewer could produce from 12 to 15 dozen pairs of gloves daily! That comes to 288 to 370 single gloves a day! That's a lot of peddling in one 10-hour day. The work was dull, detailed, repetitious, difficult and hard on the eyes. It required skill and dexterity, a strong back, strong legs - and the pay was meagre. The "sewers," of course, were women - no one else could, or would, do it. Crothers had a cutting capacity for 75 machines, but would not put on more workers until he tested the market. If all went well, and the cloth work gloves became popular, "motor machines" would be purchased "for the girls." Meanwhile, they would just have to "peddle."

1900 - 1910
BARNUM & BAILEY

Shoshone lucked out on big entertainment in the summer of 1908. The "Greatest Show on Earth," the "gigantic, stupendous, collosal, Barnum & Bailey Circus" was crossing the country on the railroad, entertaining with performances in BIG cities only. Boise and Pocatello were both on their schedule, but the distance between them was too far without a stop to feed and water the animals, so the circus people decided that the logical place to stop would be Shoshone, and since they had to get everything off the train anyway, decided to give a performance there.

The advance man showed up about the middle of July to arrange for space and food and water. He ordered wagon loads of bread and vegetables, barrels of milk, tubs of butter, whole beeves, and whole bee hives, plus hay, grain, and everything else needed for their army of a thousand men, acres of horses, elephants, camels and "wild and curious beasts of all kinds." He then made arrangements to have special trains put on to bring people to Shoshone for the show. Posters and billboards were sent out to every town within a hundred miles.

All of this was a real wind-fall for Shoshone folks, and they excitedly started to gear up to host more people than had been in the town since it was born.

The circus arrived on August 7th. At ten in the morning the street parade started and the entire colorful cavalcade took a full half-hour to pass a given spot! The parade was attended by thousands strung out along the way to the race track.

This was probably the biggest circus that ever traveled the United States. There were four special trains - not cars - TRAINS! TRAINS! containing 32 elephants, 24 Siberian camels, innumerable llamas, zebras, alpacas, sacred cows, Indian cattle etc. etc. A seemingly endless assortment of strange and beautiful creatures.

1900 - 1910

1900 - 1910

The Journal ran a few tidbits ahead of time telling about the bi-horned rhinocerous that had his entire hide rubbed full of fish oil three times a week, and both he and the hippopotamus were scrubbed down with soap and water every day. There were half-a-dozen or more babies in the zoo department: "Baby Bunting," the infant elephant, a baby camel, baby llamas, and kangaroos.

It was truly a memorable day for all who came to see the great circus.

At two o'clock in the afternoon the show was underway - three colorful, sparkling rings of lively, leaping, jumping acrobats; tumbling teams; aerialists; clowns; lion tamers; performing horses; and all the wonderful sounds and smells of the circus. Everyone was enchanted.

The "special feature" was the "Autos that pass in the air." It would have been a treat to even see an automobile in Shoshone, but to watch WOMEN performing such remarkable feats was almost more than anyone could believe! WOMEN! the audience clapped and screamed and wondered "How do dey do dat?"

They all went home tired and happy after that astonishing day when the "Greatest Show on Earth" came to Shoshone, Idaho. Memories and stories were told from generation to generation, and many a loving grandparent charmed the grandchildren with stories of the happenings they had witnessed with their own eyes!

1900 - 1910

1908 - OUT WITH THE OLD - IN WITH THE NEW!

By the end of March, the Idaho Irrigation Co. Ltd. was stone-cold dead. The old financial backers had all backed out; Boone was out; the Slick Bros. had moved everything and everybody over to a new job at Glenn's Ferry, and the Idaho Irrigation Co. project was completely deserted.

The once-promising young town of Alberta sat silent, worried, and waiting.

On May 15th, Shoshone Journal headlines announced: KUHN BROS. TAKE OVER IDAHO IRRIGATION CO.! The Kuhn Bros. were the Pittsburgh millionaires behind the big Twin Falls Northside Project, the Big Salmon River Project, and the Electric Railway. The news story went on to say "The land the State had withdrawn from the former Idaho Irrigation Co. Project has now been reinstated to the Kuhn interests, and the Kuhns' will also open up an additional 50, 000 acres."

But wait! The very next day both papers headlined: "The Kuhn Bros. have an option to take over the old Idaho Irrigation Co. and the J. G. White Co. is standing by."

Nine days later, on May 25, 1908, more headlines announced:

"THE J. G. WHITE CO., WORLD FAMOUS CONTRACTORS, WILL GO TO WORK AT ONCE ON THE IDAHO IRRIGATION CO. TRACT!"

No explanation was ever given by either paper regarding the premature announcement. Did Kuhn brothers change their minds? Why didn't they pick up their option? Or, did the newspapers just "goof" and jump the gun? All of the "action" took place in Boise and nothing was ever mentioned there about the Kuhn brothers taking over. The Statesman did report daily

1900 - 1910

arrivals and departures of V.I.P.'s in Boise, and there were a lot of comings and going and meetings at the Idanha Hotel during that time, but there was no word in the Statesman as to what was going on.

At any rate, the readers were now absolutely, positively informed that the J. G. White Co. had taken over the Idaho Irrigation Co. project.

J. G. White was the biggest contracting and engineering company in the world at the time. They had offices in London, Paris, New York, Montreal, Canada, plus more, and many field offices. They had a distinguished reputation and were famous world wide. For example, they had built a huge harbor in the Phillipines, and were working on 300 miles of railroad there; they built an enormous electric line in India, and right here in the Western United States they were constructing a huge dam and tunnel on the Snake River below Huntington, Oregon for the Idaho-Oregon Light & Power Co. The company had already completed some BIG dams - one of which was the LaCrosse Dam across the Black River in Wisconsin which furnishes water power for acres of factories, and had constructed many miles of railroads as well. The J. G. White Co. was indeed a very large, and impressive company.

Immediately, they were granted an extension of time to complete the Idaho Irrigation Co. project. Even so, it meant their crews would have to work day and night to meet the deadline.

The summer months of 1908 were taken up with red tape and details of transferring everything to the new company. Mr. J. G. White, himself, spent long hours with his engineers and accountants getting everything right, and ready to go.

S. D. Boone was given a fair and generous settlement to cover his part, plus percentages of all the work he had already completed. However, no amount of money could ever pay him for the blood, sweat and tears he shed getting the project

1900 - 1910

started and moving it along as far as he did. Only his family and close friends would ever really know the great personal price he paid for his "Magic."

The whole neighborhood came alive as professionals from all walks of life began to show up to inspect and study the new project - engineers, surveyors, attorneys, accountants, State Reclamation officers, personnel men, and more.

Of course, potential financiers were also on the scene to be wined and dined and escorted around the project.

Finally, on September 4, 1908, representatives of the old and new companies met in Hailey, and the transfer was formally executed.

A new Board of Directors was elected. Fred Gooding and C. B. Hurtt of Boise were the two local members, along with Eastern representatives of the new management. C. B. Hurtt had been one of the prime movers on the two big Twin Falls Projects, and would now be in charge of land sales for the new Idaho Irrigation Co., Ltd.

Even though the new company retained the name "Idaho Irrigation Co., Ltd.", they insisted that the name of the "company town" be changed. They felt "Alberta" would conjure up scenes of cold, cold Canada, and turn people away from the idea of a good farm with a long growing season. They decided it would be "Richfield" to suggest soft, rich soil producing riches for the owner.

So, "Alberta" was officially changed to "Richfield" on October 1, 1908. The U.S. Post Office people bucked at changing the name again; first it was "Arvada" named by the railroad, then changed to "Alberta" when Alberta Strunk was born there, and now again to "Richfield." However, the new powerful company carried a lot of weight, insisted on the change, and the p.o. complied.

A big construction company from Oklahoma City, Hales & Crane, were commissioned to do all of the canal work - under supervision of the J. G. White Co., and the J. G. White Co., itself, would build Magic Dam.

The new Idaho Irrigation Co. had 160,000 acres of land under its jurisdiction; all of the lands which had originally been segregated to the old company, including the Gooding Tract that had been withdrawn from entry during the suspension of the old company, plus 50,000 acres of new land located east of Shoshone. That 50,000 acre tract would later be named "Dietrich."

New "opening dates" were set, and preparations made to begin again to sell the lands of the Idaho Irrigation Co., Ltd.

Meanwhile, visiting parties of eastern bankers swarmed like bees all over the project. It was easy and comfortable to attach a couple of private cars to trains headed west, and gave the city-slickers an excuse to visit the wild west, with an idea of investing a dollar or two in the newest undertaking of the famous J. G. White Co.

One Shoshone Journal reporter carefully collected the names of one important group who said they were very well-pleased with the project and what they saw. Escorting this party were S. A. Farnham, who was President of the new Idaho Irrigation Co. and also Vice-President of the J. G. White Co., along with A. S. Crane and A. F. Richardson both of the J. G. White Co. The "escortees" were N. W. Halsey and F. T. Rockward of the N. W. Halsey Co., Chicago; Theo Loose, N. W. Halsey Co., Detroit; and Chas. Pettis and John Nickerson of the N.W. Halsey Co. St. Louis. W. G. Leisurling, Bond Officer, Hibernic Bank, Chicago; J. J. Bryant, Sec., Fairwell Trust Co., Chicago and J. F. Emery, Treasurer of Chicago Rawhide Co. and Director of Colonial Trust Co., Chicago. There was George H. Begg, Capitalist, Detroit; Henry G. Stevens of the Bumpus-Stevens Co., Detroit; John Anderson, Capitalist, Detroit; George E. Lawson, Vice-President, Peoples' State Bank, Detroit; J.F. Holden, Director, Security Trust Co., Detroit; Gerald J. McCoy,

1900 - 1910

Bond Officer, Security Trust Co., Detroit; W. Bruce Howard, Capitalist, Detroit; W.A. Hamilin of the W.A. Hamlin Co., Detroit, and F.S. Tilotseen, Cashier, Citizens Savings Bank, Detroit. From St. Louis came C.R. Compton, President of the Compton Co.; T.N. Dyssert, Treasurer of the Compton Co.; Fred Emmert, Secretary of the Compton Co., and F.W. Aldritch, both from St. Louis. One more - George Clark from Bloomington, Illinois. Don't know who George was, or who represented, but he was a member of the group and his name was duly recorded by the reporter.

Since this was the only list of names published, it may be assumed, I suppose, that these were the new financiers. It is also interesting to note that they all came from the mid-west, Chicago, Detroit and St. Louis.

At any rate, all of the money needed to complete the project started by S.D. Boone, was now available. All of it.

By the end of October, 1908, the new company had paid off all of the old accounts, so more than $100,000 in cash was happily circulating around the Magic Circle.

Spirits soared, and progress and prosperity were in the air wherever the Idaho Irrigation Co. showed up.

The new town of Richfield came alive! People who had been waiting for something to happen for almost a year, now burned up the mails in their efforts to supply the sudden demand for lumber, hardware, groceries and all the things needed for a lively working community.

Changes had been made in the townsite - resident lots were now 50' frontage instead of the 25' set by the first company, and the price per foot was reduced. Street names were changed also - what had been called "Reservoir Avenue" running north and south, was changed to "Main", and the old "Main Street" was changed to "Lincoln Avenue."

The Shoshone Light & Power Co. started stringing a phone line between Richfield and the dam; scores of men and

1900 - 1910

200 teams, including a carload of mules brought in from Puerto Rico, set out to start work immediately at the damsite, and the big Hales & Crane Construction Co. moved out to complete the "almost finished" canal to the Richfield Tract, and when completed would move on to the South Gooding Tract.

The Idaho Irrigation Co. announced that water would be available on both the Richfield and Gooding tracts by April 1, 1909.

In December, they started to put up a new railroad depot at the foot of Reservoir Avenue in Richfield. The Oregon Short Line added three passenger cars and a smoking car - thanks to the Idaho Irrigation Co. - which doubled the railroad capacity and made it possible for passengers to get exactly what they wanted in the way of accommodations. This change from the old mixed train, with no mail clerk, and a schedule that depended upon mail and livestock shipments, was a wonderful improvement. A permanent railroad station would soon be established where passenger, freight, mail and telegraph business could all be handled. A new side track, 1,000 feet long, would also soon be ready in addition to the siding already there.

A large office building for the company, the bank, a lava rock livery barn and a "Jap Restaurant" opened for business, along with other buildings, tents and shacks and stores.

Richfield was on the way to becoming important!

MAGIC DAM - 1908

The Big Wood River, after leaving the foothills, meanders in a southwesterly direction, is joined by Camas Creek, and - before the dam was built - flowed quietly through the broad valley where the farms of Calhoun, Rice and the others, were located. Suddenly, at the south end of the valley the river narrowed and became a torrent as it dashed through a narrow gorge, made a sharp turn, and became a turbulent, angry river. The "narrow gorge" was formed by a lava canyon on the east, which curled around sharply on the south, much as your right had would curl around a coffee mug. On the west, a solid granite cliff protruded from the shore like a huge log jamed into the river bank. If that granite cliff were your left hand, your fingers would point into the palm of your cupped right hand. The narrow space at the end of your fingers would be the "narrow gorge." It formed a natural damsite.

S.D. Boone saw it as the perfect spot for his Magic Dam.

The Slick Bros. Construction Co. had moved some of their camp to the gorge to start on the dam back in February of '08, but were not able to accomplish much before they were forced off the job when the first Idaho Irrigation Co. went broke. Slicks had planned to build Magic Dam with a concrete foundation, and a concrete core clear to the top of the dam. They intended to lay two large concrete pipes down in the open river bed, large enough to carry the entire stream without overflowing, and then build the dam on top of and over these conduits. Gates would be provided during construction, so they could be opened or closed at will.

The Slick Bros. were good builders. Had they been able to finish the job, the construction of Magic Dam would have been different - but good. They had completed the large diversion dam three miles downstream, plus 14 miles of main canal, with elaborate concrete and steel headgates. They

1900 - 1910

established a record for moving rock in the great rock cut where the canal leaves the Big Wood. Some of the heaviest blasting ever done in the State up to that time was necessary to make a place for the headgates so they would not be susceptible to damage from water or other ordinary causes. Some of that cut is more than 20 feet deep the full width of the canal. Shots were put in at a depth of 24 feet, sprung with dynamite, and the black powder poured in by the wagon load. Many of the boulders left by the blast weighed up to 7 tons each, and were then picked up bodily by the huge derricks set up alongside the canal, which swung the great rocks out of the canal and piled them 30 to 50 feet high on either side. They used 450 kegs of powder blowing out close to 10,000 cubic yards of rock.

The diversion dam has a concrete core, rock fill, and a 170 foot spillway across a concrete wall. The concrete piers and walls hold ten gates, each 6' x 16' in size. It is 1,000 feet from this dam to the main headgates of the canal.

MAGIC DAM DIARY

1900 - 1910

September 1, 1908

Today, the great J.G. White Co. is starting work on Magic Dam. Actual construction plans are far different from those of the Slick Bros. The White engineers plan to bore a large tunnel clean through the protruding granite cliff, then close the "narrow gorge" completely from bottom to top. No water will ever dash through it or over it again.

The tunnel will be horseshoe-shaped and approximately 12' x 14' - big enough to carry the full flow of the river. Controls will be installed in a concrete tower located on the upstream side of the dam.

The first step will be to bore the tunnel, and at the same time, start construction of a low wing dam just in front of where the permanent dam will eventually be. By doing this, they can raise the surface of the water so that the flow of the river can be taken through the tunnel, and at the same time, store sufficient water for next season's irrigation on the 30,000 acre Richfield Tract, and keep the company's promise to deliver that water by April 1, 1909.

October, 1908

The telephone line from Richfield to the dam is in, and busy. More men and teams are being put on the job every day. The camp, itself, is being built - sleeping quarters, mess halls, kitchens, etc. for the army of laborers, plus stables for the animals, are all located on the west side of the river. Office buildings, sleeping quarters, mess halls, kitchens, etc. for the J.G. White engineers, surveyors, superintendents, the dam keeper, and other employees, are all located on the east side.

1900 - 1910

January, 1909

The engineers receive word that the Dietrich Tract has been approved, making it necessary for them to revise the blueprints to raise the dam 25 ft. higher than originally planned. This increase will make Magic Dam one of the highest earth-filled dams in the world.

The weather is terrible during January - lots of rain and snow, and things really get bad toward the end of the month when a sudden thaw turns the Big Wood into a raging torrent discharging 4,800 cubic feet of water per second, compared to its lowest minimum summer flow of 150 inches. Work had been going well on the low wing dam when the flood hit and destroyed more than two months' work! It is a heartbreaking set-back, leaving the Herculean task of dealing with all that slippery, miserable mess in the cold, wet mud and snow. The delay will make it impossible now to impound water in time for next season's crops. They will be unable to deliver that precious water on April 1st as promised.

February 19, 1909

THE TUNNEL IS THROUGH!! It is 700 feet long, rough and raw! The men cheer and congratulate each other. Vigorous hand-shaking and back-slapping. The exhilaration is shared by the engineers and workers alike.

More good news - the heavy equipment needed for construction of the dam has arrived by train in Richfield, and is being transported to the damsite. It is a rough, dangerous trip because the snow is deep and everything must be moved on sleds hauled by multi-horse teams and mules. The average load is to haul five tons on a single sled, but much of this weighs eight tons or more. It is a 21 mile trip for the freighters, and usually takes only two days. Not so with this equipment. The

1900 - 1910

two large Marion steam shovels and three locomotives can be broken down only so far, and even then special handling is required for the heavy, bulky pieces.

The gruff voices of the freighters bellow through the crisp, cold air, and the teams sweat and strain. The big sleds side-slip and grind, spin, grip, brake and lock, until finally, the damsite comes into view.

The damsite. A teeming city! Numerous buildings on both sides of the river. More than 500 men in residence, plus countless horses and mules. Huge "stations" receiving an endless stream of supplies. Large stores of provisions neatly stacked, ready to use. Food supplies for the men. Feed for the animals. Lumber, coal, hardware, equipment, everything imaginable needed to keep this vast project moving.

March, 1909

Men are working from both ends of the tunnel, lining it completely with 2 feet of concrete.

Almost a carload of Greeks arrived to work on the dam. These men are fresh off the boat at Ellis Island. They are met by "agents" who speak their language and who accompany them to jobs. They are hired through a placement service in Salt Lake City, one of many, scattered throughout the United States. They work as common laborers under the direction of whoever acts as an interpreter.

Millions of immigrants arrived at Ellis Island between 1900 and 1910 with little more than a battered suit case and an identification tag. Those poor souls who came to work on Magic Dam suffered a long train ride right after suffering a long boat ride. But, they had work and earned good money. Others were not so lucky and ended up in the stifling ghettos of Manhattan's lower East Side.

1900 - 1910

April 29, 1909

A piano arrived at the dam today! Five minutes after it hits camp it is unloaded, unpacked, and in active operation. Superintendent McClanahan already has a piano at his home on the east side of the river, where the boys are free to gather. This new piano is for the engineers' quarters. They have guitars, mandolins, coronets, harmonicas and many other instruments there, and someone to play every one, and play it well. "Doc" Holloway and J.D. Strawn, Materials Superintendent, both play the piano. There are singers, too - Doc's baritone, M.F. Steele and J. Stewart, Assistant to the Superintendent, and a lot of others who can reel off tunes. They plan to build a club room with books and papers, and a general meeting place after the labors of the day. The piano was purchased by contributions from the office and engineering forces.

They have as comfortable quarters as can be prepared so far out in the wilderness. Baseball and tennis teams are being planned, with an eye to challenging the Hailey baseball team on July 4th. The high altitude and difficulty in finding time to practice present some problems, and there are not enough laborers available to clear the land for diamonds and courts, but that won't stop them.

May 6, 1909

Today, they blew the whole side out of the lava hill just east of the damsite! What a spectacular sight it was! First, holes were drilled 30 feet deep into the rock and then sprung with small charges of dynamite to open them up at the bottom, large enough to hold the bulky black powder. A constant cannonade of shots marked this work.

But when all that black power (1,100 pounds of it) was set off, the entire hill convulsed, roared, and violently spewed hundreds of tons of rock and earth down into the river bed on the downstream side of the damsite, exactly where the engineers wanted it to be. It will be used to fill up the "narrow gorge."

Work on the tunnel is moving along. The two-foot-thick concrete lining is nearing completion. When the reservoir is full, that tunnel will have a capacity great enough to deliver water to irrigate all of the company land. It is located so near the bottom it will come close to draining the reservoir dry.

The water will enter the tunnel through an "intake tower", and the amount of water passing through the tunnel will be controlled by two five-foot valves operated from inside the tower. The tower itself will be about 120 ft. high, hexagonal in form, with large openings all around.

July 1, 1909

A large dynamo arrived in camp this day to be used for power and light. Soon, the water in the river will be low enough so they can start to work actually filling the gorge. A double force of men - about 700 - will now be working two full 10-hour shifts.

For the past two months, load after load of cars, dump wagons, machinery of all kinds, and everything else needed to push work on the dam, have been moving onto the site. A steady stream of freight wagons arrive from Richfield, and carload after carload of coal and other provisions have been freighted in so that when the water gets low enough, there will be no delay, everything needed to finish the job will be on the grounds.

1900 - 1910

July 10, 1909

FIRE! FIRE! Saturday, six a.m. The large, main cookhouse on the west side of the river is ablaze! It is a windy morning, and the fire spreads quickly to two large dining halls. Nothing is saved. All three buildings were completely demolished. A very heavy loss. Thankfully, no one was injured in the frantic attempts to extinguish the flames.

Word of the fire is reported immediately to the office in Richfield, where every freighter and teamster for miles around is quickly assembled to start hauling lumber, utensils, stoves, and everything necessary to replace the terrible loss. No one knows for sure how the fire started, but it is rumored that hot ashes were discarded too close to the cookhouse, and the strong, gusty winds blew them back toward the buildings.

July 29, 1909

The water has abated in the Big Wood, and only the normal summer flow is coming down from the mountains. The time has come to begin the actual work of closing up the gorge. The great volume of water that has been coming down has made it impossible to work, other than to get ready to start when the volume lessened.

The low wing-dam that was re-constructed after the flood, is now closed. It is on the upstream side of the gorge, is 50 or 60 feet high, and will raise the surface of the water so the flow of the river can be taken through the tunnel and sufficient water can thus be stored for this season's irrigation on the Richfield Tract. The low dam will eventually form the upstream face of the completed structure.

The center, or core of the dam, will be formed by driving 30 ft. long sheets of heavy steel piling perpendicularly into the bedrock of the old river channel, and extending all the way

1900 - 1910

across the canyon from the wall to wall. This sheet steel is so constructed that it can be joined together by a steel web which is grooved, or dove-tailed, to match the piling, and is then driven down the entire length of the steel sheets, binding them into a solid wall of steel 800 feet from the bank to bank, and down to bedrock at the base of the gorge. This will make a water-tight steel wall to shut off any seepage that might otherwise endanger the foundations of the dam. Impervious clay will then be tamped and puddled solidly and carefully on both sides of the steel wall.

Below that, another dam is being constructed which will eventually be the lower face of the completed structure. This is where the blown-out hillside landed.

When completed, the dam will have to rise higher than the top of the gorge in order to reach the needed depth of 135 feet. Therefore, a flanking dam will be attached that will run westward across the top of the granite cliff about three-fourths of a mile. The flood spillway will be way out at the end of this flanking dam. The granite cliff will be completely covered and no one will even know it is there.

* * * * * * *

The J.G. White Co. has set up an ideal camp for the men. The cookhouse and dining rooms that were burned a few weeks ago, are now rebuilt better than before.

There are now on the job Spaniards, Bulgarians, Armenians, Japanese, Italians, and Greeks. Each nationality is quartered in its own bunk house, but all use the same dining room. Water is pumped to the entire camp through an elaborate water system.

The company maintains an excellent hospital under the care of Dr. V.K Ververkmoes, and looks after the injured men as well as if they were in the city. A fine commissary store is also provided.

1900 - 1910

The company feeds its army of employees very well - "like Delmonico's or Sherry" they say, and the crowd of visitors on the site last week were served a special luxury in the way of a trout dinner "fit for all the heathen gods that ever peopled Olympus."

The newspaper reporter quoted some of the visitors: "The J.G. White men in charge of the operation are the friendliest, nicest, cleverest and politest men that it is anyone's privilege to know."

It is interesting to note that the "visitors" quoted are young, single, women.

It must also be mentioned that many of the J.G. White men are young, single, engineers just out of college. . .

A saw-mill operating near water level saws up all material needed, from logs floated down the river. There's a blacksmith shop, stables, and a large protected area to care for the animals. There's a well-equipped machine shop - equipped for almost as heavy work as a locomotive factory, and derricks and cars and enough gear of all kinds to build a steel city. Hundreds of tons of steel and iron piping, castings, gates and other apparatus for the water control are on the grounds, not to mention all the cement, coal, etc.

August 19, 1909

The sheet steel wall is now in place, and put deep into the rocky walls of the gorge to get safe anchorage and to seal against possible leakage. At the base of the dam, trenches on either side of the steel wall are being filled with earth, and a heavy-duty pumping system then sluices the dirt into place, putting it down so that it will, when finished, have no seam nor crevice. It will be a solid structure, like masonry, no way for the water to seep through later. It is an ideal way for filling in any such place and will be as water-tight as so much putty.

1900 - 1910

September 23, 1909

The upper and lower faces of the dam are now formed. They are located several hundred feet apart - one upstream, one downstream, with the steel wall in the middle.

Two big steam shovels and three locomotives are at work rushing in the earth as fast as it can be piled in. The railway service from the steam shovels to the dam is constantly being reorganized so that there will be a continuous stream of trains pulling their earth over the dam. The two steam shovels scoop up earth from the banks, and load it into dump cars, which two or three donkey engines push out onto a trestle over the river where they are dumped onto the upper wall of the dam. Three stationary engines load dump cars with rock, and gravity rolls them out over the river where they are dumped on both the upper and lower faces of the walls of the dam, and mules haul them back. Three railway tracks lead out over the upper wall and two at the lower wall. These tracks thread the sides of the canyon on both sides of the river and are located on different levels. It will take approximately 700,000 cubic yards of rock and earth to complete the dam.

The work goes on day and night.

Skilled engineers are everywhere. They made a little survey of their own, and found that there are graduates from sixteen different universities now working on Magic Dam.

November 1, 1909

The river bed is now covered to a height of 20 feet above the top of the sheet steel wall. The work, at present, looks like two immense dams 700 feet apart - the upper and lower faces of the structure and the yawning chasm in between that is still to be filled in. There are about 235,000 cubic yards of material

1910 - 1920

in the dam at this point, a little more than one-third of the total needed for completion.

The tunnel is completed, and water is running through it.

While the dam will not be entirely completed until after the high water of next year, it will be brought up to a point where the company can store several times as much water next season as will be actually used.

November 18, 1909

There are steady jobs now for 50 men, woodcutters, wood haulers, and general workmen to clear the several square miles of the great reservoir site preparatory to filling the great lake to the brim.

January 27, 1910

A year ago now was when the Big Wood suddenly turned into a raging torrent and wiped out the low dam, seriously delaying the work, and making it impossible for the company to keep its promise to deliver water on April 1, 1909. There is more snow on the ground now than there was then, and if it goes off with a rush, the volume of water could be considerably greater. They can't take a chance on it happening again this year, so, as an insurance against such a set-back, a large flume is being built to take care of any excess of spring flood that cannot be stored behind the dam. The flume is 50 feet wide and 6 feet deep and runs over the crest of the dam.

As it now stands, the dam is about 70 feet high filled in almost level between the upper and lower faces. The tunnel will carry off about 2,000 cubic feet of water with the gates and valves set, or 4,000 wide open. The flume across the top will carry 10,000 cubic feet per second when the water reaches the height where an outlet is needed, making three times the carrying capacity of the heaviest flood-time last year. The company does not intend to be caught off-guard again.

The two Marion steam shovels and five locomotives with plenty of cars for hauling, are still in full-time operation, and an elaborate system of trackage permits the economical handling of the excavated materials.

April 7, 1910

The Richfield Recorder reporter made a trip to the dam and wrote his impression:

"There is a lake six miles long backed up behind the dam. The lake, 60 feet deep stretches way back through the hills like a giant silver shield. That dam - why it looks like they're moving a whole mountain down to fill up that mighty gorge. The dam is as deep up and down the stream as three city blocks, almost a city block high, and more than two blocks long, without counting the wings. Altogether, the place and magnitude of the job makes it look like the workshop of an army of Titans. The steam shovels, the rushing trains of earth and rock, the great cranes, hundreds of hard-working men, the placid silver lake above, and the cavernous gorge and growling torrent below the dam. What a truly wonderful picture it is to see!"

April 14, 1910

Mr. H.J. McVickers, one of the big freighters working from Richfield to the dam, is out and about the country trying to line up even more teams for the summer. He already has about 40 teams hauling regularly, and will put on more as fast

1910 - 1920

as he can find them. Several thousand tons of coal are piled up in the yards at Richfield, and as soon as what is on the ground can be freighted to the dam, an order for fourteen cars a week will be sent out. Besides the coal, a lot of heavy timbers will be needed, in addition to the seemingly endless amount of supplies and provisions for the men working on the dam.

Thousands of tons of coal for hungry engines - hundreds of tons of food for hungry men.

For example - they bake 125 pies every day "like Mother used to make." Chef Lambert tries to consider the wishes and appetites of his boarders, and with the help of his sixteen assistants, serves good, hot meals around the clock. The night work is as heavy as the day work. At present, they are consuming two beeves a day; 600 loaves of bread; 75 pounds of flour for hot cakes for breakfast; two cases of eggs (that's 30 dozen per case), and huge quantities of butter, lard, sugar, syrup, potatoes, cases of canned fruits and vegetables, and on and on.

The stream of freighters never stops. They are hauling 1,000 tons or more every month from Richfield, and this has been going on for a year and a half.

May 5, 1910

The company is getting in a lot of mules - the best blood of Missouri and Arkansas. About 50 of them have been shipped in from Kansas City this week. A number of others have been bought here at home from the Don Grant Co., and other contractors, and they now have well over 100 of the best mule teams in the West. A good mule team is worth some $500 to $700 - a lot of money tied up in that kind of property alone.

1910 - 1920

Early June, 1910

Two hundred and four settlers are now actually receiving water from the Idaho Irrigation Co. project: 71 on the North Gooding tract; 45 on the South Gooding Tract; 33 at Dietrich, and 54 on the Richfield Tract. All of this land, up until this year, was desert.

And all activity stops to watch Halley's Comet streak across the sky.

June 23, 1910

The dam ball players win! Richfield was swamped by the husky boys from the reservoir! The Richfield Baseball team came out to the damsite Sunday to meet the dam players in a friendly game. It was friendly alright, but the boys from the dam didn't give their visitors much of a chance - the score was 5 to 2. The first four men to bat for the dam scored in the first inning, and then brought in one more run in the second. The Richfield team made one score in the first inning, and not another until the sixth, and that was IT.

It was a lively and exciting game anyway, and a large, eager crowd cheered both teams.

July 10, 1910

The flume that had been built to handle any excess flooding last spring, has been removed, and the crest of the dam is being completed as fast as it can be done. At the level where the flume crossed the dam, the earth is being sluiced into place by powerful water jets, carrying it into the area between the upper and lower faces of the dam, as it is taken from the two railway tracks that bring the earth from one of the steam shovels.

The other shovel is working on the supply for the higher

1910 - 1920

level - about 20 feet higher at present. The earth for this place is carried out onto the dam on a single track, dumped, then spread into place by team scrapers. Round and round they go like a merry-go-round. It is then rolled and re-rolled by a massive steam roller. The resultant earth is packed as hard as a much-travelled road.

The earth work is extending farther and farther out over the granite cliff. When the narrow gorge was completely filled in, the dam was still not high enough to contain the water needed, so it was built higher and higher and then extended out across the granite cliff which contained the tunnel. This is considered a "shallow dam" because the actual base is the granite cliff, but it raises the crest of the entire dam up level with the area over the gorge.

The spillway is located west of this shallow dam way up on the hill back of the stables, and is the most striking measure of the real magnitude of the dam. It is far away from the main part of the structure, and actually looks like a separate affair altogether.

The lower part of the control tower has been built, and is attached to the tunnel with an intricate arrangement of concrete and special cast iron plates. The tower cannot be completed until the close of the present irrigation season. However, when completed it will contain all of the water-regulating devices - three separate sets of valves that will work independently of each other and will amply safeguard against any kind of disaster. The tower is pierced by 30 large holes, each 4 feet in diameter, plus a large portal at the normal water level, which is the level of the tunnel itself. These openings will admit the water into the tunnel. However, since the valves and gates are not as yet in place, the water supply at this time is controlled by stopping up the holes with heavy wooden plugs. It was the loosening of one of these plugs, and no defect in the dam or control tower, which started a wild

1910 - 1920

rumor a few days ago, about a leak in the dam. There was no leak in the dam, and the situation was quickly corrected with a heavy cribbing built of timbers and let down on the upstream face of the tower so that the water pressure itself would keep it in place. The actual loss of water was insignificant, and there is still far more water in the reservoir than will be needed by the new farms on the tracts.

The Richfield Recorder immediately put a stop to the rumors by explaining the situation, and assured the worried settlers there was no need to worry about what they would do if the water supply ran out before the crops were taken care of.

Under the circumstances, you probably couldn't blame the settlers for worrying - after all, the dam broke a year ago and prevented the company from delivering water when it promised. It had happened once - could happen again.

August 14, 1910

The Idaho Irrigation Co., Ltd. takes over the completed canal system from the J.G. White Co. The canals are finished and W.L. Gorton is now chief engineer for all of the canal systems. He works for the Idaho Irrigation Co. which now has full control of the tract.

The great Magic Dam is not yet completed and the J.G. White Co. is still in command there.

December, 1910

Magic Dam has now reached a stage in construction which enables the storing of 45,000 acre feet of water, enough to meet all possible demands for the first year of settlement.

Work has continued on the dam through late summer and autumn and is now, on December 1, 1910, considered complete - except for the final layer of rip-rap to be spread over

1910 - 1920

it like a blanket.

It is one of the largest dams of its kind in the world. An earthen dam, it is 143 feet high to the crest., 782 feet up and downstream at the bottom, narrowing to 20 feet at the crest. The width at the bottom of the gorge is 150 feet, and at the crest, 4,200 feet.

The lake formed by the impounded water has an extreme depth of 135 feet, extreme width of two-and-a-quarter miles, and an extreme length of between eleven and twelve miles. The reservoir is designed to hold 205,000 acre feet of water.

The concrete-lined tunnel is 760 feet long.

The concrete spillway is 400 feet wide, and then plunges over a rocky precipice 120 feet high, to the river bottom below. At the upper end of the tunnel there is a control tower of reinforced concrete, 25 feet in diameter and 150 feet high. The tower will contain the gates to control the flow of water through the tunnel.

There are four main canals in the system, with an aggregate length of 200 miles, and main laterals with an aggregate length of 400 miles. These canals range in size from a bottom width of 100 feet for the main canals, to six feet in bottom width for the smallest laterals.

The lands under the Idaho Irrigation Co. project are made up of five tracts: Richfield, surrounding the town of that name; North Gooding and North Shoshone, lying to the north of those towns; South Gooding, which surrounds the town of Gooding; and the Dietrich tract which surrounds the town of Dietrich.

For transportation facilities, these tracts depend on the Oregon Short Line which practically transverses the entire project from east to west, and of course, Richfield is one of the main stations on the Hailey Branch of the O.S.L. None of the Idaho Irrigation lands lie at a greater distance from the railroad

1910 - 1920

than ten miles, while the greater portion of the land is much closer.

Water is passed from the Richfield Main Canal system into the Little Wood River and then diverted onto the South Gooding Tract where diversion is made for these lands about nine miles east of Gooding, and water is then carried onto the lands through a main canal system approximately 30 miles long. This canal system includes a wood-stave syphon pipe five feet in diameter and 3,600 feet long. This Great Syphon is one and a half miles south of Gooding and conveys water across a valley entering the Little Wood River at this point.

Diversion for the North Shoshone and North Gooding lands is made from the Big Wood River about 8 miles below Magic Dam. The canal has a capacity to water 48,000 acres of land and will be about 35 miles long.

Water for the Dietrich lands is diverted from the Little Wood River at a point opposite the town of Richfield, and the main canal for this tract will have a capacity to water 42,000 acres, and will be about 25 miles long. Water from Magic Dam reaches this tract through the Richfield Canal, is flumed across the Little Wood and thence on to the Dietrich Land.

1910 - 1920
THE COMPANY PROMOTION

The Idaho Irrigation Co. had a big job on its hands. In addition to building the dam and canal system, it had to sell the land, and the townsites of Richfield and Dietrich. So, while J.G. White was busy constructing the dam, and their subcontractors Hales and Crane, were doing the canals, a third group set out to sell the land.

They had offices in Boise, Shoshone and Richfield, and sales were handled in all three offices.

Thousands of brochures and leaflets were printed and circulated around the country with complete information for anyone interested in an irrigated farm. They contained detailed maps showing the location of each tract, plus farms already sold and farms still available. They showed rivers and canals and ditches so that everyone could see exactly where the available land was located, its relation to other farms, and how the water got there. "The company will deliver water to within one-half mile of each quarter section, and the remaining distance can usually be cut with an ordinary turning plow."

They quoted old-timers who had, for more than 30 years been successfully farming nearby lands lying along the streams where water could be easily and cheaply applied, and cited a few examples: "The 27 acre McFall apple orchard four miles out of Shoshone has been producing bumper crops for ten years without a single failure." "Other nearby peach, pear and prune orchards have been equally productive." "This is three-crop country for alfalfa, and with small fields and skillful farming, three cuttings of alfalfa have produced an aggregate of eight and a half tons to the acre." And, "Grains raised in the area are wheat, oats and barley and the quality of the grain grown is not excelled anywhere. All garden crops can be raised here successfully - potatoes, onions, tomatoes, egg-plant, peas, beans, sweet-corn, and all other varieties of vegetables, as well

1910 - 1920

as small fruits and berries."

The cost of the land itself, was always 50 cents an acre and went to the government. However, the cost of getting water to it varied, and was set by the State Board of Land Commissioners. In the case of the Idaho Irrigation Co., the price was originally set at $35 per acre, but in December of 1910 the company went before the Land Board requesting permission to increase their price to $75 - or at least $65 - per acre. They said they were not able to market as much land as originally expected - some was too rocky, and some had hummocks that had to be leveled, and preparation of that land by the company would be much too expensive to keep it on a par with the rest. On May 1, 1911 the company was granted approval to increase their price to $50 only, and from then on, all Idaho Irrigation Co. land was $50.50 per acre, total.

Of course, if someone bought the land from them and then sold it to someone else, he could ask whatever he wanted, and the water rights went with the land. The real estate people went to work on this one, and some nice profits were quickly realized.

The brochures were clear and concise in explaining the process, and letting you know what needed to be done:

"Taking 40 acres as a basis, the expenditure at the time of filing would be:
For land, to State, 25 cents per acre......................$10.00
For water right, to Company, $3 per acre............120.00
Land office and notarial fees..1.50
TOTAL INITIAL PAYMENT............................$131.50

The lands generally are covered with sage brush. Before any farming operations can be pursued, this sage brush must be removed, the land plowed and leveled to facilitate irrigation, ditches must be dug, and the place fenced.

1910 - 1920

> *Preparation of the land for cropping will cost, about as follows:*
> *Clearing, plowing, harrowing, $7 per acre $280.00*
> *Leveling and ditching, $2 per acre 80.00*
> *Fencing, 30 cents per rod 96.00*
> *TOTAL..$356.00*
>
> *Nine-tenths of this cost the settler may save by doing the work himself. The cost of the house in which the settler may choose to live and of the other conveniences with which he may surround himself are necessarily matters left up to the individual."*

Terms of payment were set forth on a "per acre" basis: $3 per acre at time of entry; $3 per acre for the next three years; $4 per acre for the following 4 years; $5 per acre for the next two years, and $6 per acre for the last two years. Eleven years after date of entry it would be paid in full at $50 per acre.

Deferred payments would draw interest at 6% per annum. They were further advised that the cost of maintenance and operation of the irrigation system would not be in excess of 35 cents per acre annually during the time that the system is conducted by the Idaho Irrigation Co. After the system is turned over to the Big Wood Reservoir & Canal Co., (the settlers' company) this maintenance charge will be only the actual cost."

"Proving Up" carried still another set of rules:

> *"You are required to reside on the land from the day your final proof appears in the newspaper, until it has been published five times in the weekly paper. You must be sure that the two witnesses you use know that you are on your land the day publication of your intention to make final proof appears. Your witnesses will be required to testify*

under oath that they have seen in your laterals sufficient water to irrigate your crops. You are required to have water in your laterals before you publish intention to make final proof. You must have a growing crop amounting to one-eighth of your tract and have water in your laterals before you prove up. Your witnesses are required to testify to the date they first saw you living on your land and as to when you had water turned into your laterals or on your crops. You must, before proving up, have a permanent house on your land which of course means a tent will not suffice. A 12' x 14' house will serve the purpose."

There was a lot of "swearing" going on - and "legal shortcuts" taken - at least one prove-up shack sat on the line and served the purpose for two different owners, maybe more. At any rate, the job got done and the desert began to look like farm land.

A prove-up shack

1910 - 1920
RICHFIELD

The Idaho Irrigation Co. was not alone in promoting the land sales - Richfield was right in there with them, and the town folks were behind them 100%. The town population grew to more than a thousand during those two busy years. Richfield was a pretty sophisticated spot with all those professionals around.

The Richfield Commercial Club was organized with 50 active members, and they jumped right in and published a dandy booklet of their own, telling all about the wonders of the area. It was widely circulated, and members sent the Richfield booklet to friends and relatives and "desirable" folks whom they would like to have as neighbors.

They held a local contest to come up with a catchy slogan for their promotional material, and the winner was Mrs. V. V. Bower, wife of the local real estate mogul, and active socialite. "Rising, Enterprising Richfield" was used thereafter in all newspaper ads, brochures, and anything else they could get it on. Mrs. Bower won $10 for her contribution, and glowed happily in the limelight for some time thereafter.

The booklet conjured up a vision of the town - a tennis club and two tennis courts; a lively baseball team, and the large block of ground reserved for a public park. Various church denominations have been given ground for their churches, and the Methodists have already erected a "neat edifice" on the corner of 3rd and Latah.

They boasted about the 80' wide graded streets, the $25,000 water-works system, the fire hydrants, the organized fire department, the new $7,000 school and the "Richfield Recorder", their first-class weekly newspaper with a modern printing plant housed in its own concrete building. They mentioned that phone lines extend 24 miles into the country connecting with the dam site, and also with the new town of

1910 - 1920

Dietrich, forming a nucleus of farmers' telephone lines, which would spread rapidly as the lands are settled.

A strong, progressive bank was in evidence, the Idaho Irrigation Co. two-story brick office building, a newly-built depot, two lumber yards, a meat market, two liveries, two general merchandise stores, a drug store, hardware and plumbing store, a "Jap Restaurant", one confectionery, two barber shops, two real estate offices, two blacksmiths, and one harness store.

They went on to invite new businesses to move in and made a long list of what was needed: furniture stores, implement houses, physicians, dentists, wall-paper and paint stores, laundries, produce stores, warehouse, flouring mill, elevator, ice plant and cold storage, brick plant, tinshop, theatre and moving picture show, cigar factory, millinery store, gent's furnishing store, and many other lines of business that are essential parts of a growing town.

The Richfield booklet was complete with attractive pictures, one of which was the fabulous Richfield Hotel that opened on May 15, 1909. Built by the Idaho Irrigation Co., it was the ultimate in hotels. Those who spent long hours on the train, and finally arrived in Richfield were amazed and delighted to find such a beautiful edifice. The accommodations were excellent. It was a very expensive building ($35,000) with steam heat, an independent gas plant, private ice house, rooms "with baths ensuite", a barber shop, billiard room, sample room and the "best cuisine." Rates $2.00 and up.

A sample room, by the way, is a special room set aside where salesmen can display their wares.

"A white, ornate facade fronts 100 feet along the main street. A wide, breezy veranda, with quaint gas-lantern lights and easy chairs, extends across the full frontage. You enter a large, airy lobby featuring a massive stone fireplace on the right, a handsome office, wide halls and richly-tinted carpets.

1910 - 1920

At your left a piano and a wide, beautifully carpeted open staircase. Much of the furniture is of weathered oak, some mahogany, and in the rooms, mostly golden oak. In general, the rooms are tinted in strong, rich shades."

And, there were other hotels in Richfield. Ma Thomas was still running the Alberta Hotel and serving luscious pate de fois gras, pineapples, truffles, capons and the like. Fantastic "spreads" year round, all served on a long table with guests seated on backless wooden benches. Ma, herself, added color and vigor to the town. Raised in mining camps, she was a tough, honest, straightforward, no-nonsense woman who said exactly what she pleased, and HOW she pleased - and nobody argued. She wore a ring on every finger, and could out-cook anybody in the West. A rare bon vivante in the middle of the Idaho desert. Her meals were famous far and wide, and many folks made special trips to Richfield just to enjoy one of Ma Thomas' gourmet meals.

Ma's original Alberta Hotel was actually more of a collection of bizarre-looking buildings. Every so often a new one would be added in an attempt to handle the tremendous demand for accommodations when people began flooding into Richfield after the new Idaho Irrigation Co. took over. Two to ten men would share one room. Finally, on June 3, 1909, the entire huddle was torn down and cleared away to make way for the new Alberta Hotel - a fine, 2-story modern building erected on the same spot as the old, with Ma still in charge, of course.

There was another not-so-famous hotel in Richfield at that time known as the "Bedbug Hotel." . . down by the railroad tracks. . . trying to scratch out a living. . .

Those busy years of building the dam and canals generated a whirlwind of activity throughout the entire countryside. All of the towns prospered, but Richfield most of all - it was the "company town" and all of the company business

1910 - 1920

went through in one form or another. Everything and everybody needed for construction, and to keep the camps going, came through Richfield on the railroad, and every day the parade of horse or mule-drawn conveyances with anywhere from a single team up to six or more, would be coming or going to the dam or canals. Heavy-duty wagons owned by the J. G. White Co. mingled with the local drays.

People streamed into town. Potential settlers coming to look over the land, laborers heading out to construction sites; engineers, and other professionals moving in with their families to enjoy the large, comfortable homes the company built for them. Handsome company offices were built where both land and construction business were handled. They even ordered a five-passenger touring car from Boise to transport land seekers to and from the segregations. It was referred to as the "Buzz Wagon" and offered a unique and exciting experience for the riders. It was the only auto around these parts.

. . . as for the roads. . . what roads? Buggy roads.

Occasionally, the folks in the Buzz Wagon had to be rescued.

1910 - 1920
DIETRICH

The town of Dietrich was located about 20 miles below Richfield, and 35 miles below Magic Dam. The Dietrich Opening was held at the Opera House in Shoshone on May 28, 1909 and the price of land there was $50.50 per acre right from the very beginning.

In charge of the opening were two old pros, C. B. Hurtt and Bob McCollum from Twin Falls, who had already sold a lot of Southern Idaho land under the Carey Act. These two knew exactly what to do and everything moved along smoothly and swiftly. A band was on hand to enliven the day, and photos of Richfield and the Project were on display. In fact, many folks went up to visit Richfield both before and after the drawing to see the excitement there first-hand.

Dietrich townsite lots were sold on the same liberal basis as those in Richfield - on contract with a down payment of 1/4 of the purchase price, and the remaining 3/4 during the next three years with 6% interest on deferred payments.

The Dietrich Hotel turned out to be even more expensive than the Richfield Hotel at a cost of $40,000! A three-story structure with 40 guest rooms of the most modern design and appointments. Hot and cold water in every room, and a number of suites with bath, on each floor. On the main floor, a large lobby with massive fireplace, hardwood floors, a huge dining room, billiard room, sample room, barber shop, writing room, a bar, and a WINE CELLAR below! There was also a large, pleasant ladies' parlor on the second floor.

The company put on a large force of men and teams to ready the town for occupancy. Streets were graded 80' wide, and the main business street 100' wide. Business property was sold at the opening, and a bank, restaurant, lumber yard, implement store and other ventures were taking shape.

1910 - 1920

The company was busily selling and promoting; and eager folks were clearing sage brush, plowing, leveling, and seeding to get ready for the water on April 1, 1910. The area for 80 years had been widely known as the greatest sheep and cattle communities in the world, and now the Carey Act was changing all that.

The town and the tract were named "Dietrich", in honor of Judge Frank S. Dietrich, U.S. District Court, Boise, who is credited with "settling a lot of irrigation law." The decision which focused the attention of the settlers upon the jurist at that particular time, was one which prevented an irrigation company from selling more land than there was water to irrigate it.

A big white wooden sign, easily seen from incoming train windows, advertised the new community saying: "Dietrich - 30,000 acres of Irrigated Land." But some wise-acre patched a strip of white paper over the "T" in Dietrich so the sign read: "Die rich - 30,000 acres of Irrigated Land."

The locals snickered and pointed the finger at a young real estate agent for the prank.

In 1910 four carloads of prunes were wrecked near Dietrich, and Sam Peterson, restaurant owner, hauled four wagon loads of them to his restaurant and made them into soft drinks. Every available jar, and all of the sugar in Shoshone and Dietrich were used to store those prunes. After that, business was brisk at Sam's restaurant - and elsewhere.

Most of the land sales at this time had been made to people in the neighboring states - Washington, Oregon, Montana, the Dakotas, Utah, Wyoming, Nebraska, Colorado and Arizona. Most were small tracts, 40 to 60 acres, and prove-up shacks were scattering over the land.

Nothing could happen until the land was free of sagebrush - that hearty, desert perennial which lives on adversity. Sweet to smell, bitter to taste, it grows anywhere

1910 - 1920

from two to twelve-feet tall, puts out either white or yellow flowers in the Spring, and stubbornly clings to the earth with roots that grow close to the surface, but spread out in wide circles.

The innocent homesteader was often led astray by such statements as "sagebrush is easy to clear with a sharp mattock that cuts the roots below the surface. One man can do an acre a day." Hah! After one day with a mattock many a weary, sweat-and-dust-encrusted homesteader was tempted to seek out the slicker who made that statement and demonstrate an even better use for the mattock!

Other methods were certainly tried, to clear the sturdy brush, but it was the wretched mattock that still proved to be the most thorough - if a man's back held out. Some tried dragging a railroad rail over the land with a team. This was a wild, frenzied, uncontrolled experience, but it did pull up many bushes, loosened others, and was faster, and easier on the homesteader. They soon found that sagebrush no more than three feet tall could be plowed loose with a plow which had the moldboard removed, even though two such plowings were usually necessary for complete removal.

Sagebrush is primarily a desert plant which cannot stand too much moisture, and some logically reasoned that it could be flooded out --- except, there was no water yet. So much for that theory.

A few homesteaders, despairing at ever clearing their land, just freaked out and set fire to the whole mess. This method really did work, but was frowned upon by the neighbors, townfolk, animals, government, wife, kids and the family dog, until it finally burned itself out without killing or maiming or burning any other body or stuff.

"Land Grubbers" were invented later - two-wheeled contraptions hauled by a team and claimed to clear better than two acres a day. Hah! Musta been the same slicker who said one

1910 - 1920

man could easily clear an acre a day with a mattock!

Anyway, when he finally got it out of the ground, the exhausted farmer raked the loose brush into windrows, with sagebrush rakes having teeth two feet long, and set it on fire. Soon great clouds of black smoke were billowing up in many places around the countryside as the industrious homesteaders cleared their land for cultivation.

Occasionally the brush was hauled to sandy roads, and after it had been run over a few hundred times, made excellent roads. At least better than sandy.

After the sagebrush - everything else seemed easy.

The first settler to prove up on his land on the Richfield Tract was J. Ralph Nevers, one of the early 1909 arrivals who stayed. J. Ralph proved up on June 10, 1909.

In addition to the Idaho Irrigation Co. land, there were about 5,000 acres under the "Settlers Ditch and Reservoir Co." project, that was also getting ready for water in the spring of 1910. Their land was filed on as Desert Claims, and each settler had to pay his pro-rata share of the expense, as well as build the ditch. Most of that land had been taken up, tracts of 40 to 80 acres, the larger portion of which was tributary to Richfield. This was O.K. with Richfield because it would throw the trade of a goodly number of families to their city and was an attractive addition to the area.

Speaking of Richfield - the Richfield Hotel was the la-de-dah social center of the community. In 1910 it was repainted and re-done, and a new snooty French Chef named A. Joyeaux, was hired, along with a crew of "specialists in elegant foods", "Parisiane dainties and delicacies." The "Hotel Veranda East" was set aside for summer tea, dinner, and special parties. Each affair became more elaborate than the last.

Out-of-town visitors were very impressed.

"A" certainly added a touch of class!

1910 - 1920
HOW TO FARM - 101

Late in March of 1910, the Idaho Irrigation Co. started active work on an 80-acre demonstration farm adjoining Richfield on the Northwest. The place was fenced, broken up, and suitable crops put out. A residence and other necessary buildings were erected, and it was an honest-to-goodness irrigated farm.

A man from the State Experimental Station in Gooding - J. G. Pearson - was in charge, and it was the intention of the company to make it a commercial success under actual farm conditions - not a mere show place. It was set up to teach the settlers how to farm using irrigation water, to demonstrate what the land would produce, and what crops would pay best. Everybody was invited to visit the farm any time to look over the entire spread, and pick up valuable information. Pearson was an expert on irrigation, and taught by example. A similar farm was established at Dietrich. They planted two varieties of oats, one of wheat, one or two of barley and alfalfa, clover and timothy. They also took a shot at potatoes and other garden vegetables.

On April 1, 1910, water was ready for all of the Idaho Irrigation Co. lands.

Many of those who had come a year ago, had already left. The flood at the dam prevented the company from delivering water as expected, so they lost faith, said "the hell with it" and took off for greener pastures. But things looked much better in 1910 - people were bringing in high-bred horses and cows, and were ready to settle down. They arrived daily in railroad cars, all together, with horses, cows, pigs, machinery, furniture, pots and pans, clothes, blankets, the wife, the kids, the mother-in-law, assorted relatives, dogs, cats and goats.

1910 - 1920

SIGNS OF THE TIMES - 1910

Fat folks were comely. Skinny folks were homely. FAT was definitely "in." Anyone unfortunate enough to be slim and trim, was to be pitied in 1910.

But as usual, there was a remedy - Dr. Morrow's 20th Century Discovery - ANTI-LEAN! Following is one of his ads:

"ANTI-LEAN not only makes people fat, but strong and vigorous as well.

ANTI-LEAN is a medicine, not a food, and contains no fats or oils, but is purely a vegetable compound which makes people fat through the nervous system.

All lean people are neurotic to a more or less extent with a rapid heart, poor appetite, poor digestion and assimilation.

Now ANTI-LEAN quiets down the nervousness and heart action, tones up their appetite, increases their digestion and regulates the bowels. When this is done, nature will make them fat."

Also, there was the exceedingly popular "Lydia E. Pinkham's Vegetable Compound for Women." Lydia had been marketing her roots and herbs (swimming in 18% alcohol), for more than 30 years by this time, and guaranteed to cure just about any female ill - such as, inflammation, ulceration, fibroid tumors, irregularities, period pains, backache, nervous prostration, that "bearing-down" feeling and consequent spinal weakness. It did away with that "wearing feeling", extreme lassitude, that "don't care" and "want to be left alone" feeling, excitability, irritability, nervousness, dizziness, faintness, sleeplessness, flatulence, melancholy or the "blues." And, it

1910 - 1920

cured as well, "a slight derangement of the kidneys in either sex." So it was even o.k. for the gents to take a nip or two of Lydia's compound. It was a very popular drink. Er, "remedy."

Speaking of health. . .

You could buy a full set of false teeth for $5. Gold fillings were $1; silver fillings 50 cents; painless extraction, 50 cents. The false teeth were even "guaranteed to stick to you so you can eat corn off the cob, and if they don't do this, they won't cost you a cent!" There was also a 10-year guarantee with all work, and a lot of people standing around eating corn-on-the-cob - or off-the-cob. . .

Speaking of corn. . .

The Sagebrush Hair Tonic Co. in Shoshone seemed to be doing a land-office business. They never did actually "guarantee" anything, they only asked the question"Did You Ever See a Baldheaded Indian?" and that seemed to do the job. Frank Whitting had been on the road for a year, combing the northwest for business, and the Baldheaded Indian was becoming famous. It was now time to hit Kansas City, Chicago, and points east, but they had to do something about the high cost of freight. A carload of the hair tonic to Chicago would run about $600, so they decided to ship just the "extract" to Chicago, and open a bottling plant there where they could add the rest of the stuff. To ship enough "extract" to make a carload of the finished product would only cost about $5 or $6. They extracted the "extract" from the tender tips of the sagebrush, which were then dried, steamed and boiled, to extract the "extract."

All seemed to be going well with the company, when OOPS! One morning in September, 1910 the news broke: "All assets of the Sage Brush Hair Tonic Co., Ltd. have been turned over to the First National Bank under foreclosure!"

No more hair tonic. No more shampoo. No more extract. No more Baldheaded Indian. No factory. No business. No freight problems. . .

1910 - 1920

Speaking of freight...

In the summer of 1909 a great tramway was built to convey freight across the Snake River Canyon two miles below the mouth of Rock Creek and the foot of Auger Falls, near the new town of Twin Falls. It was one of the longest single-span cableways in the country, and the highest in Idaho. Snake River canyon, at the point where the tramway crossed, is fully 600 ft. deep, and the cable span was 2,200 ft. The promoters of this enterprise, George Wise, Stanley Wilson, and E. V. Berg, encountered many difficulties and delays in getting the tramway erected.

To stretch the heavy cable across that deep canyon without the advantage of roads or grades, was a dangerous undertaking. The river was unusually high that year, producing a roaring torrent, and the stream was narrowly confined at the point where the cables were stretched. But, the promoters persisted until the tramway was securely fastened and ready for business.

Produce and materials such as hay, grain, lumber, etc. could be transported over the tramway at the rate of 16 tons per day without taxing the capacity of the structure. It was no trick at all to load from a wagon on either side of the river, shoot it across, and drop it on another wagon on the other side. An ordinary load looked no bigger than a gunny sack when suspended over the center of the deep canyon.

A speedy way to handle freight...

Speaking of speed...

"Sixty miles an hour!", "going like sixty!", "doing a mile in a minute!", were popular expressions of the day. Why? Because in 1903 at Indianapolis, Barney Oldfield was the first to hit 60 m.p.h. So, it was pretty exciting when the following item appeared in all Idaho newspapers in early August of 1910:

1910 - 1920

"SPEED KINGS WILL FURNISH HAIR-RAISING SPORT FOR IDAHO!

> *Boise is to have some automobile races that will make every individual's hair stand on end and dance like an Aspen leaf. Barney Oldfield is the Speed king who had driven his racing car faster than any other man ever traveled and lived to tell of it! The only way a human being ever went faster is to be blown up by a giant explosion. Oldfield will be there in person to show what fast going is really like!"*

The paper helpfully listed railroad fares and schedules to and from Boise to watch Barney do his thing.

A short time later, there was another startling announcement: "a real honest-to-goodness "Aeroplane" will be on display at the Boise State Fair."

Speaking of Fairs. . .

In September of 1910 the Idaho Irrigation Co. went to State and County Fairs, such as Seattle, Spokane, Boise, Council Bluffs, etc. to display produce grown on Idaho Irrigation Co. land.

Here's an example of one of many telegrams received at company headquarters in Richfield:

> WASHINGTON STATE FAIR, SEATTLE, WASH.
> WE ARE AWARDED FIRST PREMIUM FOR BEST DISPLAY OF GRAINS GRASSES, FRUITS. ALSO, APPLES, POTATOES, SHELLED GRAIN, GRAIN IN SHEAF, GRASSES AND VEGETABLES SEPARATELY.
>
> MC PHEARSON

And a great honor it was - for land only five months away from sagebrush!

1910 - 1920

The Idaho Irrigation Co. won awards wherever they displayed produce that year of 1910. They loaded up the best they had and railroaded it to as many fairs as they could get to.

Speaking of railroads. . .

On December 1, 1919, the Oregon Short Line let a contract to the Utah Construction Co. to build approximately 71 miles of new road from Richfield to Camas Prairie. The new railroad will pass right by Magic Dam.

1910 - 1920
J. O. JONES AT MAGIC DAM

Perched like two birds atop the huge load of supplies, the young engineers, Walker and Jones burrowed and wiggled into fairly comfortable positions. The driver barked a command, six horses dug in, and the giant tandem sled lurched forward.

J. O. Jones was on his way to Magic Dam.

The early morning was crisp, cold, dark, and November, 1910. And, if all went well they could reach the dam by nightfall. The road was well worn by two years of heavy traffic, but still very rough, and covered by a heavy blanket of snow-- enough to deliver this load on runners instead of wheels.

Walker had met Jones at the train in Richfield last night, and they stayed at the elegant Richfield Hotel. Walker had been working for the J. G. White Co. for several months now. He and another classmate from the University of Kansas were graduated a semester ahead of Jones and immediately hired on to go to work on Magic Dam. Jones stayed at the University to finish, but kept in touch with the others. A couple of weeks ago, Walker sent him a J. G. White job application saying there may soon be an opening for another engineer at the dam, and would he be interested? He certainly was! Fired the application back by return mail, and promptly received a telegram from the company to "come out immediately."

Now, he was here and Walker was telling him about the work presently being done at the dam, most of which is on the long, shallow dam. Some work still remains on the control tower gates and of course, the final blanketing of the entire surface of the dam with rip-rap.

Walker tells him about the famous engineers who have, at various times, inspected and approved the work at Magic. Some of the best-known experts in the United States, such as A. C. Crane, Hydraulic Engineer for the J. G. White Co., and

1910 - 1920

designer of many important power plants and hydraulic works in the U.S. and abroad; T. F. Richardson, formerly of the Metropolitan Water Works Commission Staff of Massachusetts; the famous Fredrick P. Stearns of the Panama Canal Commission, and J. A. Ockerson of the Mississippi River Commission.

When they arrive at the dam, they are warmly greeted, and Jones is shown to his quarters: "a rather flimsy building of one-inch boards covered with tarpaper", he noticed, with three beds to a cabin, and a sheet-metal, trash-burner-type stove for heat. Meals were served to the engineers and superintendents in a smaller building adjunct to the main mess hall. It could seat about 20 men, contained two long trestle tables with backless benches alongside, and enough room for the waiters to serve both sides.

There was a small store where razors, tobacco, cards, and various personal items could be purchased. One family lived in a tent by themselves on the west side - the father was a teamster who hauled wood for the camp. The Dam Superintendent, Lathrop Crosby, lived in the large, five-room house with his wife and two children, a boy 2, and a girl 4 years old. Otherwise, there were no "residents."

A young Japanese boy did the laundry week by week for the engineers and superintendents, and was supposed to police the grounds daily, going from one end of the damsite to the other, picking up trash. He spoke only Japanese, but was trying very hard to learn English from an old hygiene book someone had given him. Often, Jones would hear odd-sounding, vaguely familiar English medical terms coming out of him.

There were about 75 to 100 "special" laborers on the job. "Barcelonians" from Spain, they were. When the White Co. came out from New England to begin work on the dam, they brought these Barcelonians along with them. Most spoke English fairly well, and all were top-notch men, honest and

1910 - 1920

hard-working, and completely trusted by the company. They functioned as the "core" of the laborers, and could be counted on to lead and direct new and inexperienced men.

Whenever additional laborers were needed, they were supplied by a company in Salt Lake City which acted as a job placement office for the J. G. White Co. All one had to do was make a phone call, order the number of men wanted, and they would be sent up on the railroad - anybody they could get, new immigrants, old immigrants, out-of-work miners, railroaders, hobos - anybody with a strong back looking for a job. Some would come in , look around, and disappear. Others would stay on - some for only a short time. All were given meals.

After the dam had been topped out, there was an inspector covering each face of the dam 24 hours a day. They changed inspectors every eight hours, so the patrol was constant. Jones had been on the damsite for about three months, when he was gingerly awakened one morning about 3 o'clock, by one of these inspectors who told him that water was coming under the dam! Jones sprang to life, rushed over to awaken Crosby, the Dam Keeper, and then reported the leak to the J. G. White office in Richfield.

Crosby immediately opened the gates to the tunnel - wide open, so the water could drain out faster than it was coming in. First, they had to find out how much was coming through, so they built a water-tight fence downstream, that was built in such a way as to measure the flow, and it was found that there was a very considerable flow coming from under the dam.

Within a few days, as quickly as the train could get him there, an expert arrived from Boston - a man with a great deal of experience in earth-filled dams, Mr. Fredrick P. Stearns, who had previously visited the site. Stearns ordered 4" pipes to be driven vertically from the crest of the dam on down to the base, into the original material from which the bottom of the canyon

1910 - 1920

was formed. The pipes were spaced about 20 ft. apart from the east end of the dam to the west end. When they hit the elevation of the original surface at the bottom of the canyon, they ran into trash of all kinds - small sticks, brush, etc. Each pipe was cut off about a foot above the ground after it reached the point where it could be driven no further. There were 14 pipes in all.

Stearns ordered the reservoir to be completely drained. Then, on the crest of the hill above the dam, above Crosby's house, he built a concrete-mixing station where they mixed water and cement (no sand). Each time a batch of water and cement was mixed, and after it had all drained into the vertical pipes on the dam, they put 300 lbs. per square inch of pressure behind it to force as much of it as possible to disperse horizontally at the base of the dam.

In one of those pipes near the tunnel, it was so open at the base where it should have been tight, they forced 300 barrels of cement into that one hole. The leak was believed to have been in the loose rock and debris around the upper end of the tunnel.

Mr. Stearns recommended that this treatment be given to each of the holes, and to the amazement of the crew, not only did it seal the bottom of the dam at the base of each of these holes, but some found its way under the tunnel, and appeared to be seeping out from the crevices along the canyon wall for several hundred feet below the dam.

It was during the time that J. O. Jones was at Magic Dam that the heavy rip-rap blanket was put down. The upstream face is 3 feet thick with massive blocks of lava rock thoroughly imbedded in gravel. About 200 laborers sent up from Salt Lake did the work, (a carload of Greeks) with the help and direction of the Barcelonians.

One event Jones could never forget, happened during the cold winter weather when the ice was still on the reservoir.

1910 - 1920

The engineers decided it would be a good time to make a topographical map of the surface of the bottom of the reservoir, and to do that, it was necessary to make soundings at regular intervals. They decided to lay lines over the surface of the ice, then chop holes at regular intervals through which they could lower a tape by means of a weight on the end of the tape, and thus measure the depth.

While he was working on this, Jones was wearing rubber boots because the only others he had were leather, and would soon be wet through. Those rubber boots were not very good insulation against the ice, and he froze both feet! Says "I never did recover", and carried with him that life-long reminder of Magic Dam.

His pay? $40 per month, from which they took $25 for food. The payroll was made in Richfield.

He left the site only once during his eleven months at Magic, and that was to attend the big July 4th celebration in Hailey in 1911. It lasted two or three days and the paper reports more than 2,000 visitors at the celebration that year.

Engineer Jones resigned in November, 1911 to return to some unfinished business at the University of Kansas. The dam was nearing completion and people were being laid off, so he felt it was time to go.

He taught in the Engineering School at the University of Kansas from 1912 to 1955, with a brief time away during World War I, and with a 6-year span in the 20's teaching at the University of Minnesota.

He received a Master's Degree from Cornell University in Ithaca, New York in 1915. During World War II he was acting Dean of the School of Engineering at Kansas University. Married in 1914, he and Mrs. Jones moved to Santa Barbara to be near their daughter, Alice Ann Stephenson, and her husband, Dr. W. A. Stephenson.

Mr. Jones had many memories of Magic Dam - the long

1910 - 1920

strings of beautiful trout caught by some of his fellow workers below the dam; the ice cream they made with ice from the Ice Caves; the many good times they had singing - someone would suddenly burst into song, and within a few minutes would be joined by other voices. He recalls playing a card game that he learned at the dam, and had never played it before, or since, where they counted 1 cent for every five points, and a fellow could lose $15 or $20 an evening! He remembered the busy piano and Victrola in the engineers "lounge."

We sincerely appreciate his sharing these memories with us. He sent a detailed tape of his time at Magic Dam and provided the following pictures.

Mr. J. O. Jones passed away in February, 1982 at the age of 97.

1910 - 1920

Note: On March 23, 1911, after numerous careful and constant inspections, the seepage through the outside of the tunnel lining was pronounced free of leaks and other imperfections, and the engineers and State Inspectors officially proclaimed Magic Dam to be safe and complete.

R.I.P. HARRY WILSON

Mr. Harry Wilson died June 1, 1912.

Mr. Wilson was the French-Cherokee Indian who jumped off the cliff at Shoshone Falls on March 2, 1905 during the opening of the Milner Dam on the Snake River.

No one had ever before made that leap - nor has anyone done it since.

Harry was working at Arrowrock Dam the winter of 1911 when he became ill with pneumonia and was taken to St. Luke's Hospital in Boise. After several weeks, he was permitted to leave the hospital, only to return in a short time with serious heart trouble.

He spent the last six weeks of his life at St. Luke's.

He had no money, no known relatives, no friends, no visitors. He was cared for by the County.

He carried with him until his death the medal on which was inscribed:

"HARRY WILSON JUMPED SHOSHONE FALLS MARCH 2, 1905."

The medal was buried with him in the County Cemetery.

1910 - 1920
TIDINGS OF 1911

Thrills at the dam! The Idaho Irrigation Co. is running an 18 ft. steel launch around Magic Reservoir. A twin-cylinder engine that will make 15 miles per hour is being used for many purposes by the company, and folks round and about are invited to visit the dam and have a boat ride. Everyone is welcome, and arrangements are being made to care for visitors on a commercial basis. The dam promises to be popular as a pleasure resort and public accommodations will soon be provided for those who wish to make the trip. The fishing is fine - a young lad just recently caught a record-setting - 7 1/2 pound trout.

Farmers are unhappy. The reservoir is full, the rain continues to pour down and there is just too much water. Here they went and paid for all that dam water, and now don't even need it.

Approximately half of the Idaho Irrigation tracts have now been sold and are being worked.

Richfield continues to flourish. On July 4th they throw a gigantic day-long celebration. First, they rouse everybody out of bed at sunrise with a 21-gun salute! Next, a gigantic Industrial parade, followed by a baseball game between Richfield and Soldier. At the park, politicians orate, patriotic poems are presented, original patriotic essays read, the Gettysburg Address by a lucky 5th grader, and the Carey Band played music all day.

In the afternoon, another ball game, this time Richfield vs. Shoshone, plus bucking contests, horse races, water fights, sack races, climbing greased poles to get the two $1 bills on top, pie and watermelon-eating contests, and games, games, games for everyone - men, women and children, and "plenty of prize money."

A table-sagging supper was served to one and all, and

1910 - 1920

the dark was greeted by a gigantic fireworks display. Dancing from 8 to 12 in the evening, with music furnished by the Carey Orchestra. "Orchestra"? Yes, in the daytime it is the "Carey Band" - at night it is the "Carey Orchestra." A valiant, dedicated, fat-lipped group.

* * * * * *

Back in 1909, Idaho adopted local option over the regulation of intoxicating liquor. In 1911, a search-and-seizure law was enacted for enforcing the intoxicating liquor laws. Richfield and Shoshone both went "dry."

Following is an item taken from the Richfield Recorder along toward the end of 1911:

C.J. BAUGH LIQUOR DESTROYED! ALL WET GOODS TAKEN FROM BAUGH DRUG STORE POURED OUT ON ORDER OF DISTRICT COURT!

On Court Order Monday, they publically destroyed all booze that was taken from Dr. C. J. Baugh on a Search-and-Seizure warrant. The goods seized were of every brand and kind and totaled about 106 gallons of intoxicating liquors as follows: 185 bottles of beer; 54 quart bottles of whiskey; 161 pint bottles of whiskey; a 30-gallon barrel of whiskey and 20 gallons of alcohol. Dr. C. J. Baugh came in here last spring and opened what he claimed to be a drug store but which finally turned into as near an open saloon as is possible for a man to run in a dry town, and any person who wanted booze could get it there without a prescription. It is claimed by friends of the doctor that the prosecution was brought about through spite work but any person who spent the last summer and fall in Richfield knows that his place became a regular

1910 - 1920

> nuisance after he had been in operation only a few weeks.
>
> There are seven other charges against the doctor, but it is not at all probable that any more of these charges will be prosecuted as he has paid a $500 fine and is now serving a 90-day sentence in the county jail in Shoshone.

So, Richfield is finally (hic!) "dry."

* * * * * *

Another news bulletin - the papers all have been announcing the coming of a huge Demonstration Train touring all of Southern Idaho to help the farmers learn how to irrigate, what to plant, when to plant, the best crops for their area, etc. The train is actually an Irrigation College on wheels teaching the best known methods and principals to follow in agriculture, horticulture, and stock raising. State and Federal governments, railroads, and reclamation companies all join forces to help the settlers - and they need help, desperately. Irrigation is new to them, and takes some special know-how. They came and bought land expecting farming to be simple now that they would not have to depend on Mother Nature for water. But, irrigating proved to be much more complicated than they had ever dreamed, and many are bitterly disappointed and ready to leave.

The Idaho Irrigation Co. helped in every way it could with trial farms and experts brought in frequently to work with and teach the new settlers the vagaries of irrigation. Now, they are being offered even more good advice from the experts after having struggled through the 1911 growing season. The Demonstration Train saved many a discouraged land owner.

* * * * * *

1910 - 1920

Richfield is still booming and slogans are a big part of the advertising programs of the day. Lemon Bros. Hardware, in promoting their brand new store quipped: "We meet you on the LEVEL, And act on the SQUARE, when you come here - for your hardware." And, the Byrne Bros. Packing House enticed customers with "Where you save all of the hog but the kink in its tail, and the squeal."

The clothing firm "Alexander's" opened the first clothing store in Richfield with a big sale - for example, $17.50 good wool suits for only $10.00. And MORE!

By the end of 1911, Richfield would again be host to large crews of workers - this time it was railroad personnel.

1910 - 1920
THE CENTRAL IDAHO RAILROAD

It all started late in 1910 when visiting officials representing every department of the railroad met in Richfield to lay plans, set up headquarters, and arrange for "dirt to fly" in the Spring of 1911. The new road, called the "Central Idaho", would connect Richfield with the Pacific Coast!

The proposed 220-mile Central Idaho would be only one link in the main line across Idaho and Oregon. Plans were likewise underway to start work on the "Oregon & Eastern", the east/west road through Oregon with its western terminal at Coos Bay, and its eastern terminal at Ontario/Payette where it would link up with the Central Idaho.

By June 1911, the Utah Construction Co. was in full swing setting up grading camps along the line and breaking ground in several places. 500 men and 250 teams were in the field with others being added fast. Sixteen camps were established at the Richfield end of the job, so that tracks could be laid quickly to haul out men and supplies, and particularly the materials needed for the two big bridges over the Big Wood River and the Malad. (Camas Creek was at that time called the "Malad River")

They also set up a second camp in the southwest corner of Richfield, near the one already there. This camp would be headquarters for all railroad business. They were also doing a lot of work around the depot - clearing, leveling, building, etc.

Meanwhile, out on Camas Prairie, two gents named Perkins and Leonard were busy laying out a 160-acre townsite in the heart of the prairie. Perkins was a pioneer who tried hard to get the railroad to go nearer the old town of Soldier, and was successful in getting it within two miles, instead of the five on the original survey. But the engineers could not do the impossible to bring the main line to the town, so the town moved to the railroad.

1910 - 1920

On July 12, 1911, they opened the new "Soldier" with a celebration, bar-b-que, and lot sale all rolled into one. W.Y. Perkins was president of the new townsite company, J. McMillan, manager (from Twin Falls), and V.E. Cunningham, Secretary.

They advertised their new town:

"Located on the Central Idaho railroad now being built by the Oregon Short Line, 35 miles north of Gooding, 45 miles northwest of Richfield and 30 miles west of Hailey, the hub of 250,000 acres of tillable land that will produce 40 to 60 bushels of all wheat without irrigation. Soldier Creek is the gateway to the Sawtooth range of mountains in the Stanley basin and the headwaters of the Salmon River, opening up a fine bed of timber and rich productive mines that will receive their supplies at the new town of Soldier. Choice lots available from $50 to $500 per lot - terms 1/3 cash down, balance in one or two years at 6% deferred payments."

The opening was well attended and a social success as well as a financial success. People were enthusiastic about the new Central Idaho Railroad, and vigorously supported the towns along the line.

Two other gents, Mikelwait and Lisle, were promoting still another town at the end of the first leg of the Central idaho. They named it "Prairie City," but the post office said "no," so they changed it to "Hill City."

One of these Hill City promoters, Chas. Lisle, was a reporter for the Shoshone Journal, while at the same time selling Gooding townsite lots back in 1907. When the second Idaho Irrigation co. took over, Chas. Lisle moved to Richfield as the first Editor of the Richfield Recorder. Those two jobs - newspaperman and town promoter, must have been

1910 - 1920

compatible, because here he was again, working on a newspaper and promoting a new town at the same time.

Building a railroad was no small task, and it took as many men, mules and machinery to build the Central Idaho as it did any other railroad, and Richfield again became the headquarters town for a big construction job. The dam workers had barely moved out when the railroad men moved in.

In July, 1911, the Richfield Recorder gives us a glimpse of the activity at that time:

> "During the past week five carloads of mules have been shipped in from Kansas City by the Utah Construction Co. at an expenditure of $75,000, besides the mules they had when coming here, several hundred head of work stock, together with the trainloads of machinery to be used on the works. Another big camp of more than 100 men has been established at Mile 16. 61,000 ties have been unloaded at Richfield and soon to come are 100,000 more, plus carload after carload of bridge timbers and several loads of rails. The depot will soon be moved across the track from where it is now, and a level strip of ground on the south and east will be parked, which will make it one of the most beautiful depot locations in the State of Idaho."

An immense tracklaying machine that could lay close to two miles a day with a full crew, was put to work, and by September 15th, track to the dam was completed. Subcontractors were Eggleston and Matthews - whoever they were - just for the record.

Work stopped on the railroad in January, 1912. The weather shut everything down. They had reached the Blaine Station located 12 miles east of Soldier, and regular service was maintained from Richfield to Blaine, where stockyards would soon be built.

1910 - 1920

The stations had already been blue-printed out along the line, and named.The first station out of Richfield was "Rowson," second, "Burmah," third, "Magic" (at the dam where they also built a water tower), at mile 29 the station was named "Macon," at mile 34, "Blaine," at the town of New Soldier, the station was named "Fairfield," next was "Corral," and finally, "Hill City."

The name "New Soldier" never did stick to the town that moved to the railroad, but the railroad station named "Fairfield" did.

The following year, on September 12, 1912, the completion of the first leg of the Central Idaho was celebrated at Hill City. Mrs. Ellen Finch, a 61-year-old, was the lucky lady chosen to drive in the golden spike - except, it wasn't really a golden spike, it was a bronze spike, and Mrs. finch didn't drive it very far. And when she finished, she was not presented with a golden spike either, she was presented a breast pin made of solid gold in the shape of a spike.

Upon completion of the driving ceremony, cheers went up, and the celebration began! More than 600 people were there, and there were fun and games all day long. Prizes for the oldest couple, the most humorous family (?), races of all kinds, a prize fight between John Carpenter of San Francisco and Jesse Day of Boise, and of course, the feature of the day - a baseball game, this time between Hill City and Corral. Corral won 8 - 5.

It was a wonderful, glorious day, and to top it off, the crowd unanimously and enthusiastically resolved to celebrate this event annually forever more at Hill City on September 12.

At that time, there were two hotels in Hill City, a General Store, Post Office, two saloons, a lumber yard, and assorted shacks and tents. Everyone was certain Hill City would continue to grow and prosper - at least "until the Central Idaho Railroad was constructed on to Boise and beyond."

But, it never was.

1910 - 1920

The track at Hill City simply looped out onto the prairie and circled back to connect with itself, then head back to Richfield.

The bright plans to connect Richfield to the West Coast simply vanished in the wind across the prairie.

Nevertheless, the "Hill City Road," as it came to be known, continued to operate. Trains went up regularly on Monday, Wednesday, and Friday - back on Tuesday, Thursday and Saturday and the freight business was good.

And, there was considerable passenger traffic, too.

1910 - 1920

THE TURBULENT TEENS

The new settlers on the irrigation tracts were floundering and struggling, working day and night to clear the land, build the house and barn, irrigate and propagate. Even though twice as many proved up in 1912 as did the year before, the tracts were far from being sold out, and most of those were not able to meet their payment when due. So, the Idaho Irrigation Co. asked, and got, permission from the State Land Board, to defer the settlers' contracts with the company for five years. There seemed to be no limit to what the company, and the State, would do to make this venture a success. Everybody was trying hard.

One farmer brought in 75 head of Holstein cows from Wisconsin in the hope that a dairy would be profitable. Another invested heavily in pigs; chickens were running all over the place; and several local men got together and formed the "Richfield Percheron Horse Breeders Association." Percherons were considered the best and most profitable stock on the farm, and were well represented on the Richfield Tract. Through Robert Burgess & Sons, famous importers and breeders of horses from Winona, Illinois, they purchased a beautiful Percheron horse named "In-Quiet," whose breeding went back to the most famous horses of his line. He was imported from France, and had been a great prize-winner there. "In-Quiet" arrived in Richfield on June 31, 1912 and folks came from far and near to view the magnificent beast. He was purchased at a great price - $4,000, and it was the intention of the association to take him to the State Fairs, show him off, publicize his background, arrange for stud service, and win all the prizes at the fairs.

On August 1st, one month after he arrived, In-Quiet died from pneumonia. Even though he was insured, the enthusiasm for horse breeding died with him.

1910 - 1920

* * * * * * *

The settlers were surprised and pleased to find that the potatoes they were growing were unusually large, well formed, and excellent in texture. Better than they had ever grown, or ever seen grown from other States. They were amazed and pleased with this product. One happy farmer, R.L. Young, got to wondering how much his beautiful sacks of potatoes were selling for on the other end of the line, so he put a little note in every sack asking the buyers to write to him telling him how much they paid. And they did - $1.50 to $2.50 a sack! Young was not so happy after that - he was only getting 38 cents a sack.

* * * * * * *

It was during the teen years that Idaho began to really promote the "Idaho Potato," and Idaho's only folk lore figure came to life - "Old Jim." Jim was a champion grower of Idaho potatoes, but refused to sell customers a mere hundred pounds because it was against his policy to cut a potato in half.

* * * * * * *

In 1910 and 1911 the City of Hailey issued its very own automobile license plates! Made of steel with baked-on enamel, they had the town's name and date painted in white on a blue background.

In 1910 nine of the plates were sold.

Don't know how they made out in 1911, but it was not until 1913 that the State of Idaho began collecting a fee for all automobiles using State roads.

* * * * * * *

1910 - 1920

During the time the J.G. White Co. (the largest construction company in the world at that time) was completing its work on Magic Dam, another construction company was being born right here in Idaho. It, too, would one day become the largest construction company in the world, and it, too, would one day work on Magic Dam. Harry W. Morrison and Morris Knudsen formed a partnership in 1912, and decided to pool their resources and go into business. Together they had a dozen teams, a few plows, scrapers, wheelbarrows, picks and shovels, and $600 in cash. They called their new company "Morrison-Knudsen."

* * * * * * *

Meanwhile, in July of 1913, the Twin Falls Northside Land and Water Company (the Kuhn Bros.) went into receivership. The Kuhns had invested millions in developing the land located just south of the Magic Circle. They had promoted the Great Shoshone and Twin Falls Power Project at Shoshone Falls; had started to build the North Side Electric Railway which they planned to run all over Southern Idaho; and were in the middle of the huge North Side Irrigation Project when the Panic of 1907 hit. Even though things were going fairly well for them in Idaho at that time (they were forced to pay in scrip, though, just as the Slick Bros. were), some of their other enterprises failed, and they were hurting. Even so, they managed to continue in Idaho and had opened the Hazelton-Eden tract and were nearing the Jerome-Wendell and King hill tracts, when they finally went belly-up. Jerome was their company town, just as Richfield was the company town for the Idaho Irrigation Co. Their Idaho Southern railroad was never electrified as they had planned, but it did operate in a limited way between Gooding and Jerome, and from Milner to

1910 - 1920

Oakley. The failure of the Kuhn Bros brought to an abrupt end the dream of that far-reaching electric railroad.

* * * * * * *

A rooming house for Basques exclusively was thriving in Shoshone. Domingo Sabala, owner, catered to Flock Masters only, and there were lots of them in and around Shoshone - several hundred decent, dependable, trustworthy people most welcome in the area. The sheep industry was big business.

* * * * * * *

There was, however, another "element" which was not so welcome. The following statement by Sanitary Commissioners Smith and White appeared on the front page of the Shoshone Journal in August, 1913:

> "The Chinese Restaurant conducted in Shoshone is one of the worst places we have examined. We have had trouble with this Chink at Idaho Falls and other places and have fooled with him just about as long as we care to. In addition to the unsanitary condition of the place, the moral conditions of his place are equally bad. That is a condition over which we have no authority but trust that Shoshone officials will lose no time in cleaning out this dump. He maintains a woman waitress there and she has a sort of loving stall in the rear of the place and conditions are vile to say the least."

No further information was printed as to what happened to the restaurant after the Sanitary Commissioner's report. We may never know whether the restaurant was shut down - or business picked up.

1910 - 1920

* * * * * *

We do know that buckets were being picked up. Buckets were a big part of everyday life, and it was mighty frustrating when a fella needed his bucket only to find that someone had walked away with it - or just plain misplaced it somewhere. The stable boys therefore figured out their own way to stop the pail pilferers, they drilled a big hole in the bottom of each bucket, then carried a cork or two in their pocket, and it worked! Nobody burgled a bucket with a hole in the bottom. Sure, once in a while somebody with a cork might take your bucket, but it cut way down on bucket burglaries. And they were praised for their resourcefulness in the Shoshone Journal and basked in the limelight for a few days.

* * * * * * *

Be that as it may, it was the beginning of the end for both stable boys and horses. Idaho was growing up and changes were coming fast. On April 17, 1913 it was reported that there were now 3,000 autos and motorcycles licensed by the State; road maps were on the drawing board, and the legislature enacted a law of the road. Henry Ford's motor company was producing an astonishing 1,000 Model T's per day, and he was keeping his promise to produce a car everyone could afford. The cost of a Tin Lizzie dropped steadily from $850 in 1909 to a low of $260 in 1924.

By 1919 Idaho had only 5 miles of paved roads and only 108 miles that were even surfaced.

* * * * * * *

Meanwhile, back inside the Magic Circle, Mr. Chas. J.

1910 - 1920

Lisle, then editor of the Richfield Recorder made a day-long trip on Magic Reservoir. His lovely account of the trip was published in the Idaho Club Woman publication. It is printed here in its entirety so that people today can know what it was like in 1914, even though Charlie's statistics are a bit fuzzy in spots:

How would you like to go by motor boat clear out of the range of the locomotive whistle, the school or factory bell, the clang of hammer and the grind of wheels – out to where the beavers gnaw down their little trees just as they did in Hiawatha's day? Out to where the wild ducks nest in swarms, and the big blue herons keep their solitary vigil over their young, and the coyotes and the otter and the mink and all manner of keen-eyed little wild things peer at you from every side? Out where the trout swim in shoals, and where the water is rippling with their play? Out where the smell of spring is in the air, the clean breath of running water invigorates like wine, where titanic cliffs and distant mountains frown or smile as may be the mood of nature – would you go with me to see all these things, and enjoy them?

The Magic Reservoir – that's an awful, utilitarian word to use for such a beautiful thing in nature; reservoir, a tank or tub or hand-made receptacle to hold a little muddy water, or some common stuff that has no part or parcel in beauty!

But that's the official name; it is the artificial lake formed by the Idaho Irrigation company in Blaine county, to store the waters of the Malad and the Big Wood rivers for irrigating 120,000 acres of fertile land in Lincoln and Gooding counties. The dam that holds the water is 142 feet high – the highest earth-and-rock-fill dam in the world. And the lake itself covers almost 4000 acres, and has a shore line of 30 miles. It was essentially sordid in its conception – it would hold so much water, which would irrigate so much land, at such and such a price and profit per acre.

But incidentally, a thing of beauty has been created. The once wild, impassable canyon, where the birds could scarcely fly through the thickets, is now made into a beautiful lake, as fair as the oldest, coldest gem in all the mountains. At the lower end, the canyon walls are obliterated –covered by the flood of pent-up waters. But higher up, where the cliffs are taller and more rugged, and the backwater ceases and becomes alive with the swift current of the streams that feed it, there is water to

1910 - 1920

carry one's little craft for the most beautiful sail in all the west

From the junction of the two rivers, six miles from the dam, one can first sail up the Big Wood river – as we did. It is five miles up to the end of slack water. What a wonderful five miles it is! Wild ducks of a dozen varieties swarm on the river, their summer nesting place. They skitter ahead of the boat, not leaving the water, until the last, after you have followed them for a mile or two, they wheel and sail back past you, with a squawk and a derisive grin – for it is the closed season, and they know the calendar by heart! Herons rise and sail away; all kinds of little wild creatures – otter, mink, muskrats, rockchucks, chipmunks, and occasionally a coyote – peer around the bases of the cliffs. They do not fear the puffing little boat – they seem to not know the fear of man.

There are some picturesque cliffs up the Big Wood, but the river itself, and what it contains, is the chief source of interest. At one place the water has overflowed a large thicket of quaking aspens and other forest growth; and a colony of beavers – there must have been dozens of them in all – have taken possession. Rank after rank of trees have been cut off for their food, and dams, and playthings or whatever seems most good in the beavers' eyes.

Trout leap out of the water as you pass, singly and in shoals. A great eagle sails overhead; and smaller birds sing and fly through the thickets along the river. The water gets colder and more alive with every foot; you near the end of the slack water, and come at last to where the full open current fills the banks. It is too much of a stream to navigate with a launch – there are too many rocks, too many swirling eddies, too many shadowy places where death and destruction lurk – and you must turn back.

But all is not lost even if you do come here to your journey's end, where nature hangs out her sign of "No Thoroughfare." For you can retrace your way back down to the junction of the two rivers, and go up the Malad for even more picturesque wonders.

The Malad canyon is steeper, deeper, laid out on a more titanic scale. You will seem to be sailing straight for a giant cliff that looks to be the end of all travel; so huge that, even though you are going against both wind and current, you seem to be sliding straight down hill to be wrecked against the rocky mass that over-towers you. But nothing like that happens; you find a river a thousand feet wide at its base, curving magnificently around into another vista of a mile or two.

The cliffs stand up in a towering rocky wall on either side, several hundred feet high. Many places they seem to hang over

1910 - 1920

the water – though that is probably only an optical illusion. However, they are such as would be impossible to scale by any means known to man or beast.

There are not a few rocky islands in this great artificial lake. Some of them are huge, single rocks as big as a church; others are more earthy, and some have vegetation growing. They offer delightful places for landing; though there is little there but the landing!

As you go farther up the canyon, the walls are closer together, and the stream naturally smaller; and you begin to notice the current – for you are nearing the end of the slack water. It isn't quite so safe boating; for there are unseen rocks that may reach up and with their stony fingers clutch the unwary boat. Twice we missed the main channel, and scraped on boulders; once the propeller shaft was bent badly enough to give the boatmen a Swedish vibratory treatment all the way home – and you'd think that they had the St. Vitus dance for the next week! But by taking a row boat, or a flat-bottom launch drawing only a few inches of water, one could go two miles farther than we did, and see the deepest gorge, the most precipitous cliffs of all the route.

That thirty-mile ride is well worth the taking. It is at its best the last of May or early in June, while the reservoir is still at its utmost height, and the water flowing over the great spillway at the dam. All the water of both rivers is at that time going over the 140-foot spillway around the end of the dam. It makes a cataract second only to the Great Shoshone Falls. Later in the season, as the flood waters abate, and the stored waters are drawn off for irrigation, the reservoir shrinks in volume, so that by late summer it isn't to be compared with its spring beauty.

There is a comfortable guest house at the dam, and visitors can always count on accommodations there. If one cared to bring his own boat, and a little portable motor of the type so common nowadays, he could have a long, delightful stay. There is the most wonderful trout fishing below the dam; in the reservoir itself, the water is too deep, and is not such as trout usually inhabit. In the fall, duck shooting is good all over the reservoir and along the lower river.

It is seven years since work first began on the irrigation project of which this reservoir is the foundation; and the lake was first filled to the brim only three years ago. In that time, the system has proved to be one of the finest water supplies in the whole West – and the beautiful blue lake, hand-made, but with the settings marvelously supplied by the higher power that rules all, is today one of the real beauty spots of the whole state.

1910 - 1920

On July 9, 1913 Zack T. Spelling was granted a patent on 80 acres of land on the West Side of Magic Reservoir, just east of the Magic railroad station on the Hill City Branch. Zack was the very first to get a patent on land on the West shore. Two years later, George B. Starcher got the second patent on 120 acres directly north of Zack's place, which put him about on Myrtle Point, except that it wasn't called that then.

* * * * * * *

In the meantime - out in the real world - the movie industry was coming into its own. It was now the custom to hire a nimble-fingered piano-player to accompany the wild, silent films and add to the excitement. Old Nimble-Fingers also got to lead the between-reel sing-a-longs when everybody in the audience got to bellow forth.

* * * * * * *

In January of 1914 the Golden Rule Store in Shoshone had a big sale on unmentionables. The ad mentioned: "Men's union suits, fleece-lined 98 cents, all wool, $1.98. Ladies union suits 69 cents and 89 cents." Also, ladies house dresses 98 cents and $1.49, plus AB Naptha and Crystal White soap - 6 bars for 25 cents.

Midwinter excursions to California via the Oregon Short Line cost $46.70, round trip from Shoshone to Los Angeles through Salt Lake City.

* * * * * * *

May, 1914 - the Shoshone Journal reports that trout are getting so plentiful at Magic Dam the Sportsmen are anxious! Fishermen are at the dam daily. On Sunday the count runs into the hundreds. Of fishermen that is. The reporter claims to have

1910 - 1920

seen more than 100 trout taken by a single party of anglers, and not one of the catch was less than a foot long. Most were from 15" to 18", and there are more fish there every year, he said.

In July, it is reported that the "King," aka "Goliath" was caught in the Cottonwoods. Three feet long, he was, and carried five broken hooks identified by fishermen. One angler identified his hook on a cast made 25 years before. (That would have been back in 1889. Come on.)

* * * * * * *

In September of that same year, there was much talk about a new resort to be built on the Wood River at the Cottonwoods, with cabins and summer homes being planned. Ed Gill and his brother Wes of Jerome had already built a cabin near the dam site with two double bunks, a cook stove, table and a dozen chairs. Their automobile line carried two or three parties up there every week and the cabin was rented out every time. No fancy hotel prices here, but figure to pay the Gills very well for their investment - $30 a month. The tenants actually feel the Gills are doing them a favor as they happily haul in fish by the truckload, as both above and below the cabin, are the famous reaches of the Big Wood River - chock full of trout!

* * * * * * *

November 3, 1916 - the first carload of sugar beets was shipped out of Richfield.

* * * * * * *

In 1917 one of the big excitements inside the Magic Circle was the discovery of Salt Petre near the old town of Soldier. John Finch, Sr., one of the Lightfoot boys, and others, located the

1910 - 1920

deposit and claimed to have offers from some Salt Lake City investors. Salt Petre is of commercial importance in the manufacture of gun powder and pyrotechnics, among other things.

* * * * * * *

In 1917 the big excitement outside the Magic Circle was the United States' entry into the war in Europe which had been going on since 1914. Until 1917 America had managed to stay neutral, but when German U-boats (from the German Unterseeboot, "submarine"), sank a number of unarmed American ships, everybody got up-in-arms and yelled "Kill the Kaiser," and "Let's get the Hun," and Congress passed a law authorizing compulsory military service on May 18, 1917. Before this, all of our wars had been fought by volunteers. (Except for a few instances during the Civil War when men were drafted only when quotas could not be filled otherwise). By June 5, 1917, 9,500,000 men had registered - practically the entire young manpower of the United States. 41,921 of them were from Idaho.

America went to fight in a war that had convulsed Europe for nearly three years. On one side stood France, Britain, Russia, Italy and eight other "Allies." Opposing were the "Central Powers" - Germany, Austria-Hungary, Turkey and Bulgaria. Since 1914 they had been battering each other with the largest armies ever assembled in Europe. A nasty war that created "no-man's land," trench warfare, miles and miles of deep, filthy ditches and tunnels, endless barbed wire barricades, and muddy wastelands littered with shell holes and rotting corpses. Into this mess marched our young, idealistic, patriotic Americans and the whole country was behind them, supporting them with Liberty Bonds and songs. The French affectionately dubbed them "Yanks."

1910 - 1920

More than 115,000 Yanks died there, and countless others were wounded.

New weapons were developed during that war - deadly gas by the Germans and accompanying grotesque gas masks. The British built big, lumbering tanks with metal tracks that could roll over everything. Even though the British are given credit for those famous "tanks," the original idea came from America. And in the beginning, that new war-machine had nothing about it that was warlike. It started out as a big, strong automobile invented by Benjamin Holt of Stockton, California, and it was manufactured in the West. It was built to do certain kinds of farm work, on rough ground where neither horses nor oxen could be used. Because it had enormous pulling power, it was called a "tractor," and since it crept along very slowly, it got the name "Caterpillar Tractor." It could easily force its way over stones and through brush and up and down steep places where an ordinary automobile would have been upset and knocked to pieces. In doing this the tractor could drag gangs of heavy plows which would break up the hardest soil and prepare it for raising crops of wheat and corn.

An English military officer happened to see this go-ahead machine, and hit upon the idea that this was just the sort of thing needed in the war against the Germans. He bought several of these tractors, and before they were assembled, had the parts boxed up and shipped to England. There, some alterations were made, and the whole thing was covered over with plates of steel. All work was done secretly so the Germans would not find out what they were. Luckily, a report got out that they were "water-carriers," when in reality they were forts on metal tracks, built to carry men and guns.

They were sent off by night to the battlefields of France, and when the soldiers there caught sight of them they laughed and ridiculed the awkward way in which these new "water-carriers" stumbled along. They nicknamed them "tanks," and

1910 - 1920

predicted that they would get wrecked in a hurry. But, the "tanks" astonished everybody by beating down and breaking through German barbed-wire entanglements, and utterly destroying the enemy's nest of machine-guns, whose shower of bullets could do no harm to the men inside the slow-moving monsters with walls of steel. They stopped at nothing, and went straight across trenches or down into them and out again without tipping over.

During the last year of that war came the airplanes. Glamorous-looking aviators with goggles, leather helmets and long, white scarves, piloted their spindly bi-and-tri-planes in air attacks and dog fights. Army aviators who shot down five or more enemy planes were designated "Flying Aces." Major Edward (Eddie) Rickenbacker became the "American Ace of Aces" with 26 victories. Squadron 94, which he commanded, was credited with shooting down the last enemy plane to be felled during the war.

Place names - little known up to this time, became commonplace and unforgettable - Verdun, Chateau-Thierry, Belleau Wood, the Argonne Forest and others. New words came out of that war - "camouflage," "barrage," "convoy," "tank," "sabotage" and "civvy."

New songs were written and belted out with gusto to arouse one's patriotism or bring a few tears - "Over There," "Yankee Doodle Boys," "Smiles," "It's a Long Way to Tipperary," "Keep the Home Fires Burning," "You're A Grand Old Flag," "When the Yanks Come Marching Home," "Oh! How I Hate to Get up in the Morning," "How 'Ya Gonna Keep 'Em Down on the Farm (After they've seen Paree?") "Hinky Dinky Parlay Voo?" "K-K-K-Katy!" and "Mademoiselle from Armentiers" with lots of unprintable verses.

In Europe and America both, women joined the labor force to replace the men sent to the fronts. Many worked in factories, but others drove trucks and busses or tilled the fields.

1910 - 1920

Thousands of nurses tended the wounded, both on and off the battlefields. Their contributions provided feminists with a strong argument for post war sexual equality. They could do the work of men - and still take care of everything and everybody at home.

At 11:00 a.m. on the 11th day of the 11th month, 1918 the Armistice was signed.

The Great War to end all wars, was over.

However, along toward the end of that war, beginning in the Spring of 1918, the terrible flu epidemic swept over Europe and the United States, killing scores of people. It seems that every family was hit. In small towns like those inside the Magic Circle, schools and churches were turned into temporary hospitals. The suffering was terrible. The epidemic came in three distinct waves, the first began in May of 1918, and most of those cases were fairly mild with few complications and few deaths. The second wave, starting in the Fall of 1918, was agonizingly severe and a great many died. The third wave, ending in May of 1919 was somewhat less severe than the second, but still resulted in many, many deaths.

More people were killed by the flu, than by the war.

* * * * * * *

While all of this was going on in the world, problems were multiplying on the Idaho Irrigation tracts. Back in 1910 when the first irrigation water was delivered out of Magic Reservoir, there was plenty for everybody, but only a few farms were ready to receive it. In 1911 it filled to the brim, holding 181,000 acre feet - theoretically enough for the entire segregation. Everyone was ecstatic!

However, in 1912 and '13 it did not fill up with water and what was there was gone before the harvest. Many disappointed, hard-working folks just pulled up stakes and left

1910 - 1920

the country, and the company was stuck with more and more land. Like just about every other Carey Act Project, too much land had been segregated for the amount of water available, so the size of the tracts were reduced. Also, they discovered that some of the land was too high to irrigate, so that too, was taken out of the segregation.

In 1914 Magic again filled to the brim, but '15 was a complete disaster - only 1/3 full. . .the exodus continued. In 1916 it again filled to the brim, and the company decided to raise the level of the reservoir by building a series of gates out over the spillway to increase the capacity to 191,000 acre feet. In 1917 it filled right up to the top of the gates. Not so in '18 and '19 and the troubles began again. Weather cycles and the capriciousness of Mother nature continued to subject the system to alternating floods and trickles.

* * * * * * *

Note: When the U.S. first entered the war in 1917, a large delegation from the Magic Circle area went to Boise to ask the Governor for guards to protect Magic Dam and the canal system from any kind of German trickery. Their request was denied.

* * * * * * *

On November 9, 1917, readers of the Wood River Journal were shocked and saddened to see the headlines "S.D. BOONE PASSES AWAY." The report went on to say that Mr. Boone had been stricken about 8:00 a.m. that morning and died within the hour from a sudden attack of paralysis. "Mr. Boone appeared to be in his usual good health yesterday, and he certainly had no suspicion that his end was near as he talked about the war,

1910 - 1920

spoke confidently of our ultimate victory, and planned to take part in the upcoming drive for YMCA subscriptions."

It praised his many accomplishments, his active participation in community affairs, and stated "He was one of the very foremost of our citizens in every respect and his demise is a great loss to the community."

There was no mention of his greatest contribution, and the one which would affect the lives of thousands of people - Magic Dam. Without his initial efforts, drive and imagination, it may never have existed.

Even if it had - it would not be "Magic."

1920 - 1930
THE ROARING TWENTIES

In the aftermath of the War To End All Wars, America cavorted into the Jazz Age. Endless parties, flappers, bootleg gin, and easy boom-time money. Prohibition, which became U.S. law in 1920 was doomed from the start. Too many Americans wanted to drink, and there were never enough Federal Agents to locate and destroy all the illegal booze in the country. Bootleggers and gangsters ruled the underworld with a flashy, pin-striped-army of their own, operated thousands of speak-easies, and mowed each other down on the streets with machine guns.

In 1920 women won the right to vote and the "Flapper" became the new emancipated woman - the symbol of freedom and daring. She shortened her skirts to above the knee, rolled her stockings below the knee, wore skimpy underclothes called "scanties," smoked and drank in public, used cosmetics to excess, bobbed her hair, donned a close-fitting hat called a "cloche," wrapped her coat tightly around her new boyish, flat-chested body, and wiggled off to dance the Charleston with her boy-friend, who showed up in diamond-patterned knee socks, knickers, a coat to match, and a bow tie, or maybe long pants with spats.

The "flaming youth" of the '20's played hard at having a good time.

The American car culture picked up speed in the '20's. Prit near everybody could afford a Model T, and as sales and production increased, Ford kept lowering the price, and in 1925 a "Runabout" sold for only $265. During the Tin Lizzie's 19 years on the market, its incredible popularity did much to put America on wheels. Besides, the "T" was FUN. It could go practically anywhere, and if a hill were too steep to climb, it could be turned around and backed up handily. The high seats offered a grand view of the countryside, and it was easy to fix.

1920 - 1930

A raw egg was usually carried right in the tool chest in case the radiator should spring a leak. All you had to do was crack it open, drop the egg into the radiator and the hole was soon plugged by the egg fragments cooked in the hot radiator water. Sometimes it took two eggs.

The "T" was black. That's all - just black. But the Model "A" introduced in 1927 as the successor to the "T" was available in colors! The Roadster sold for $395 and was the ideal car for the flaming youth. Other big, powerful, fancy cars were on the market at that time, but it was the Ford that wiggled its way right into the family circle, was given a name, and became one of the family - just like the kids and the dog. Everybody made jokes about the Ford and Henry Ford himself so loved the Ford jokes he offered to pay $100 for any new story that made him laugh. He received hundreds! Ford jokes poked fun at every aspect of the "people's car" for example: "A lady sent all her tin cans to Detroit and got back a Model T." Lizzie, as in "Tin Lizzie" was one of hundreds of names lavished on the Model T. What became known as "Lizzie Labels" were really one-line Ford jokes painted on the outside of the cars - the grandmothers of today's bumper stickers.

The Roaring Twenties were a time of excess. Stunts and fads took hold - gold-fish eating, marathon dancing, flagpolesitting, ouija boards, miniature golf, crossword puzzles, and marriage ceremonies in airplanes and other strange places for such rites.

America was listening to jazz on the gramaphone, victrola, or later on, the crystal radio set. One educator said "If we permit our boys and girls to be exposed to this pernicious influence, the harm may tear to pieces our whole social fabric." And a physician warned "Jazz affects the brain through hearing, giving the same results as whisky."

On October 6, 1927 the "talkies" burst on the scene with Al Jolson in "The Jazz Singer," the first successful commercial

1920 - 1930

talking film. Theatre owners all over the country fired their nimble-fingered piano players, and silent films and vaudeville were soon replaced by the talkies. Jolson made popular such songs as "Swanee," "Sonny Boy," "My Buddy," "Mammy," "Toot, Toot, Tootsie," and other members of his family, plus "Tea for Two," "Ain't She Sweet?" "California, Here I Come," "Yes, We have No Bananas," and numerous other jumpy, jazzy tunes.

"Three O'Clock in the Morning," and "How Dry I Am" were especially popular during those bad Prohibition days.

* * * * * * *

Did any of this wild stuff go on inside the Magic Circle? Not much, but the influence was there. Small town folks mostly just enjoyed reading about the big city hi-jinks, and they welcomed the new songs on sheet music and records and soon reflected the current trend in popular music. Eventually, the "talkies" came, too and were shown weekly at the schoolhouse, or church basement, or one of the town theatres like the Rex in Shoshone. And before long, the new shipments of house dresses available at the Golden rule were shorter, and kids started rolling their bulky lisle stockings or twisting them tightly at the tops to form a hard knot to keep them up. The new Butterick patterns offered new shorter styles for the young and daring, and women started bobbing their hair. It was a lot easier to take care of.

But the farmers on the Idaho Irrigation tracts continued to be plagued with problems during the twenties even though the economy of the Magic Circle had improved during the "War to End All Wars." High prices and patriotic urgings had greatly expanded the farm market, but when the war was over, excess productivity led to the collapse of farm prices, starting in 1920. Idaho potatoes that commanded a price of $1.51 a bushel

1920 - 1930

in 1919 brought only 31 cents in 1922, and other crops dropped the same. Such a severe market collapse left many unable to meet their mortgage payments, which in turn caused a rash of bank failures, and again, discouraged farmers moved away. Fluctuations in snowfall still controlled the amount of water in Magic Reservoir making every year a guessing game, would there be enough water?

In August, 1920 there was an ambitions scheme to tunnel clean through Galena Summit to supply the headwaters of the Big Wood river with water from Alturas Lake. The plan never got off the ground, but there was a lot of talk and planning and desperate grasping at straws.

By 1921 it was time for the settlers to take over the operation and maintenance of the Idaho Irrigation system. One-half of the capacity of the segregation had been sold so the entire system passed into the hands and control of the farmers on the tracts. They received shares in proportion to their water rights, plus perpetual rights in the system.

They named themselves "The Big Wood Reservoir and Canal Co."

It was quickly shortened to "Big Wood Canal Co."

Having already suffered through many short-water years, the new canal company was determined to do everything possible to conserve water. In 1924 they constructed a 10-mile by-pass canal at the Cottonwoods on the Big Wood. The contractor was Morrison-Knudsen, and Harry Morrison himself had active charge of the work. It cost $250,000 and did save a goodly amount of water formerly lost at that place in the river. But while the by-pass helped the situation, it did not eliminate the problem, and continued low-water years made it apparent that a more stable water supply was necessary.

Now, it happened that just a year before this by-pass project, the American Falls Reservoir District was organized, and the Secretary of the Interior o.k.'d "The American Falls

1920 - 1930

Project," one of the largest reclamation projects in the U.S. at that time. The American Falls dam construction started in 1925, and the reservoir first filled in June of '27. Somewhere along in there the Big Wood Canal Co. discovered that some of the water in that American Falls District had still not been appropriated, so they whipped right in and nabbed it for the Shoshone and Gooding lands. They were awarded four-seventeenths of the storage capacity of the American Falls Reservoir!

So what? American Falls was so far away from their segregation it was almost laughable! How could they possibly afford to transport that water over such a long distance? There was a lot of opposition and sour grapes, both at home and in Washington D.C. The whole plan seemed about on a par with the scheme to tunnel through Galena to tap the waters of Alturas Lake.

However, there was one man who was convinced it could be done, United States Senator John Thomas, who had just been appointed to fill the seat of Senator Frank R. Gooding, who died in June, 1928. Thomas got right busy looking into the possibilities, and the idea to divert the water out of the Snake River at Milner Dam Diversion seemed to be workable. Why Milner? Because that was the last spot on the Snake river where water could be diverted by gravity. Anything past that would have to be lifted by pumps, onto the land.

First, Senator Thomas managed to convince his colleagues in Washington, and then, because of his enthusiasm and encouragement, he finally received the whole-hearted support of the planners of both river decree lands, and the Wood River Canal Co. lands.

Thanks to Senator Thomas's untiring efforts, the U.S. Government agreed to undertake the project. The "American Falls Reservoir District No. 2" was created to facilitate the plan, and to create a legal entity to deal with the government as well as the land owners, and to operate the new canal system, levy and collect assessments, etc.

1920 - 1930

So, the canal was built. It turned the water out of the Snake River at Milner and brought it 76 miles across the lava. It cost four-million dollars, was completed early in 1932 and was called both the "Milner-Shoshone," and the "Milner-Gooding" canal. The water it carries irrigates only the lower half of the old Idaho Irrigation Co. project - the upper half still receives water from Magic Reservoir. By putting the lower lands under the American Falls Reservoir it assured the upper lands of a good supply of water every year out of Magic, which could then carry large hold-over storage.

At least, that one big problem was finally solved.

But there were others. . .

In 1928, just before John Thomas was appointed Senator, there was a freak accident up at Magic Dam. Les Bushby, a long-time Richfield resident and ditch-rider for the Canal Co., tells how it was:

"The missus and I were married March 5, 1928 and were staying at the old Alberta Hotel when we heard about the accident caused by that big silo with the control catwalk out to it. Ice was thick around the tower. They got a thaw and the water raised, and ice froze around that tower and pushed it over some on the upper side. It looked like they were going to lose all their water, but they got out and cut that ice away and the tower settled back some. Then they got two divers here from the coast and another ditch rider and I went up to watch them because we had never seen deep-sea diving before. They were operating under some 80 feet of water down there. Cold, cold water, too. They went down and they were using Oakum, and they caulked that crack and pretty well shut that water off under that pressure down there. They could only work for about eight or nine minutes and then that diver would come up and the other one would suit up and then he

1920 - 1930

would go down and work eight or nine minutes. They wouldn't let anyone else work the bellows."

"After that tower tipped, it never did settle back in place true, and the gates would bind and it took two men to work those gates instead of one."

Leon Grieve, Watermaster at the Big Wood Canal Co. was later told it took 125 turns of the wheel to raise one of those big gates one inch.

* * * * * * *

Other events were happening around the reservoir at that time during the '20's. On the West Side of Magic Reservoir land was being patented. In addition to Zack Spelling in 1913 and George Starcher in 1917, David Murray received his patent in 1918 on the land presently occupied by the resort area. Lyle P. Salisbury got his in 1920 just north of Starcher, and George Webb got his patent in 1922. However, these patents remain something of a mystery, because Les Bushby claims when he went up to the dam to watch the divers in 1928, there were absolutely no buildings nor signs of life anywhere on the shores of the reservoir. The only building there, he said, was Ed Dayton's (the damkeeper) house on the East edge of the damsite.

* * * * * * *

Elsewhere in Idaho other important "firsts" were made during the 1920's: Radio broadcasting began in Idaho in 1921 at Boise High School. Harry Redeker, a science teacher, and his students constructed the pioneer transmitter, which was licensed in July, 1922 with the call letters KIDO, making it the first standard broadcasting station in Idaho, and one of the few west of the Mississippi.

1920 - 1930

* * * * * * *

In 1926 Morrison-Knudsen was one of six companies building Hoover Dam, and M-K also worked on the San Francisco Bay Bridge.

Also in 1926 the first Federal Air Line was established in our neck of the woods. It flew from Pasco, Washington, through Boise, to Elko, Nevada. The first pilot heading for Boise was blown off course and landed in a field in Owyhee County, which did not do a lot to promote air travel here. However, the following year Charles Lindberg thrilled the world with this non-stop flight from New York to Paris. "Lucky Lindy," the "Lone Eagle," and the "Spirit of St. Louis," became the revered symbols of the air industry, and made flying seem respectable and safe.

The same year Lindy made his flight, the spectacular Twin Falls-Jerome bridge was completed, making it a joy to drive from the South Side of the mighty Snake River to the North Side, or vice versa...

* * * * * * *

During the twenties a strong Basque culture grew and flourished in the Wood River Valley, and Ketchum again came into the limelight. Sheepmen began to drive their bands through the valley to summer grazing in the mountains, and the sheep industry kept growing until Ketchum became the largest sheep and lamb shipping station in the United States and was reputed to be second only to Sydney, Australia as the sheep shipping center of the world!

* * * * * * *

1920 - 1930

The "Roaring Twenties" came to a screeching halt when Wall Street's $15,000,000,000 slide in 1929 plunged the entire country, and the world, into a deep economic depression.

1930 - 1940
THE GREAT DEPRESSION

The Great Depression of the 30's was the worst economic crisis in our nation's history. Agricultural prices, on the downward slide since 1921 slumped disastrously. Thousands of farmers were thrown into bankruptcy, and even though some managed to stay on the land as tenants or sharecroppers, most of them just gave up altogether and faded into the population. Shutdowns of failing industries threw millions of factory hands out of work, and International trade losses aggravated the situation.

13 million Americans were out of work, and those who still had jobs had their wages slashed. About 40% of American families had annual incomes of less than $1,000, and in places like the coalfields of Kentucky there was seldom enough to eat. Some families were living on weeds.

Manufacturing output slid back to 1916 levels. Between 1929 and 1932 more than 86,000 businesses went broke, more than 6,000 banks buckled, and by 1933 twenty-four states were entirely without banks.

The United States was technically bankrupt.

Armies of jobless men and boys roamed the country looking for work, stowing away on freight trains and haunting hobo jungles. Any kind of work - chopping wood, clearing away trash and garbage, digging ditches, anything, just for a meal.

In cities all across the country hungry people stood in endless bread lines. Soup kitchens were filled to capacity and beyond. Dismal shantytowns, better known as "Hoovervilles" would spring up near the railroad yards in virtually every city, their ranks swollen by a steady influx of poor families thrown out of their homes for nonpayment of rent. "Hoovervilles" were so named to insult then President Herbert Hoover whom they felt was not doing anything to alleviate the situation.

1930 - 1940

To make matters worse, the Great Plains were beset by a two-year plague of dust storms. From Canada to Texas, millions of acres of crops were ruined, leaving behind a vast dust bowl of barren earth. Out of this wasteland emerged a bedraggled stream of so-called "Okies" in rickety cars and jitneys piled high with all their earthly goods, rattling westward toward the still-green valleys of California, where they hoped to eke out an existence as field hands and day laborers.

The country was sick. Business was very, very bad. People were frightened and desperate.

Franklin Delano Roosevelt was elected President of the United States on March 4, 1933.

Eight days after his inauguration he began his "Fireside Chats." Carried by radio from his White House office into the living rooms of America, he talked about his plans for a "new deal for the American people." He explained what he planned to do, and reported on progress. He opened every "Chat" with "My friends. . ." and talked to them as if they were. It was a big psychological boost for them, and they listened carefully - with hope.

First thing Roosevelt did was declare a 4-day bank holiday and close all the banks. The country had to do business with whatever cash was in circulation, or make do with credit, barter, or scrip. It was the beginning of "The Hundred Days," a period during which FDR proposed, and Congress passed, fifteen major pieces of legislation. His plan was to "prime the pump" and pull America out of the Depression by positive Federal action. His "New Deal" strongly appealed to the troubled masses, and despair turned to hope as the hundred days came to an end.

To give an idea how things were inside the Magic Circle - in September, 1933 a wage scale was published in the Shoshone Journal: Single hands, 28 cents per hour. Teams, 17 cents per hour. Man and 4 horses, 62 cents per hour. The jobs were filled immediately.

But the New Deal had something for everyone. Desperate farmers, plagued by low prices and overproduction, were helped by the Agricultural Adjustment Administration (AAA) which paid them federal subsidies for crop reduction, marketing quotas, and loans. In 1933, to hasten AAA's effectiveness, farmers were paid to plow under 10 million acres of cotton, and slaughter some 6 million hogs, and 100 million pounds of pork were distributed to families on Relief.

The Public Works Administration (PWA) provided loans and grants for the construction of bridges, highways, dams and other works. It was created to boost consumer buying power and stimulate independent activity by providing federal jobs on some 34,000 public projects.

By April, 1935 the Works Progress Administration (WPA) was in operation. Under its 11 billion worker umbrella, some 8.5 million skilled workers of every kind, were put to work for the public good. More than 651,000 miles of streets and roads, 78,000 bridges, 125,000 public buildings as well as parks, airports, public utilities and recreational facilities were built, refurbished, or improved by the time the WPA was phased out in 1943. Small town projects included schools, city halls, and post offices. WPA workers repaired buildings at air stations and did ground maintenance. Those who had no special skills worked as laborers, or helpers, carrying ladders, digging ditches and other menial jobs. They received $50 lump sum the first month and after that, $20 a month, and were damned glad to get it.

The Civilian Conservation Corps (CCC) was created to provide useful work for unemployed young men and to get them off the streets. Often called the "Tree-Planting Army," they did dozens of other jobs as well, and learned new skills in doing

1930 - 1940

them. The "C's" were sent to a camp, issued olive-drab uniforms, and lived the army life. Three good meals a day, their time was tightly scheduled, and they worked hard. Every camp had an educational advisor to encourage and assist them to complete their high school education, and they received free medical and dental care. The pay was $30 a month - $5 went to the enrollee, and the other $25 was sent home to his folks. The young men were proud to be able to help their families get off Relief.

The CCC's thinned trees and planted them, built barbecue pits, rock walls, walkways and sturdy buildings in the parks, helped widen vital roads to fire lookout towers, put up telephone lines, replaced washed-out bridges, developed wildlife refuges with animal shelters and nesting sites, and spent many a sweaty day clearing a firebreak with a brush-hook, or protecting a stream channel against erosion by embedding stones in the mud. One of their projects was installing concrete markers, with medallions in the top, at certain places along the old Oregon Trail.

Thousands of public works projects were undertaken by the estimated 4 million young men who served in the CCC between 1933 and 1942 when it gave way to manpower needs of the military for World War II.

More than 28,000 young men from Idaho were enrolled in the CCC, and more than 37,700 others served in the State.

Arthur M. Schlesinger, Jr. said it all when he wrote "The Civilian Conservation Corps left its monuments in the preservation and purification of the land, the water, the forests, and the young men of America."

FDR's New Deal also included the Social Security Act which offered protection against penniless old age and provided aid for the disabled. And, it also included the Home Owners Loan Act which put the credit of the government behind mortgages that millions had been unable to meet, and saved their homes.

1930 - 1940

And, he did something else - in 1933 FDR tilted his long cigarette holder heavenward, smiled, and said "I think it's time for beer." And so it was. Americans crowded into liquor stores, bars and cafes to buy their first legal alcoholic beverages in 13 years. Except in Idaho, where it didn't happen until 1935 when our Legislature finally passed an act repealing the Prohibition Act and providing for the sale of intoxicating liquor through State dispensaries.

Roosevelt's New Deal "Alphabet Soup" programs were ladled out all over America and out of the ashes of the Depression rose factories, schools, office buildings, highways, dams, public parks, forest and land improvements. America was indeed perking up - but the hard times hung on. Even with such tremendous effort, by 1938 there were still some 10 million jobless Americans. The economy finally improved only after the big business boom brought on by the outbreak of World War II in 1939.

Meanwhile, Idaho was a leading beneficiary of many of the New Deal programs, ranking first in Rural Electrification Administration (REA) expenditures; second in Civilian Conservation Corps (CCC), and fourth in Public Works grants. Also, many Idaho farmers received benefit payments under the Agricultural Adjustment Act (AAA), and Works Progess Administration (WPA) programs were everywhere.

The Depression knocked the sheep industry off its feet, too. The high cost of feed, and the declining market cut deeply into the number of sheep and lambs shipped out of Ketchum, and it never did recover to where it had been during the 20's.

The irrigation tracts inside the Magic Circle suffered terribly. Mont Johnson, who has lived on the Richfield Tract longer than anybody else in the world, says that during the 30's the Federal Land Bank and Continental Land Bank wound up owning 75% of the land around there. The banks were left holding the bag when the farmers they loaned money to went broke.

1930 - 1940

However, when the Milner-Gooding canal was completed on May 10, 1932 and the water flowed abundantly from the American Falls reservoir, the old Idaho Irrigation Co. tracts began to look pretty attractive again. No more water shortages now that the upper half would be served from Magic Reservoir and the lower from the Milner-Gooding canal. That canal, by the way, went UNDER the Little Wood River via an inverted siphon, and OVER the Big Wood via a concrete flume.

There was still one big problem for the Big Wood Canal Co. - the leaning tower at Magic Dam. The aging gears and heavy gates were complaining more and more, and the stress brought on by the tilt made it extremely difficult to control the water. The foot bridge leading out to the tower collapsed in 1933, making it a damp and precarious undertaking for the dam keeper to even get out to the tower. As if that were not enough, the old concrete-lined tunnel was seeping more and more, and the whole business seemed to be crumbling. Something had to be done about the tower - and maybe the tunnel, too.

Fortunately, that was about the time FDR took office and soon there was all that New Deal money floating around for public works. The Big Wood Canal Co. immediately applied for $180,000 PWA funds to fix the tower and the tunnel, and after months of hand-wringing and paper-shuffling, it was approved on June 29, 1934. $180,000 with 21 years to repay at 5% interest. Plans were made for a new needle-valve control system that had to be approved by a PWA engineer for Idaho and PWA engineer in the Federal offices in Washington, D.C. and an Irishman named Thomas H. McCarthy from New Mexico was brought up to oversee the project.

Morrison-Knutsen got the bid. The same M-K who built the by-pass canal in the Cottonwoods in '24; had a portion of the contract on the Milner-Gooding canal in '31; and now everybody was happy to have their popular, respected, friend-contractor do the major repairs at Magic Dam.

1930 - 1940

Work began October 1, 1934 and was completed by January 15, '35. The inside surface of the old concrete lining the tunnel, was first cleaned, and all disintegrating concrete removed, pressure grouted to cut off all leaks and a big new, clean, solid steel pipe was installed inside the tunnel. That pipe is 3.8" thick and 11 feet in diameter, and runs the full length of the tunnel. The old leaning tower was torn down to below where it had buckled, and trash racks were placed over the intake tunnel. Finally, two gigantic 60" needle valves were put in at the tunnel outlet, and a completely new control system was installed in a valve house built over the top.

Les Bushby, who had watched the deep-sea divers caulk the tower after it tipped, was back up at the dam working on those repairs. Les says, "Most of the ditch riders went up to work on that project. It had been a dry year, and water ran out about the last of August. Those big needle valves were molded back in Birmingham, Alabama and came in on a flatcar. Oh, they weighed a heck of a lot. they came in at the Magic Station, where they had a siding and water tank, and unloaded them there. This construction company from Boise made a big kind of a sled business with poles under it and pulled them off carefully with two big cats and brought one of them across at a time."

The new control system worked like a charm

Needle Valves

Herb Mingo at the controls.

1930 - 1940

* * * * * * *

Elsewhere around the Magic Circle, little events were happening here and there. CCC camps were scattered about, and most of the young men inhabiting them came from big cities in the East. Most had never been out of the city, and Idaho was another world to them - wide-open spaces, strange landscapes, and unfamiliar animals, work, and people.

* * * * * * *

In 1933 Tracy Coker, A Shoshone school teacher, wrote a novel about Jim Hawk, his French-Shoshonee wife Ee-dah-how, and her brother, Eagle Feather. They took refuge in the ice caves to get away from other nasty Indians who were after Jim. And the story goes on to say that Jim named the big room in the cave "Ee-da-how's Cathedral." Later, Eagle Feather ventured out of the cave and got shot and Jim buried him standing up in a big crack in the ice in the cave. And, that's how the caves came to be known as the "Shoshone Indian Ice Caves" - because Eagle Feather was iced in there. And the name stuck. And people actually claimed they could see old Eagle Feather looking out at them when they visited the caves.

Well, Coker's book was very popular, and widely read, and it got the Shoshone Chamber of Commerce all fired up about the ice caves, and they decided to fix them up to make them into a tourist attraction. The Chamber gathered a group of volunteers and went up to the ice caves one Sunday and built ladders to get in and out easier, a walkway or two, and cleaned it up some. Their enthusiasm carried them on to try to officially name them "Ee-da-how's Caves." No luck. Then they requested Congress to establish the "Shoshone Ice Caves, National Park of Idaho." No luck. Then they asked to make the caves a national monument. No luck. Finally, the caves were designated an

1930 - 1940

educational project with $22,000 appropriated by the government to be used for trails, walkways, a caretaker cabin, and a road in from the main highway.

They finished all this by June, 1936 and a "Mr. Hopper" took over as the new cave caretaker and guide. He and his family moved into the new cabin for the summer and guided visitors through the caves. Two summers later, Hopper noticed that the ice seemed to be melting inside the cave. It seems that after Hopper had left for the season, three CCC youths decided to make a new entrance to the caves and chopped and blasted a big hole, ending up in a collapsed section of another tube above the ice caves. But, this new opening allowed the wind to blow from one end of the caves to the other, and the ice really began to melt in earnest - drip by drip, dribble by dribble, splash by splash.

The government abandoned the whole business in 1939. Vandals burned the cabin down, the parking area and cave turned into a public dumping ground, the road slowly disappeared under the sagebrush, and nobody cared.

The enthusiasm of the Shoshone Chamber of Commerce did not die with the ice cave caper. They were determined to get as much of that public works money as possible. They managed to wrangle government land for a 9-hole golf course three miles East of Shoshone along the North Side of the Richfield highway. RFC Relief workers did the work, and 112 trees were planted on the course. Golfers shot around this new playground until the maintenance got to be too much, and it, too, finally disappeared under the sagebrush, and nobody cared.

Folks up around Silver Creek asked for a dam to be built on Silver Creek three miles West of Picabo to impound 10,000 acre feet of water in a storage reservoir. No luck.

And, the community of Carey was still struggling with their problems. Way back in the 1880's the settlers rushed into the Carey Valley and made their homes, and in ten years all of the naturally irrigable land had been homesteaded. During those early years, the streams maintained a constant flow, and water was plentiful, but as time went on and more and more land was brought under cultivation, the water became scarcer and scarcer.

Fields became parched and brown in the fall, logging wagons crossed fords more easily, and sheep trails turned into dusty paths. The Spring sun sought out the southern basins and mountain slopes, and since there were fewer trees to absorb the heat, the snows were rapidly reduced to water that rushed pell-mell down the trails, over stump-land and into logging roads, denuding grassy areas and carrying away valuable top soil. The water, needed later in the season, ran off even before the farmers had plowed their land.

In desperation, the people of the valley formed the Little Wood River Reservoir Co. and filed on water in Muldoon Creek and Fish Creek. This was back in 1916, and the company spent $100,000 making surveys, getting engineering data and other preliminary work. But in April, 1918 the State engineer investigated the two sites and told the company to forget any plans to build a dam on Muldoon Creek. It would cost about $100 an acre-foot, he said, and recommended that they concentrate on Fish Creek where it would be only $35 or $40 an acre-foot. So, after spending all that money, the company was back to square one. They dissolved the Little Wood River Reservoir Co. and formed The Carey Valley Reservoir Co., and the debts were assumed by the new company. W.F. Rawson, Edward B. Arthur and Heber Q. Hale were named directors of the new company and Geo. C. Thompson, president of the Atlas Development Co. of Salt Lake City, outlined a plan for building and financing the project. Money to build the dam was to be raised through the sale of 40,000 shares of stock, each share to give the holder one acre-foot of water when the dam

1930 - 1940

was completed. At first, shares were $40 each, but later the price went up to $60.

The Fish Creek Dam took five years to build, and during that time many of the stockholders lost their farms because they were unable to pay the mortgages they had been forced to put on their land to raise the money to pay for the water stock and construction. Work was halted several times for lack of funds. However, in January, 1922 the Utah Home Fire Insurance Co., the Beneficial Life Insurance Co. and the Deseret Savings Bank, joined together and agreed to supply the money to finish the project.

The completed dam was 1,800 feet long, 105 feet high and built of concrete and reinforced steel, capable of impounding 14,000 acre feet of water. Total cost, $452,858. The nine-mile-long main canal with the four main laterals, cost $96,000 and was supposed to irrigate 17,241 acres of land - but they soon discovered, as usual, that there was not going to be enough water in the Fish Creek Reservoir to take care of all the acreage under cultivation. The usual problem - too many years when the reservoir did not fill.

So, they wearily decided that another dam would have to be built, this time on Little Wood River 15 miles north of Carey. The Carey lands were incorporated into the Little Wood River Irrigation District, and plans were set in motion for the construction of the second dam. But, money was again the problem - and that brings us up to the New Deal years of Franklin Delano Roosevelt.

In 1935 the Works Project Administration approved construction of the Little Wood dam and made an initial grant of $185,000 to be matched by labor and money from the people. Wonderful! Hopes ran high! But not for long - all of the money was spent for building houses for the workers and for a road to the site! All of that $185,000? Yes, all of it!

Nevertheless, the government made two more grants to

1930 - 1940

the project - one for $120,000 another for $165,000. Work progressed by spurts. In 1940 the WPA was taken off the job and the stockholders had to bond themselves for an additional $130,000 to complete the system.

The first water was delivered from the Little Wood Reservoir in 1941. The dam is 77 feet high and 1,000 feet wide at its crest. It is earth filled, and capable of impounding 12,724 feet of water. The engineers on the project were H.E. Echols and Roy Buck, and the contractor was Dan J. Cavanaugh of Twin Falls, with Duffy Reed as foreman.

* * * * * * *

During the Depression years the once-proud, luxurious Richfield and Dietrich Hotels faded, sagged, became weather beaten and dilapidated until they took on a ghost-like appearance. No visitors, no money, no fancy French cooks, no maids, no maintenance, no management. In April of 1934 the east end of the Richfield Hotel was fitted up for the Richfield Women's' Club to use as their meeting place. A month or so later, the Methodists from Gooding offered to buy the hotel and move it to Gooding. The taxes against it were $1,157.03 and the minimum for which it could be sold by the county was 90% of that.

Too much for the Methodists, so the women's club continued to hold it down for their meetings.

The Dietrich Hotel had already been taken over by the Dietrich Methodists for their meetings, but after the Gooding Methodists failed to negotiate a deal for the Richfield Hotel, they made an offer for the Dietrich Hotel and got it! So those Gooding Methodists disassembled it and hauled it over to Gooding to be used in construction of the Methodist Parsonage there.

1930 - 1940
THE SUCCESSES

Not everyone was down and out during the 30's. One industry grew and flourished during that time - the movies. Americans turned out in unprecedented numbers to see their favorite fantasy acted out and to escape from their daily woes. Two wonderful hours of dancing away depression blues with Fred and Ginger in frothy, romantic, rich and elegant musicals, or cooing and giggling over the antics of two new saccharin child superstars like Shirley Temple and Mickey Rooney who were always putting on a "show" in a barn somewhere. And, there were tough-guy-gangster-types by the dozen, smart-alecky Jimmy Cagney, who also danced; swarthy Humphrey Bogart who didn't; super-ugly Edward G. Robinson who was easy to hate, and sinister George Raft with the evil eyes.

Comedies were plentiful, too, ranging from the zany carryings-on of the Marx Brothers to the boozy, nasty, W.C. Fields, Laurel and Hardy, The Three Stooges, and on into more sophisticated comedies like "It Happened One Night" with Clark Gable and Claudette Colbert.

Kids swarmed to the Saturday matinees (5 cents or 10 cents admission) to watch Hollywood cowboys shoot and gallop their way across the silver screen and kiss the horse instead of the girl.

The bill usually included a newsreel, a cartoon, a short feature, and sometimes a weekly cliff-hanging serial that shocked your sox off every week, and forced you to come back next week to see what really happened; and finally, the "feature." Tarzan movies were very popular during the thirties and encouraged kids to learn to swim and swing from the trees.

There was something for everyone at the movies, plus additional incentives like "Bank Night" when money was given away to the lucky ticket holder, and if not money, then dishes or pots and pans or whatever.

1930 - 1940

Hollywood was the capital of the Movie Kingdom. Hopeful actors and actresses arrived daily to "break into the movies," only to end up waiting tables or washing dishes just to stay alive. Fame and fortune eluded most of them, but the few who made it made it BIG! All America knew everything about "The Stars," and they were all rich, rich, rich.

So - "prosperity" was evident during the Depression as well as "adversity."

As for the "old money" in America - anyone "born with a silver spoon in his mouth" usually just kept it there, and there was really not much change for them.

1930 - 1940
THE WOOD RIVER VALLEY

The Wood River Valley has always been a favorite of the humans who found it and loved it for one reason or another. The base of the valley is 6,000 feet above sea level, and the circling heights stretch from 8,500 to 12,500 feet. The Sawtooth mountains protect the upper end of the valley from cold, northern gales, and in the winter the sun is warm and the snow is deep.

The Indians called it "Heavenly Heights." When they were finished with the camas harvest they would move up to gather wild berries, hunt, and enjoy the lovely summer months there. When fall began to turn the leaves to gold, they would migrate South to the Hagerman Valley to spend the winter. Long after their ancient way of life was destroyed and they were herded onto the reservation, many of them still managed to visit their beloved Heavenly Heights during the summer.

When the trappers moved into the valley, they loved it because of the many beaver and other valuable fur-bearing animals, but hated it because of the "sickness" they experienced. They named the river "Malade" on their crude maps to remind themselves, and warn others, of the poison hemlock that made them ill. The trappers were there to take what they could get and didn't have time to look around at the scenery.

The Missionaries and Oregon Trailers missed the Wood River Valley completely, being in too much of a hurry to get to their destinations.

The gold seekers, like the Trappers, loved the valley for what they could take out of it, and the cattle and sheep ranchers appreciated it for the economical summer pasture.

Did the railroad workers love it? Some did. Many Irish and Chinese stayed on to make their homes in Ketchum, Hailey and Bellevue. And we know the big railroad barons loved the

1930 - 1940

Wood River Valley because they loaded up family and friends and hauled their private railroad cars clear across the country just to enjoy the hot springs, the scenery, the gold and silver mines, and the excellent hotels. Prominent and wealthy people like Thomas Mellon and his son Andrew Mellon, Jay Gould, the Strahorns, E.H. Harriman and his family, etc. Harriman was the brilliant railroad magnate who, in 1898 formed a syndicate which then acquired the bankrupt Union Pacific Railroad. He shaped it up and made it pay, and in 1903 assumed the office of President of Union Pacific. Not long after that he repossessed the old Oregon Short Line for Union Pacific, and not long after that, Harriman and his entourage came out to inspect the new acquisition. It is reported that his young son, Averill, was a member of the party - he was about 13 or 14 years old, and it was summertime.

Years later - in the mid-1930's - that same Averill Harriman shook the sleeping Wood River Valley awake, and introduced it to a new class of the rich and famous.

He founded Sun Valley.

1930 - 1940
SUN VALLEY

It all began in 1932 when tall, handsome W. Averill Harriman stepped in as Chairman of the Board of his family's Union Pacific Railroad. He was a man of action, and changes came thick and fast. He immediately put on the new sleek Streamliners before any other railroad had them, thus offering slick, comfortable accommodations, more elegant and attractive car interiors, and lower prices in the dining cars, so that Union Pacific passengers could travel in style and luxury at less cost, and arrive in half the time.

But he didn't stop there. He figured U.P. needed some kind of exclusive attraction - something to create a reason for large numbers of Americans to travel on Union Pacific to the far west where his trains often ran half-empty. Other western railroads offered natural attractions - Santa Fe had the Grand Canyon, Canadian Pacific had Lake Louise and Banff, and Southern Pacific had lavish Palm Springs.

He was well aware that the great winter-sports centers, like Switzerland's St. Moritz, were thriving; that the first Winter Olympics were being held at Lake Placid, New York, and that America was becoming obsessed with the new sport of downhill skiing. Sports centers were opening, ski fashions covered the pages of magazines and newspapers, and department store windows were full of ski gear.

Well, now, the Union Pacific railroad cut through and around more mountains that it could count and Harriman decided some of them had to be good for skiing. All he had to do was locate the best place - as long as it was on or near the Union Pacific road.

He contacted the most knowledgeable winter-sports enthusiast he knew - Count Felix Schaffgotsch, who came from a long line of Austrian winter-sports lovers. He was a skilled downhill skier and had toured most of the elite ski resorts of

1930 - 1940

Europe. The Count had once been employed in Harriman's investment-banking house and frequently reminisced about the famous Austrian ski trains that met the channel boats to take passengers off to lavish resorts in snow-covered high country. When Harriman told him about his plan to build such a place in America, the Count was enthusiastic, and agreed to search out the perfect place for such a resort.

He headed West on a Union Pacific Streamliner in October, 1935 to find the American St. Moritz.

Six weeks, seven states, and a thousand mountains later the Count was ready to throw in the towel. It was tough exploring in winter. Roads were often blocked, forcing him into whatever conveyance was available. He used dog sleds, skis, snowshoes, horse-drawn sleighs, snowplows, toboggan and whatever, to check out dozens of possibilities. Interestingly, some of the areas he visited and rejected, have since become veritable monuments in modern American skiing - for example, he turned down Aspen, Colorado because it was too high for the average person's comfort; Alta, Utah, for being too close to Salt Lake City and its crowds; Jackson Hole, Wyoming and Lake Tahoe, California for being too remote. Other sites were too cold, too windy, too steep, or too heavily forested.

He finally just gave up, said good-bye to his most recent U.P. escort, Freight Agent Bill Hynes, in Boise, boarded a Streamliner, and headed back to New York to break the bad news to Harriman. Hynes, after putting the Count on the Streamliner, headed for the Bottle Club at the Hotel Boise, where he met his friend, Joe Stemmer, Director of the State Highway Department, and told him all about the Count's failure to find the American St. Moritz. Stemmer listened sympathetically, and it began to dawn on him that the Count had not seen the Wood River Valley. Stemmer shouted, "You didn't show him Ketchum? Hells bells! Get him on the phone in

1930 - 1940

Denver and yank him back to Ketchum, the one place he hasn't seen, and God's own choice for a ski resort!"

They did, and the Count came back and waded through the snow and found his perfect place one mile north of Ketchum. A small valley, surrounded by mountains which were largely untimbered, and perfect for plenty of good ski runs. The Sawtooth Range curtained the valley from the cold northern winds, and the entire area was bathed in brilliant sunshine. The snow was ideal for skiing - powdery and light with no surface crust. The Count was ecstatic! He wired Harriman, "It contains more delightful features than any other place I have seen in the United States, Switzerland, or Austria for a winter-sports center."

Harriman came out within a few weeks to check things out for himself. The 60 miles of track from Shoshone to Ketchum were still in use and intact. Built originally to haul tons of heavy ore in the old mining days, they also transported the men and materials for Magic Dam, for miles of canals, for the Central Idaho railroad, for millions of sheep and lambs during Ketchum's heydey as the sheep capital of the nation, plus the many tons of produce hauled out and furniture, rugs, lumber, fabrics, ribbons and laces hauled in for the residents. Now, the sturdy "Ketchum Branch" was destined to transport the rich and famous to the new Union Pacific winter wonderland.

Harriman later said "When I arrived in Ketchum I remember vividly getting off the car and putting on my skis in powder snow, and I fell in love with the place then and there."

He went immediately to inspect the "perfect spot" selected by Schaffgotch. It was the Brass Ranch, and he wasted no time in buying it - 4,000 acres (give or take a few) at the depression price of $10 per acre. He accepted without question the Count's suggestion about where to locate the lodge - right on the exact spot where amazed residents had seen him sitting in the sunlit meadowland in a deck chair. It was in this way he determined where the windows and sundecks on the lodge would get the maximum winter sunshine. The Count knew what he was doing.

No time was lost. Plans were drawn, and other experts were hired to start immediately on all phases of development.

Charlie Proctor, a member of the U.S. Olympic Ski Team of 1928 was put in charge of selecting the sites for ski runs, and Steve Hannagan, the flamboyant press agent who sold Miami Beach to millions as a balmy winter escape, was put in charge of "projecting" the new winter resort to the public.

Hannagan and one of his staff arrived in Ketchum in March. "We looked around," Hannagan remembers, "and all I could see was just a godforsaken field of snow. I thought they must be crazy! All I had on was a light tweed suit - I was used to the sun down at Miami Beach, and this was colder than hell. 'This is strictly ridiculous,' I said, but we walked around some more, with my shoes full of snow, and then the sun came out. Soon I opened my coat. Pretty soon I took it off and opened my vest. Then I began to sweat. You know, the temperature goes up to 97 there in the sun and still the snow doesn't melt."

Nevertheless, he really hated cold, and when you think of winter sports, you think of cold. When he was promoting Miami Beach he often commented that if he ever started a town there he would name it Sunshine, Florida. Hannagan knew how important a good name was. Now, he wondered what in the world he was doing in the middle of Idaho in winter, and wondered what he could possibly do to attract mildly intelligent people to the middle of this veritable icebox just to slide down hill on two boards. Standing there in the snow, in that sun-drenched valley the name hit him - "Sun Valley!" Now that sounded warm!

His over-all advertising campaign was based on "roughing it in luxury," and all publicity was tied to the brilliant

1930 - 1940

mountain sunshine. Sun Valley's first poster picture was of a young man on skis, stripped to the waist, wiping perspiration from his face. The photo was made in a New York studio, the "snow" was really Borax, and the "sweat" was Vaseline, but it was an unusual picture, and similar ones were used again and again in Sun Valley brochures. It was Hannagan who coined the term "snow tan" to indicate what the young man was getting with his shirt off.

Another Hannagan touch was bathing beauties. When he promoted Miami Beach, which he sold to millions as a balmy winter escape, he did much of it through a wide distribution of photos of bathing beauties basking in the sun. He did the same thing at Sun Valley, except he draped them around the outdoor heated pool, with snow piled around outside and steam rising from the top, and the bathing-suited beauties basking in the sun cozily and comfortably. It was all very effective and unique, and exciting.

Old-time Ketchum-ites watched all the comings and goings with exaggerated winks, patronizing smiles and elbows to the ribs, convinced that this whole business would probably be another short-lived chapter in the roller-coaster history of the Wood River Valley.

But within a few weeks more than 200 people were busy at work on the huge Sun Valley Lodge, a double Y structure, four stories high, made of concrete, which had been poured into rough-sawn pinewood forms. What emerged looked so much like wood, few people could tell it from the real thing. Labor was cheap during those Depression years. Men wanted jobs and were willing to work for forty-three cents an hour and board - and Union Pacific fed them well.

The lodge was built at the mind-boggling cost - by Depression standards, of $1.5 million. It was designed to cater to the upper income groups and the rates ran from $6 to $25 a day, European plan. Other attractions were quickly added - a

1930 - 1940

movie, bowling alley, luxury dining, an orchestra, sleigh rides to a remote cabin for a fantastic meal, an outdoor heated pool, and more.

And the big problem - the really, really big problem of getting the skiers up the mountain so they could ski down, was solved beautifully. Union Pacific engineers brain-stormed all of the possibilities of the T-Bar, the J-Bar, aerial tramways like those in the Alps, etc. "Whatever method you use," said Hannagan, "it HAS to be comfortable!" And it was Jim Curran, a young engineer who had helped to build an aerial conveyor to transport bunches of bananas onto ships, who came up with the idea of attaching chairs to banana hooks. After six months of trial and error, the first two chair-lifts in the world were erected on Proctor and Dollar mountains.

Sun Valley opened on December 21, 1936, and Hannagan had done his job well - it was a sell-out! The rich and famous came from the East Coast, the West Coast and in between. Hannagan had a lot of friends in Hollywood, and imported film celebrities by the dozen - Jimmy Stewart, Gary Cooper, Ingrid Bergman, Clark Gable, Bing Crosby, Claudette Colbert, and more. From the East Coast came friends of the Harrimans - "old money," society names like du-Pont, Vanderbilt, Studebaker, Armory, Gloria Baker, heiress to millions, and more.

It must be mentioned that Averill Harriman had kept his finger on every phase of Sun Valley's development. It was a special project of his and he supervised everything closely.

By the end of the first season, it was obvious that Sun Valley could also attract plenty of less prosperous skiers, so Harriman commissioned the Challenger Inn, where rates were from $3 to $7.50 a day. This made it possible for a couple, out from New York, to enjoy a terrific two-week stay for about $500, including the $23 train fare.

He named his new addition "The Challenger Inn" to

1930 - 1940

publicize his latest streamlined train named "The Challenger." It opened in the winter of 1937. A rambling Alpine style building with 230 guest rooms. It also housed a Camera Shop, Drug Store, Telegraph office, Gift Shop, Cafe Continental and "The Ram," a popular dining and dancing night spot.

The resort continued to grow, both in size and popularity. The fun and games never stopped. All year long there was bowling, billiards, ping-pong, and numerous other forms of indoor recreation in the game rooms.

Outside, the main activity was skiing, but one could also enjoy ice skating on a large artificial ice rink next to the lodge, swimming in the heated pools, horse back riding, skeet and trap shooting, hunting, fishing, tennis, bicycling, sleigh rides, dog sledding, golfing, you name it.

Sun Valley stayed open winter and summer and people flocked in to enjoy and experience.

Ernest Hemingway first arrived in September, 1939 with "For Whom The Bell Tolls" half completed. He finished it in Suite 206 of the Sun Valley Lodge. Like everyone else, Hemingway fell in love with the area. He bought a large home just outside Ketchum, and brought his family out in 1940.

The world remembers Ernest Hemingway as a writer, Nobel Prize winner, fighter, boxer, deep-sea fisherman, or big game hunter on African Safari, but the Wood River Valley folks reminisce about the husky, robust man who hunted in their fields, shopped in their shops, walked in their streets, spun tales in their bars - a great and famous man, but more important, a friend and neighbor. This was his "home."

* * * * * * *

In 1941 hannagan pulled off his greatest coup for Sun Valley. A major motion picture was made in and about Sun Valley - the "Sun Valley Serenade," starring Sonja Henie, John

1930 - 1940

Payne, Milton Berle and The Glenn Miller Orchestra. The picture gave Sun Valley its very own song, "It Happened in sun Valley," and more than any other publicity, it put Sun Valley on the map.

Sun Valley's guest register soon became a world-wide "Who's Who."

1930 - 1940
MAGIC VALLEY

In 1937 another Idaho "valley" was christened when some of the executives of a Twin Falls Newspaper (THE IDAHO EVENING TIMES later changed to TIMES-NEWS) got together to dream up a more attractive name for the area, which had always been referred to as "Southcentral Idaho." They wanted something catchy, easy to pronounce, and easy to remember.

While brainstorming the idea, someone pointed out that it was indeed a huge valley - from the Sawtooth Mountains on the North to the rolling hills on the South. So that meant they must also decide the boundaries for the new valley name. After much discussion they included eight counties - Blaine, Camas, Cassia, Gooding, Jerome, Lincoln, Minidoka and Twin Falls.

By this time, the word "magic" had been around for a long time - the Carey Act Lands were promoted heavily using the word to describe what happens when irrigation water meets the rich, fertile, virgin lava soil. Newspapers used it frequently in their ads and stories.

And, of course, that dam up there was named "Magic Dam" a long time ago. . .

So, when someone said "How about Magic Valley?" Silence. Then, "Yes!", "Right!", "Good!", "That's it!" They all agreed!

And so it was. The newpapers, radios, magazines, and every flyer, leaflet, map etc. referred to the area as "Magic Valley."

But remember this - Mr. S. D. Boone named his project "Magic Dam" before anyone else even thought about it. . .

1930 - 1940

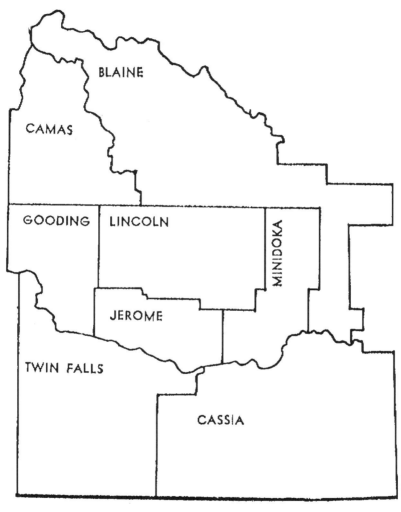

The Magic Valley

1940 - 1950
WORLD WAR II

In the fall of 1939, America was still fighting the Great Depression. But, in Europe, another fight was going on - Hitler's army invaded Poland, and Britain and France declared war on Germany.

America watched - and followed this European action in the newspapers, radio and on the News-Reels at the movies.

America watched - as Hitler's "Blitzkrieg" (lightening war) rolled across Poland, France, Belgium, the Netherlands, Denmark and Norway, and bombed London 57 nights in a row during the fall of 1940.

America watched - as Japan overran Burma, Thailand, Hong Kong, Malaya, the Netherlands East Indies and the Phillipines.

America watched - as Germany, Italy and Japan joined together in a 10-year military and economic partnership, and set out to create a new global order.

America watched - horrified - on Sunday, December 7, 1941 as a huge Japanese air fleet attacked the U.S. Pacific Fleet at Pearl Harbor and in less than two hours sank or badly damaged seven battleships, three cruisers, two destroyers and four auxiliary vessels. They also wiped out the island's air defenses destroying most of the planes before they even got off the ground. Altogether, 2,403 sailors, soldiers, marines and civilians were dead, and another 1,178 had been wounded.

America watched and listened as an outraged President Roosevelt took to the air-waves and described December 7th as "a date which will live in infamy." Congress immediately declared war on Japan. Three days later, Hitler declared war on the United States to show support for his ally, Japan.

America was in, and immediately began to assemble all of her resources, a tremendous multi-million-dollar effort involving more than 16 million men under arms, 300,000

1940 - 1950

aircraft, 85,000 tanks and more than 20 million tons of shipping. America armed herself and managed to provide aid to Britain, the Soviet Union, and China, plus other allied nations, while at the same time fight a two-front war in Europe and the Pacific.

Draft Boards all over the country went into action and young men left home in droves. On the home front, women turned the manpower crisis into a work crusade and six million women flooded the labor market. Some joined the military, and the WACS, WAVES, SPARS, and Marine Corps released more than 200,000 men for combat. Some of those women became pilots, engineers, chemists, economists, lawyers and doctors. Others cleaned blast furnaces, serviced cars, ran giant cranes, greased locomotives, cut precision tools and filled in wherever they were needed. In the shipyards and aircraft plants women worked on everything from assembling navigation equipment to welding and riveting. "Rosie the Riveter" became a national symbol. Before the war, jobs outside the home had been considered "inappropriate" for a women with a household or children to care for, but the demands of war quickly pulled down those barriers against wives and mothers in the labor force.

And finally, it was the war that wiped out the Great Depression by giving employment to practically everybody from teenagers to old folks, many of whom had never worked before. Whole industries turned to war production - auto makers turned out planes and tanks, appliance and electronics manufacturers built radar devises, shells, etc. Farmers, the group hit hardest by the Depression, saw their income triple. Nightclubs and restaurants drew huge crowds of big spenders night after night - servicemen on leave and civilians making more money than ever before. Trains were jam-packed with soldiers and sailors on leave, and families and sweethearts traveling to meet them somewhere.

The marriage rate jumped, and three million children were born each year in '42 and '43.

1940 - 1950

Ration books were issued to everyone on the home front - gasoline, shoes and foods suitable for overseas shipment were carefully rationed, while tires, typewriters and the like were available for civilion use only when "priority claims" were justified. Even at that, if one had enough money almost everything was available on the Black Market. Nobody was hurt much by rationing - it was just another inconvenience of the war.

But, one group in America was deeply hurt by the war - the Japanese-Americans. After the attack on Pearl Harbor, prejudice against those easily identifiable people living on the West Coast, led to many acts of violence, so, on February 19, 1942, President roosevelt authorized the Army to take control of civilian affairs there. Commanding General John L. DeWitt, immediately issued an order to round up all Japanese in Washington, Oregon, California and Arizona and move them to ten relocation centers inland. 110,000 Japanese-Americans were cruelly uprooted from their homes and businesses and allowed to bring with them only what personal possessions they could carry.

One of the ten centers was located just outside the Magic Circle in the sagebrush desert north of the North Side Canal. Officially, it was called the "Minidoka War Relocation Center," but the town that was established in the center was called "Hunt," in honor of Wilson Price Hunt who had led the Astorians through the area way back in 1811.

Morrison-Knudsen quickly constructed the dreary, tar-paper-covered buildings. The residential area was three miles long, contained 36 blocks, and each block held 12 barracks for living quarters plus one dining hall, a recreation hall and a laundry building that also contained toilet and shower facilities. The camp was surrounded by barbed wire and patrolled by Military Police guards.

The first Japanese arrived on August 10, 1942. One

1940 - 1950

month later there were 8,948 and almost 60% were American citizens.

On opening day of school ten teachers faced 775 pupils. 97 different elementary schools in Oregon and Washington were represented. 77 students in one 20' x 30' room. No blackboards. No chairs. Only a few second-hand, 20-year-old textbooks. The first desks were two-inch planks nailed to dining hall tables, but, those amazingly resourceful people managed to cope. Less that six weeks after school started, 1,400 copies of the high school newspaper, "Hunt Hi-Lites" were distributed. The peak enrollment in the high school was close to 1,500 students. The enrollment for the three years at Hunt High School totalled 3,881 and 695 seniors were graduated from the school.

Their first "harvest" consisted of 17 baskets of radishes from the project gardens that first year. They also built a beautiful park and picnic grounds with overhead decoration, foot-bridges with handrails, and there were carefully tended flowers and vegetables everywhere. All of the water for the park had to be hand-carried by buckets from the North Side Canal.

They put together a baseball team that beat every team around, and they earned the respect of the soldiers guarding them as well as the people in the nearby communities.

During its three years, the Hunt Center supplied 1,201 men to the United States Armed Forces. Of that number, more than 300 were volunteer members of the famous all-Japanese-American 442 Infantry Combat Unit described as "the most decorated in United States Military History."

There were 82 casualties among the Hunt G.I.'s.

The total construction cost for the three year Hunt project was $5,992,909 which included buildings, railroad spur, more than five miles of perimeter fencing, and eight sentry towers.

1940 - 1950

The military police withdrew from the premises on September 14, 1945 but it was a month later before the last Japanese-American left. It took three more months to close the center completely. In addition to taking inventory and attending to dozens of other small details, the camp staff had to find and identify the pets that had not been around when the time came for their owners to leave, and ship them on to the owners. Also, the Center had to be completely vacated, even to moving the graves of those who had died there, so the graves were relocated - even as the people had been.

The premises were officially transferred to the Bureau of Reclamation on February 4, 1946.

Today, all that remains at the site of Hunt is a portion of the main gate. The buildings have been scattered throughout the area and the site itself is now a tract of fertile farms developed by the veterans whose numbers were drawn in a land opening in the late 1940's.

* * * * * *

On April 17, 1952, in impressive demonstration was conducted on a virgin farm owned by John Herrmann at Hunt. Under the direction of the U.S. Soil Conservation, 1,500 workmen and 200 machines leveled, plowed, and ditched a 128-acre tract. They dug a well, installed the pump, built fences, planted a wind-break, and constructed a two bedroom house - <u>ALL IN ONE DAY!</u>

Thousands of spectators witnessed the evolution of this incredible accomplishment.

1940 - 1950

SUN VALLEY GOES NAVY

The attack on Pearl Harbor threw the whole country into turmoil. Nobody knew for sure what they were expected to do - but everybody felt they had to do SOMETHING!

Magic Circle people quickly formed Home Guards and Civil Defense Units, and gathered together to make plans to help defend the country if necessary. Their theory was that the first line of defense against the Japanese would surely be the Rocky Mountains. Consequently, deep mine tunnels were designated as bomb shelters for protection against enemy air raids, and elaborate, and far-reaching blackout practices were held often.

As in World War I, they were afraid of possible sabotage of Magic Dam and again sent a committee to the Governor to ask for protection. This time, an order was issued by the Fish and Game Department to close the area around the dam and forbid trespass on property owned by the Big Wood Canal Co. "due to the unsettled International situation."

Rumors were rampant. Lies and gossip were whispered and passed along about "the foreigners" at Sun Valley - the Austrian ski instructors. Someone started the rumor that they were sending secret messages to Germany via short-wave radio, and their fears were multiplied when they sat around and remembered that Sun Valley's "discoverer" Count Felix Schaffogotsch, was a Nazi who had served as an officer in Hitler's army, and they also knew that the brother of one of the ski instructors was also a Nazi who had returned to Germany to fight for his country. All of this became pretty ominous and as a result, three Austrian ski instructors were arrested and jailed in the Salt Lake County jail. But, after a thorough investigation two were released, and the one whose brother was a Nazi soldier was the only one to actually spend any time in detention. The two who were released joined the United

1940 - 1950

States Army. One served in Italy where he was wounded, and the other served in the Pacific where he earned the Silver Star for rescuing wounded American soldiers during the Battle of Corregidor. The strange thing about all the rumors - nobody ever stopped to question why Germany would be interested in anything going on in the remote Wood River Valley. And would it be important enough to relay via short-wave radio? In wartime nobody trusts nobody.

In the meantime, Sun Valley's founder, W. Averill Harriman was serving as Lend-Lease Coordinator in London and hob-nobbing with President Roosevelt, Prime Minister Churchill, and other high powers. Mr. Harriman has a long and proud record of service to his country.

And what about Sun Valley itself? Well, just before the 1942-43 season, the lodge closed and the rich and famous and everybody else disappeared. Everyone's attention was turned to the war effort.

In June of 1943 the United States Navy moved in. The lodge was turned into a rehabilitation hospital for war wounded. The first wave of patients were malcontents and war-weary sailors who were sometimes quite neurotic. The gambling casinos in Ketchum at that time provided an outlet for some, but also caused discontent and problems for the town folks. Frequent fights, drunkenness and out-of-control situations almost daily. But these were our fighting men and their behavior was tolerated. However, as the war progressed the malcontent and neurotic were replaced by ambulatory wounded, and the sailors' overall behavior was much better.

And their social life was much better, too. The USO stepped in to provide entertainment. Young, single women from 16 to 22 or so were permitted to attend dances, picnics, and whatever else they could think of, as long as chaperones (older, married USO hostesses) were in charge. The girls had all been carefully screened by the USO staff, and were all

1940 - 1950

guaranteed good girls. No bad. Occasionally they were even bussed to Sun Valley, some from as far away as Twin Falls, to spend a week-end socializing with the land-locked sailors. These weekend affairs were very carefully planned, very carefully chaperoned, and very carefully executed. No hanky-panky. The girls were housed in Chalets and Chateaus on the Sun Valley grounds and all doors and windows were locked up tight at curfew. No one - absolutely NO ONE - was allowed in or out after that time. Except for those who managed to jimmy open the windows and slide to the ground on tied-together-sheets from two stories up.

Swing and jitterbug dancing were all the rage, and music was usually provided by a "Juke Box" which offered an infinite assortment of Big Band sounds. Harry James, Glenn Miller, Tommy and Jimmy Dorsey, Woody Herman, Stan Kenton etc. were all household names. Skinny Frank "Swoonatra" was adored by screaming, fainting teenagers who saved the dirt he walked on. There were many other popular singers as well, such as "Der Bingle" Crosby, Spike Jones, and the Andrews Sisters who would belt out "Don't Sit Under the Apple Tree With Anyone Else But Me," and everybody danced.

The Juke Box was not an entirely new creation. Coin operated pianos were popular in saloons and restaurants since the early 1900's, and there were other coin operated music boxes as well. The flamboyant Juke Box really came into its own in the late 30's, about the time Prohibition was repealed, and picked up speed during the war. By that time high volume sound had been perfected, the music-box was electrified, and the "Juke Box" was born. Put a nickel in the slot.

The name was actually a kind of generic term since the machines were manufactured by several different companies - Wurlitzer, Nickelodeon, etc. The word "Juke" came from an African dialect meaning "misconduct" or "disorderliness," and "Juke House" was a brothel where lusty, raucous music was

1940 - 1950

played. Someone, somewhere, dubbed the new high volume electric record player "Juke Box" and the name stuck.

There was a Juke Box in every kind of gathering place. A ponderous, magnificent monster, lit up like a Christmas Tree with strips of vivid reds, blues, greens and yellow lights oozing into one another around its belly and crawling up its sides, while it rumbled out new songs, or oldies. It was wonderful to be able to call up any kind of music any time you wanted it. Good music.

Popular songs were a great morale-booster for American Servicemen and frequently expressed what they wanted to say to wives and sweethearts half a world away - "The More I See You", "'Til the End of Time", "Sentimental Journey", "White Cliffs of Dover", and on and on. And, many of the songs were written just for the fighting men "This Is the Army, Mr. Jones", "When the Saints Go Marching In", "Boogie Woogie Bugle Boy", etc. The Navy sang "Bell Bottom Trousers" - not a new song, but had been revived and cleaned up from an old ditty dating back to the Civil War during the hey-day of America's Clipper ships. It could not be published during the Victorian days because of its raunchy lyrics, so it remained exclusively sailor property until it was re-written, sanitized and "decent." It took eighty years to get from an unprintable sea chanty to a delightful popular song during World War II.

* * * * * * *

April 12, 1945 - President Franklin D. Roosevelt dies suddenly of a massive cerebral hemorrhage. Harry S. Truman, Vice-President, steps in as President of the United States.

May 8, 1945 - V-E Day. The war in Europe is over!

July 16, 1945 - The first Atom Bomb ever, is exploded in a blinding flash in the barren desert of Alamagordo New Mexico by the U.S.

1940 - 1950

<u>August 6, 1945</u> - The second Atom Bomb ever, is dropped on Hiroshima, Japan by the U.S. 260,000 Japanese killed. The city is gone. The world is shocked.

<u>August 9, 1945</u> - The third Atom Bomb ever, is dropped on Nagasaki, Japan by the U.S. 78,000 killed. The city is gone, the world is shocked.

<u>August 14, 1945</u> - Japan surrenders.

<u>September 2, 1945</u> - V-J Day. The war with Japan is officially ended.

* * * * * * *

Servicemen the world over are finally free to go home and put their lives back together. It is estimated that 400,000 Americans lost their lives in that war, and worldwide, some 16 million military personnel and 18 million civilians had died.

WWII produced, in a crude form, what we now know as the "computer." It also gave us radar and jet aircraft and it ushered in the Atomic Age.

Immediately after the war there was a dip in the U.S. economy due to the conversion from war to peace. But after this adjustment, the post war years were a time of unprecedented prosperity in the United States. After fifteen years of hard times (the Great Depression followed by the war), young people wanted more than anything to build a happy, secure future for their families. They were determined that their own children would have all of the comforts and advantages they had missed. The G. I. Bill of Rights offered millions of vets the opportunity to get a free college education, a good job, and a comfortable home. By 1946 nearly half of the two million college students were war veterans, and millions more were buying their own homes with a little or no money down and 30 years to pay.

The '40's decade ended in a tremendous flurry of

1940 - 1950

production - automobile production, home production, washer, dryer, kitchen appliance production, and baby production. From 1946 to 1956, 37 million babies were born in the United States, and a torrent of consumer "needs" flooded the market - new things to assist the new families.

And, the television industry exploded onto the American scene. In 1948 there were 29 commercially operated T.V. stations in the United States, and manufacturers turned out a million sets - most of them with 12-inch screens. Advertising revenues were estimated at $8.7 million. Television was here to stay.

And, the 37 million babies grew up right along with their favorite baby-sitter - the tee-vee.

* * * * * * *

Meanwhile, back in December of 1946, Sun Valley opened to the public, with a magnificent Grand Opening Gala! The old crowd happily returned with love and enthusiasm. Nobility, movie stars, old-money, new-money and no-money showed up at the beautiful resort for a gigantic party. Handsome, carefree ski-bums mixed and mingled with the rich and famous and everybody had a glorious time. Pictures of Ernest Hemingway bird hunting with Gary Cooper circulated in magazines and tabloids throughout the land, plus hundreds of fun-filled photos of famous folks frolicking at Sun Valley - Paul Newman, Marlon Brando, Lucille Ball, Ingred, Clark, Claudette, queens, kings and aces. The list went on and on. Sun Valley was once again the swankiest, ritziest, poshest, expensivest, resort in the whole wide world.

* * * * * * *

Two years later, another ski resort made a quiet debut inside the Magic Circle. On Soldier Mountain, eleven miles

1940 - 1950

north of Fairfield, Bob and Sten Frostenson put up a rope-tow as a hobby. Soldier is 10,000 ft. high, usually has a heavy snowfall, and offers excellent skiing. The small resort quickly became popular and soon was taken over by LaVard Hansen who added more rope-tows and a J-Bar. The Soldier Mountain Ski Area was underway...

1940 - 1950
GLEASON'S LANDING

Remember back in 1936 when Sun Valley first opened? When thousands of famous people the world over heard about the magnificent destination resort and all the luxuries it offered?

Well, that same year - 1936, also marks the opening of the first "resort" on the shore of Magic Reservoir. There was no big celebration, no publicity, no luxuries, and no people. Just Ed. Ed Gleason was the first to officially open the Magic Lake Recreation Area because he filed a mining claim on the West Shore and put up a building on the site. O.K., so it was just a shack, but it was the first one, and Ed did it.

Ed Gleason was an avid angler who had been fishing the Big Wood River, up and down, for years and years - even before the dam was built. In 1936 he was fifty-three years old, had arthritis in both knees, and needed crutches to get around most of the time. He had once been a U.S. Deputy Marshall in Nevada; held the office of Sheriff in Jerome County; and in 1936 was living in Jerome figuring Income Taxes for a living.

His Mining Claim was located on a barren spot on the west shore - and just happened to be nice and convenient for fishing. It was just a skip-and-a-hop off the Old Cottonwoods Road, and not impossible to get to. Ed moved in, dug a good-sized hole to mine from, built a shack to sleep and eat in, and a comfy chair to sit in and fish right from the shore. It was sunny, and warm, and wonderful.

So wonderful, that before Ed hardly had a chance to sit, several others joined him. And, to pass the time of day, Ed would sometimes tin-snip trolling-spinners out of the metal headlight reflectors from old cars. These sold like hot cakes to the visiting fisher-folks, and before long Ed was also stocking line, hooks, sinkers and stuff to sell in case of emergency.

Fishing at Magic was not new - people had been maneuvering around the shores ever since the water first rose

1940 - 1950

behind the dam. In 1937, while Ed was just getting established in his shack, several tents were clustered at the North end of the lake, and according to Everett Vineyard of Eden, there was a turkey farm below the dam where the road passed from the highway to the East Side.

Anyway, the word about "Gleason's Landing" quickly spread along the grape-vine, and more and more folks stopped by to fish and socialize. Along in the late 30's somebody arranged to have the nearby CCC boys work on the bumpy, road/path leading from the Cottonwoods Road to Ed's place, making it even easier to get to Ed's good fishing spot.

Two friends of Ed's (Mack Gray and Giff McDonald) came along and each put up a small cabin on Ed's Mining Claim, and in 1940, when Everett Vineyard asked him about putting up a cabin, Ed said "Just go ahead and build anywhere on my Mining Claim." And he did.

Meanwhile, Ed added a board or two to his place and pop, candy, and ice in addition to the fishing tackle. Ice? Yes, he put doors on the "mining hole" and stored ice - sometimes from the frozen reservoir, and sometimes from the ice house at the Magic Dam railroad stop. Glenn Hall from Boise, an old friend of Ed's tells how one of the railroad men told Ed that if he ever broke the lock on the railroad icehouse he would have to arrest him. But - that same railroad guy showed Ed that if he "just pulled out those two big nails holding the lock and took out what ice he needed, and then put the two nails back in place, he couldn't do anything about that." So Ed did.

He hauled drinking water in 10-gallon cans from a Spring on a nearby ranch. "Barrel Springs" was named because of Ed's water carrying. They had to knock both ends out of a barrel and ram it into the Spring so that it would fill up with water to be transferred to the cans. That's when the little spring came to be known as "Barrel Spring." What kind of a barrel was that? Who knows?

1940 - 1950

So Gleason's Landing continued to expand. Folks would put up any kind of tarpaper shack, or haul in an old shed or whatever. Many were without glass in the windows or doors in the doors - all they really needed anyway, was a place to sleep at night, and a little shelter from wind and rain. No trees to speak of - just a few scraggly fruit trees still surviving from an old farm now submerged in the reservoir.

But, those who loved to fish, loved the place, and it continued to grow, just a hap-hazard scatter of shacks. Nobody owned the land, so nobody kicked them off. They just went on happily fishing, enjoying and multiplying.

As time went on, Ed added three little cabins to his "resort", and a few row boats to rent out. You could rent one of Ed's cabins for $1 per night. Two rooms including one table and two chairs and one bed in the other "room." Bring your own blankets.

Finally, in late 1945, the war was over, and the government and everybody else began to ready themselves for peace-time living. Up until that time, the U.S. Grazing Service and the General Land Office held a kind of joint jurisdiction over public lands. But, in 1946, these two agencies were combined to form the Bureau of Land Management, and new laws, new rules, and new blood were added to organize, control, and manage public lands for the U. S. Govmint.

So, it wasn't long before the new BLM came across the casual congregation at Gleason's Landing. The population had increased considerably during the war, and since there had been such a shortage of materials during that time, it was a motley mixture of sheds, shanties, lean-tos, shacks and by now, a used Quanset Hut, or two. . .

Something had to be done of course, but what? Many of those dwellings were on government land close to the waters' edge, so the BLM pondered the situation and decided that "legally" they were "Squatters"

1940 - 1950

A Squatter is someone who just up and "settles" on land without having title to it - usually government land. Such settlement must be for a considerable length of time, and the land must be visibly improved, such as by the addition of a dwelling. Well, Gleason's Landing had been there for almost ten years, and there were certainly a goodly number of "dwellings." So, in 1950 the BLM surveyers moved in to lay down a "grid" dividing the government land into lots.

A Public Notice was issued that these lots would be sold at public auction under the Small Tract Act of June, 1938. Some of the shacks ended up being smack-dab on the dividing lines so the owner was given the option of either moving his dwelling, or buy both lots. It was agreed all around that if you already had a shack on a lot, nobody else would bid against you.

The appraised value of each lot at the first sale was $100.

Well, "Magic Fishing" became more and more popular, and in 1959 the BLM held its second auction of lots. This time, their notice mentioned that electrical power was available (power poles had been installed in 1957), and domestic water could be obtained at reasonable depths, from wells. It further informed that TWO resorts were operating in the area, and a small air strip was situated nearby. The air strip land had been donated by Harold Croft who owned a plane and operated a nearby ranch.

As for the TWO resorts mentioned - Glen Hall tells how the second one came about: "Ed Gleason always kept his money in a cigar box right on the table in his shack - made change right there and kept the money from his sales, boat and cabin rentals. And, everybody who came there to fish knew and saw the cigar box full of money. Among them was a man named Hap Wilson from Boise. Wilson was fascinated with all the money Ed took in and decided to build a place just like it next to Ed's. He called it the 'Rainbow Lodge' and it was located at first, on the road

1940 - 1950

coming in - which put Gleason's in second place and nearer the water. Gleason controlled his own area which included a good stretch of beach. Well, Wilson would stand out in front of his place and wave down people coming in, and usher them into his place. If anyone asked 'is this Gleason's place?', Hap would say 'sure is'. Well, this made Gleason mad as a Hatter when he heard about it and refused to let any of Wilson's customers on his beach, and that went for Wilson, as well. So Wilson managed to buy 10 acres of land from Rancher Newman so his customers would have some place to park, because by this time people were pulling in house trailers and campers and needed somewhere to park them."

So the feuding began and the competition for customers was brisk indeed.

And, so was business.

And both places were soon taken over by new owners.

Wilson sold to a man named John Jack, who soon sold to May Janicek. It was May who was instrumental in developing the area. Along about that same time Ed Gleason sold his entire operation to two young couples - Don and Ada Bopp and Frank and Ownie McCleary, who brought a great deal of energy and optimism to improving their newly acquired resort.

When they bought it there were four rental cabins in place, plus Gleason's "store." They kept adding cabins until they had a total of 14 to rent out, plus a number of parking spots for house trailers. They kept adding to and enlarging the "store", and were soon offering meals, drinks, dancing, cabins, rentals, fishing tackle, boat rentals, gasoline and a friendly place for fisher people to gather, sit and relax, lift a beer or two, sing, dance, discuss the fish they caught (or didn't) and gossip.

By 1959 there were somewhere around 125 shacks, shanties, trailer houses, Quanset Huts, as well as neat, attractive cabins lined up on the government subdivision on the West Side of Magic Reservoir. The Shoshone Rod and Gun

1940 - 1950

Club even constructed a unique club house out of railroad ties which still stands there, sturdily, even though the club has long since disintegrated.

In 1964, owners Bopp & McCleary, pulled huge quantities of sand and dirt up out of the reservoir to make a road along the water's edge.

Bill Newman, a sheep rancher, controlled most of the land behind the government subdivision and the sheep were running and grazing and gamboling on his land. I'm told that the sheepherders never did have anything to do with the fisher people and vice versa. Their only contact was to wave to each other when the fishers were maneuvering through the sheep to get to the water.

In 1959 when the government was selling lots, and people were buying and building, Sidney L. Craig, S.B. Smith and their wives, bought 13.6 acres of land from Rancher Newman, which directly adjoined the government subdivision. But, instead of selling the lots, Smith and Craig decided to LEASE their lots on a 99-year basis. According to Harold Hoover of Twin Falls, they offered them at prices ranging from $100 to $250, depending on size and location. They further stipulated that "the buyer agrees to pay $1.00 to $2.50 per year to the sellers to apply on the property taxes."

A third person, Dewey Davis, was also involved in the deal in exchange for a lot or two. Dewey agreed to run water lines from the well Smith and Craig were putting down, so that anyone buying a lot could also buy water. The buyer would have to pay to connect to the trunk line plus an annual amount for his share of the electrical bill. Every lease showed the exact amount each lot holder would have to pay.

Smith and Craig 99-year leased a lotta lots.

Their subdivision was called (surprise!) The Smith and Craig Subdivision.

Might mention that they never bothered to have it

1940 - 1950

professionally surveyed. They just "stepped off" the area, drew a big map on a piece of cardboard and numbered out the "lots." A rather casual operation - but nobody complained.

Soon people were building and summering on their leased land. All went well until along about 1966 when a Blaine County Assessor dropped by, saw all those lots with cabins and other "improvements" and the taxes soared! OOPS! That meant that Smith and Craig would be responsible for all those new higher taxes for 99 years! Besides, taxes have a way of escalating automatically, and the situation was beginning to look pretty bleak for Smith and Craig because those lease agreements only required the lot owners to pay the $1 - $2.50 per year which wouldn't even come close to covering the new taxes...

So, they came up with a plan. They would simply deed the lots over to the leaseholders and everybody could pay their own taxes, and before the leaseholders even knew what was happening, Quit-Claim Deeds were falling like snow all over the Smith-Craig Subdivision. Each lessee received a deed to his property. No more 99-year leases here. You own your own lot now, so pay your own taxes. The well was also dealt over to the lot owners to be responsible for. The new owners immediately changed the name to the "West Side Subdivision."

* * * * * * *

During those developing years of settlement, special places on the West Shore were given names such as "Barrel Spring." Some are still identified by those early names while others have been distorted or misspelled, but survive nonetheless.

There's "Metcalf Spring," named after the Metcalf family who farmed there at one time, and today's maps show "Pofferman Spring," which is probably really supposed to be

1940 - 1950

"Palfreyman" because Louisa Palfreyman owned the property from which the spring springs forth.

And, there's "Jake's Neck" just northwest of the resorts on the bay which was named after Jake Rosseler in Shoshone because it was his favorite spot to fish. Not many know it as "Jake's Neck," but they should, because Jake Rosseler was well known among the original dam builders. He was the same Jake Rosseler mentioned earlier in this book whose wedding was so nicely written up in the Shoshone Journal. Jake owned and operated a well-drilling company in Shoshone for years, and his drilling rig can be clearly seen in pictures of the dam under construction.

The Rosseler family still lives in Shoshone, and George Rosseler, Jake's son, tells how his father hired 20 men to pick rocks out of the way so the big rig could be moved from Shoshone to the dam. There was no sign of a road at that time and it was a rugged, grueling process to get it across the desert and lava beds to the dam. Jake Rosseler spent much time both at the dam, and fishing at this favorite spot, which his friends dubbed "Jake's Neck."

"Magic Resort" is Gleason's old place, and is so identified by today's map makers. Further on down on the shoreline toward the dam is a place called "Myrtle Point." Actually, the whole name-thing appears to be a series of misunderstandings or not hearing too well. It seems that back when Ed Gleason was settling in, there was an elderly man named Randall who lived in Murtaugh. Every Spring he moved onto that particular spot in his sheep wagon, and just stayed right there until summer was over and the cold weather set in. He suffered from arthritis, and the warm sun helped to ease his pain. He loved to fish, and it was because of him, and the fact that he was there every year, that some folks began to call the spot "Randall's Point." However, some others, who did not know his name but did know that he was from Murtaugh,

1940 - 1950

started to call it "Murtaugh Point." Well, this passing around of his name and his home-town somehow got all scrambled as it passed from one to another and eventually came out "Mertle," or "Myrtle," instead of Murtaugh because they didn't know the story and were just repeating what it sounded like. Finally, the map-makers just settled on "Myrtle Point," because that was the most commonly used name.

Other identities are probably bouncing around but are not yet seasoned enough for the map makers. People coming to fish the West Side of Magic have their own ways of directing friends and relatives to where they are supposed to meet. Paper plates tacked on fence posts are common, with notes like "Bill and Flora - TURN HERE, or "We are at Gull Island," or "Turn at the Dam Road," or "NOT HERE" - go to the next turn-off," signed "Fred and Irma."

There are many "turnoffs" from the Old Cottonwoods Road so it's easy to take a wrong one. Dirt roads, winding and twisting. Some are dead-ends and you have to back out. Not an easy thing to do if you happen to be towing a trailer and/or boat and your wife told you not to take that turn in the first place.

MAGIC CITY

1940 - 1950

Over the water on the east side of the reservoir, almost directly opposite Gleason's Landing, people were skittering down the high, steep, embankment to a flat apron of land where they could fish from the water's edge. The trail going down was narrow, winding, and treacherous, and at first, no one dared to drive it, so they scrambled and slid and tumbled on down.

"The Clay Banks" had always been considered good boat fishing and when those avid anglers found they could get there on foot, nothing could stop them.

So, along about 1946 or so (almost ten years after Gleason sat down in his comfy chair) John Segetti built his resort on that piece of land at the bottom of the Clay Banks.

He, too, stocked fishing supplies, candy, pop, beer etc., built a few small "cabins" to rent out along with a few boats.

Fortunately, hauling all that stuff down the steep embankment helped to improve the rustic "trail", and before long a few courageous souls were brave enough to drive on down. Next thing ya know they were bugging Segetti to sell lots so they could build their own cabins.

Segetti named his resort "Magic City."

In 1954, Mr. & Mrs. Gus Stertman bought Magic City from Segetti, and by that time electricity was available. Mrs. Stertman says the "cabins" were just tarpaper shacks divided into rooms - no windows - just open, "like a sheep shed."

One of the first to build his own cottage, Robert Hinkley, put down a well and reached usable water at 125 feet. The Hinkley cottage had a kitchen, bedroom and large living room with picture windows over-looking the water. They planted trees and fixed things up around the place.

Others soon followed, and ultimately there were more than 40 privately owned cottages.

1940 - 1950

The Stertmans' owned and operated Magic City for eighteen years. It became more and more attractive - grassy lawn, beach, boat launch areas, R.V. hookups, restaurant and bar, shade trees and a much better road going up and down.

Magic City changed ownership several times after the Stertmans', and continued to attract fisher folks year in and year out.

Update

THE NORTH SHORE

Commonly called Hot Springs Landing, the North End of the reservoir is where Camas Creek, the Big Wood River, Rock Creek, and Poison Creek all kind of come together, so there's not much room for any large area development.

The first "camps" were people in tents enjoying the hot springs, and there were quite a few coming and going. However, in 1956 when the new Highway 68 was built, Dick Comish of Hailey, built a resort there. He advertised the location as "The North End of Magic Reservoir, 1/2 mile South of Highway 68. Turn west off Highway 93 at the foot of Timmerman Hill, and take the newly improved State Highway 68 (U.S. Highway 20) only six miles!" He had boats, motors, and cabins for rent, plus meals, room for trailer parking and fishing tackle. He invited all to "stay overnight or for as long as you wish, in a comfortable cabin with parking available. He offered cold beer, soft drinks and plenty of sound fishing advice.

Several years later it was sold to Dr. Alden Parker, and still later, it was deserted and fell into a state of disrepair.

In the late 60's and 70's some "Hippies" spent a lot of time in and around the Hot Springs area. Water-skiing was the big attraction, and it was during that time period that it really became a disgrace - strewn with garbage, the buildings torn apart and scattered.

The Fish and Game Department uses the north shore to replenish the supply of fish in Magic. They back the truck right out on the shore, and turn thousands of fingerlings into the water.

These rainbow trout living in Magic are a unique, special treat. The fish feed on the millions of tiny fresh-water shrimp found in abundance in the reservoir, and produces a pink meat not found in stream trout.

Update
THE SEICHE

WHAT HAPPENED HERE???

Boats were scattered over the docks and up on the beach like toys! Some were filled with dirty water, some were sideways half up on the docks, and some half under the docks!.We were dumbfounded!

It was early in the morning, and we were among the first to arrive at the jumble (on the West Shore of Magic). Our boat had been properly tied up at the dock the night before, and now we found it tipped sideways on the shore, half-full of muddy, filthy water.

Someone said "the lake turned over last night." Someone else said "this has happened before, no wind, no rain, nothing - the lake just turned over - like a tidal wave. . ."

Nobody knew what caused this "tidal wave." Some said it had to do with the phase of the moon, others speculated it was caused by the sudden warm weather. Someone said they heard this same thing happens on Lake Mead, and other lakes as well, not necessarily just man-made lakes. But nobody knew what caused it.

One of the members of the Coast Guard who patrols Magic, said "large swells seem to rise right out of the bottom of the lake and big waves roll into shore." He didn't know what caused it either.

Now it happens that I have a nephew (Michael Hoernemann) a graduate of Anapolis, whose studies include Oceanography. So I wrote to him telling about "Magic turning over." He replied immediately, explaining the "cause" both in scientific terms and at a level I could understand - hopefully.

The name of this occurance is SEICHE (pronounced Say-sh).

Update

"A Seiche is often described as being similar to water sloshing back and forth in a very large dishpan. Although the effect is similar, the situation is a bit more complicated."

One of the "causes" he mentioned is the one I think fits Magic. He says "water heated by the sun gets slightly lighter, and stays at the surface. Incoming cold water is heavier and goes directly to the bottom. The volume of incoming water can contribute to a Seiche."

(Note: When this happened at Magic, the weather was very warm and of course, cold water was coming in from both Camas Creek and the Big Wood River.)

"Water rises at one side, while subsiding at the other. The frequency of alteration can be minutes or hours. In Magic, it would probably be only a few minutes. Actual rises and drops in water level depend greatly on bottom contours. Funneling effects can make the changes larger in a small area, while a broad gentle bottom would spread the effect over a wider area."

"A seiche, at a point of maximum effect, could look very like a 'tidal wave'. Water withdraws, becoming very shallow or even exposing the bottom. The water then suddenly rises rapidly in a rush, going well above the normal level."

Mike suggested that if seiches do occur in Magic Reservoir, it would make an excellent study project and theses for a graduate student in physical sciences. A controlling factor on the effects of seiches is the bottom profile of the lake. Since this is a man-made lake, excellent data should exist on bottom contours such as found in old surveyors maps of the area. The data could all be nicely programmed on a computer. The program could predict the points along the shore of maximum and minimum effects.

Of course, seiches are a natural phenomena, and nothing can be done to prevent or even to accurately predict them.

Update

So now you know. Now you have a name for the "lake turning over" and if you want to know more all you have to do is look up "seiche."

1970 - Present

BAJA MAGIC

Up until the '70's the fisher folks had it all their way on Magic Reservoir - friendly, comfortable resorts on the West Side - friendly, comfortable resorts on the East Side - friendly, occasional resorts on the North End. Boats of all kinds puttering around the water, and float tubers in cowboy hats quietly casting about.

Then about 1979, a Ketchum business man stood at the crest of the hill on the East Side Clay Banks and said "Baja."

"Baja"??? "Yes" he said "A bunch of us go down to Baja Mexico every year to windsurf. We've got pictures, and when you compare that place with this - it's uncanny!"

So "Baja Magic" was discovered.

How on earth did this favorite fishing spot become a popular sport from the sunbelt? For the same reason it is prized for its trout - Magic is deep and narrow with relatively clear water, mild summer temperatures, and easy access to population centers north and south. It is protected from the north by high bluffs and volcanic rock, and is open to the southwest, hence, it gets fairly restrained winds, but few violent weather disturbances.

Windsurfing combines many of the attributes of at least four other sports - sailing, skiing, surfing and water skiing. The main parts of a sailboard include a board, a mast, a universal joint connecting the two, a triangular sail, and a wishbone boom similar to that used in some early sailing vessels. However, it is skiing that those locally involved usually refer

1970 - Present

to, in their comparisons. Both sports deal with a planing surface, speed, acceleration and power turns.

Before long, Cremin Huxley and Richard Sampson bought Baja Magic, and it blossomed like a huge, colorful flower with enormous triangular petals skimming over the water. An estimated 300 boards are in the Ketchum-Sun Valley area alone. An excellent off-season sport for those now living in the area who learned to surf or sail in California - and the ski bums like it too. . .

All equipment needed for water sports is now available for rent on the site - sailboards, fishing gear, fishing boats, canoes, paddleseats, paddle boats, camping sites, RV hookups, a restaurant and bar, and even a coin-operated hot shower. Public boat ramps and docks are available, making it a good place to water ski.

Newcomers to Baja Magic are trained to windsurf on dry land first, with a sailboard simulator that mimics the action of the waves and wind. The resort keeps a rescue boat ready on the beach, just in case a sailor or swimmer gets into trouble out in the water.

Several competitive events are held during the summer - such as the six-mile race from Baja Magic to the Dam and back.

1970 - Present

SUN VALLEY AND ELKHORN

In 1968 Bill Janss bought Sun Valley, and during his ownership many changes and additions were made. An Olympic sized pool was added; a large shopping mall was built between the Lodge and Challenger Inn; also tennis courts; more ski lifts and runs were opened; Lodge apartments and many condos were built. . .

* * * * * * *

In 1971 Elkhorn Village was started a mile-and-a-half from Sun Valley. A joint venture by Sun Valley Corporation and Johns Manville Corporation, it opened on Christmas 1972 with a 144-room hotel, convention facilities, an Olympic-sized pool and tennis courts. shops, offices and restaurants were built around an ice rink at that time, but the ice rink was later scrapped and planted into lawn. . .

* * * * * * *

In 1977 Sun Valley changed hands again. Earl Holding, owner of Little America Hotels and Board Chairman of Sinclair Oil Corporation, purchased Sun Valley and up-graded just about everything. Planted hundreds of trees, refurbished the restaurants, and remodeled the Lodge in time for Sun Valley's 50th anniversary. Ski runs were increased and made better, and Sun Valley continued to grow, improve, and attract more and more people. . .

* * * * * * *

In 1984, Milton Kuolt, owner of Horizon Airlines, bought Elkhorn Village, and developed even more of the Village area.

1970 - Present
WESTSHORE LODGE

The West Side of Magic from the shore to the mountains, is a broad sweep of barren desert land with plenty of space for development. So, when the BLM put some of it up for auction, Don and Dorla Farnes bid, and bought, 20 acres along the Old Cottonwoods Road.

They cleared the sagebrush, built a restaurant and bar, opened officially on October 10, 1984, and invited everyone with the announcement "Magic is open year - round, and so are we!"

They quickly added a new, heated 4-unit motel, a 13-hookup RV park, and Paul Hoppe built a Gazebo in the front yard. There's a playground for the kids, snowmobiling, a tubing hill, fishing licenses, gas, propane and everything else you might need or want during your stay at Magic - in case you forgot something.

Later on, across the road they developed a 15-acre subdivision for year-round homes including a well-house, fire house for a pumper truck, a hangar with 1,300 ft. of air strip for Don's Ultra Lite sports plane, and a par 3 golf course.

They cope with the drought years when the water in the reeservoir is down, and welcome the years when it fills.

Don is a tireless worker and promoter for the West Magic area, and has even managed to get the road paved from Highway 75 to West Magic - a great improvement for the fisher people coming and going.

Carved into the desert two miles from the Magic shoreline, "Westshore Lodge" is a good example of the kind of cheerful optimism shared by Magic's hard-working entrepreneurs.

1970 - Present

Westshore Lodge Area

1970 - Present
MAGIC DAM ELECTRIC

Construction of a hydroelectric project began at Magic Dam in 1988. The Magic Reservoir Hydroelectric Inc., owner of the power rights was required to get approval from the Blaine County Planning and Zoning Commission; the Bureau of Land Management; the Idaho Fish and Game Department and the U.S. Army Corps of Engineers.

The 9-megawatt hydroelectric generating plant utilizes water released from the reservoir for irrigation and flood control work. The plant will operate for less then four months during the irrigating season, and at other times throughout the year when water is released from the reservoir.

The old tower base

This project was approved with the condition it not interfere with existing water rights.

The commissioners required that a formula from the Department of Fish and Game be used to replace any fish destroyed through the turbine or machinery: and they want copies of the oxygen monitoring system reports, and fish mortality reports, to be sent to the Blaine county's Planning and Zoning commission.

The county also requires a full-time experienced operator at the location while the facility is operating.

An 800 ft. spillway was built in addition to the generating plant.

Electricity generated from Magic Reservoir is sold to the Idaho Power Co.

1970 - Present

DAM FOOLS

It's been more than a hundred years since there was an organization called "Dam Fools" inside the Magic Circle. (Remember the Damphools in Bellevue marching up to Hailey to bury the hatchet in a gallon of buttermilk?) Never found out why they were called Damphools, but we do know how the Magic Dam Fools came to be.

Along in the early '70's Chuck and Rosa Lee Harmon and Ross and Loretta McNurlin would get together at West Magic about every weekend - year-round - boating in the summer and snowmobiling in winter. Rosa Lee tells the story:

"Dorothy McMullock, then owner of West Magic Resort, would jokingly complain about the noisy, smelly machines, and we would threaten her that we would form a club so she'd really have a reason to protest. Finally, she told us to put our money were our mouths are or shut up. So, I typed a 'Notice of Intent' to form a Snowmobile Club and brought it to Magic the next weekend. Seventeen people signed up! We sent notices to meet February 3rd, 1979 to select a name and start the club. We decided it would be a Recreation Club to benefit all persons visiting Magic Reservoir. 'West Magic Lake Recreation Club' was the name chosen. (I suggested 'Dam Fools' but it was voted down.) However, mysteriously, when the membership cards were printed 'Dam Fools' was the name."

By May there were 140 members. The first Winter Fun Days and the first Boat Parade were held in 1980.

The Dam Fools provide a First -aid station with oxygen, splints, bandages and other supplies available to the public in case of emergency.

1970 - Present

Their charitable work began when they raised money for the Elks' Childrens' Rehab in Boise; helped purchase a wheelchair for a young man in the Bellevue area; provided a day of fishing for children from the Idaho Youth Ranch, plus cash contributions for Christmas. Since then, Christmas baskets, Rainbow Gold (children with cancer), and Veterans Homes have joined thir list.

They put together a yearly calendar of events for all members, like snowmobile races in January with chili and hot dogs; a "men's cook-off in April; "clean-up day" in the park area; Mother's Day breakfast, boat parades, and memorial Services at the Monument. Something is planned every month along with the meeting.

As of 1999 the "Dam Fools" have members from ten States, Germany and Canada - in addition to Idaho. Some years there have been as many as 600 - 700 members.

All are welcome to join. . .

BURREN WEST

1970 - Present

Magic Reservoir and the surrounding area have never claimed to be a "scenic wonderland." But, it's very easy to get to the water, and kids just out of diapers can toss in a line from the shore and catch a fish - and so can Grampa sitting nearby in a folding chair. Boat fishing and float-tubers are a bit more "scientific" and sophisticated, but they all go home with the same fish.

When people "find" Magic, they fall in love with the laid-back, friendly atmosphere, and keep coming back. Some move right in and stay, which brings us to Ken and Jane Moore and the new "Burren West Resort".

In 1979 the Moores' moved to Twin Falls from Wisconsin, and Ken spent many Autumns deer hunting in the area around Fairfield. Along about 1991 they started thinking about a "weekend place" not too far from their home in Twin Falls, and it happened that on one of the hunting trips, a friend took Ken to the resort area at West Magic. He liked what he saw, and so did Jane - this was exactly what they were looking for. When a cabin came up for sale they bought it, and from then on spent almost every weekend at Magic - winter and summer.

In 1994 they purchased the Rainbow Lodge and trailer park from Hal and Gail Quinn, and started removing and improving. They drew their own plans for a bar, grill and store, and hired Owen Scanlon, Architect from Hailey, to do the final plans.

They broke ground on April 15, 1998. The new building is closer to the water and set at an angle to get the best view of Magic and the mountains. A 6,000 sq. ft., 2 story building with a bar, restaurant and store on the main level. A balcony the length of the building overlooks the water, plus a full deck with terracing down to the water. The lower level has a banquet/meeting room and storage area.

1970 - Present

They named it "Burren West".

"Burren?"

Yes, "The Burren" is a strangely austere and even bleak place on the West Coast of Ireland's spectacular, jagged coastline, where the limestone grassland gives shelter to an extraordinary collection of wildflowers. When the Moores visited Ireland in 1993, they toured the western coast, driving through "The Burren" and visiting the Cliffs of Mohr. Jane especially loved the many wildflowers that appeared after a rain, and the high desert area around Magic Reservoir remined them of "The Burren". In the entry of their pub and grill they have a framed photograph of "The Burren" in Ireland with a full explanation as to how they named their place "Burren West."

Burren West

THE END

As I worked my way through scraps of information pieced together from everywhere, I realized that our "Magic Circle" is "Idaho in Nutshell". We've had Indians on Camas Prairie, and an unbelievable mix of nationalities who've lived, worked, and died in the Magic Circle. We've had explorers, trappers, traders, miners, the Oregon Trail folks, railroads, the second-largest sheep and wool production in the world, cattle drives and cattle ranches. We've got stands of timber, mountains, rivers, lakes, dams, and desert, and a world-famous ski resort, Sun Valley.

The world-famous J.G. White Co. built Magic Dam, and Idaho's own world-famous Morrison-Knudsen re-tooled and repaired it.

The Magic Circle people even tried to get the State Capitol moved to Hailey because it is more "centrally located".

We've had TWO organizations with practically the same name the (Damphools and Dam Fools) a hundred years apart, and we have the Ice Caves and lava flows still holding onto all the "robbers loot" stashed there years ago - according to legend.

But, most of all, we have beautiful irrigated farms and wonderful people farming them.

The Magic Circle people have survived wars and drought, depressions and money Panics, and a terrible struggle getting those irrigated farms in shape, getting water to them, and managing through the dry years.

Mother Nature is still in charge of whether Magic will "fill this year" ...or not, but either way, the fishing and water sports will go on winter and summer, and the shores of Magic are becoming more popular and populated.

I'm finally closing this book on St. Patrick's Day in the year 2000 with an ancient Irish farewell:

May the road rise up to meet you,
May the wind be always at your back,
May the sun shine warm upon your face,
And the rain fall soft upon your fields,
And until we meet again,
May God hold you in the palm of His hand.

Betty Murphy Bever

* * * * * * *

"The past belongs to the future, but only the present can preserve it."

Anonymous